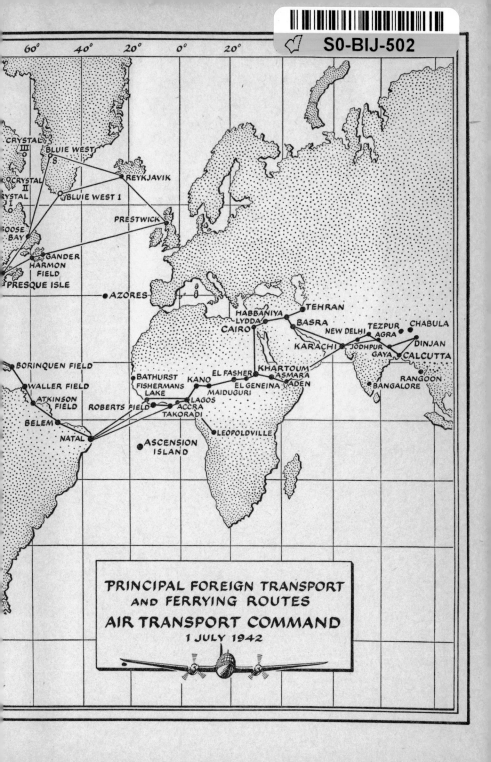

PRINCIPAL FOREIGN TRANSPORT
AND FERRYING ROUTES
AIR TRANSPORT COMMAND
1 JULY 1942

THE EAGLE
IN THE EGG

books by
OLIVER LA FARGE

ALL THE YOUNG MEN
LAUGHING BOY
SPARKS FLY UPWARD
LONG PENNANT
THE ENEMY GODS
AS LONG AS THE GRASS SHALL GROW
THE COPPER POT
WAR BELOW ZERO
[with Cory Ford and Bernt Balchen]
RAW MATERIAL
THE EAGLE IN THE EGG

scientific

TRIBES AND TEMPLES
THE YEAR BEARER'S PEOPLE
THE CHANGING INDIAN [editor]
SANTA EULALIA

THE EAGLE
IN THE EGG

by

OLIVER LA FARGE

lieutenant colonel
air force reserve

HOUGHTON MIFFLIN COMPANY
THE RIVERSIDE PRESS CAMBRIDGE
BOSTON
1 9 4 9

9/9/49 Personal 2.53

The Riverside Press
CAMBRIDGE · MASSACHUSETTS
PRINTED IN THE U.S.A.

29973

FOREWORD

BY GENERAL H. H. ARNOLD

SIMULTANEOUSLY WITH OUR ENTRY into World War II, overwhelming demands came pouring in to Washington from the
four corners of the earth, for United States military aircraft.
Everybody, everywhere, wanted our planes, and wanted them
NOW. Since neither ground nor sea transportation could be
expected to cope successfully with the time element of these
demands, there remained but one other alternative: air transportation. Thus, we of the Army Air Forces found ourselves
faced with the necessity of creating an air transport organization
that, overnight, could, and would, be expanded to extend to
the four corners of the globe, delivering military aircraft,
equipment, personnel, and cargo to near and far places — in
many instances, over air routes of which no man had heretofore
dreamed.

For this colossal task we had to have a particular caliber of
personnel. Imagination, initiative, boldness, daring, infinite
resourcefulness, technical know-how, capacity for unrelenting,
grinding hard work — these were "Must's." Above all, this
personnel must be undaunted by any obstacle or difficulty in
their path, whether it be the Hump on the India-China route;
the North Atlantic, with its blizzards; the deserts, with their
sand and heat and uncharted vastnesses; the dense tropical
jungles, with their explored, and unexplored, dangers.

How the Air Transport Command, and the organizations
encompassed within that title, met this challenge, is an everlasting glory to its personnel, and to the country that fathered

a breed of their kind. No one can read Mr. La Farge's account
of this achievement without being deeply stirred, for it is the
unembellished record of a gauntlet flung to the Impossible —
and left uncontested.

H. H. ARNOLD,
General of the Army.
Commanding General, Army Air Forces
during World War II.

FOREWORD

BY LIEUTENANT GENERAL
HAROLD L. GEORGE

FOUR YEARS have done little to dim my memories of the A.T.C. As I travel across the United States and abroad, scarcely a day passes that I do not meet, in an airport or train or hotel, some person who served in the A.T.C. "I was a Hump pilot," he will say, or a crew chief in the South Pacific, or any one of a hundred jobs in as many places. In these brief meetings I find always the warmest satisfaction. For when I think of the A.T.C. and its great story, I find that the statistics, the jobs done in the Arctic, in the jungles, all over the world, have a way of fading. It is the faces which come back to me, the faces and voices of men and women to whom no effort ever seemed too great, no problem too impossible of solution.

Often, during the war years, I called my staff together to tell them of some new and difficult mission which had been given the A.T.C. — always something that had never been done before — no pattern to follow. Knowing what they faced, that they must work without precedent, against time, and under the most trying circumstances, I always marveled at the assurance, the courage, and ability with which they accomplished each new task, from the first planning in Washington to the final execution usually in some remote part of the world. These were the people who, together, accomplished what has since been recognized as one of the great and unforgettable performances of the war. To have been associated with those people was one of the finest and most rewarding experiences a man could have.

Out of World War II have come many lessons. None, I think, is more urgently in need of attention than the demonstrated importance of air transportation as an essential arm of our national defense. We know now that anything, in any volume, can be carried anywhere in the world by air. This fact, proved by the A.T.C., is being further emphasized today in Operation Vittles. We know, too, that any new war of the atomic age will come upon us with stunning swiftness. Then, more than ever before, there will be an immediate demand for airlift, large-scale airlift, in sustained support of our striking forces. In short, no military effort can hope to succeed without adequate air transport, organized and equipped in advance. Our military air-transport service must be maintained on a strong, global basis; an experienced, going concern which can be rapidly expanded in time of national emergency, one unified command to serve the entire military establishment the world over.

No one is better equipped than Oliver La Farge to tell the story of the A.T.C. As the A.T.C.'s chief historian, Colonel La Farge was intimately familiar with the command: its people, its development, and its performance. His book will be read with great interest by all who cherish those American qualities of spirit, vision, and resourcefulness which have always carried this nation to victory through every emergency that has confronted it and made it today the greatest power for peace in all the world.

HAROLD L. GEORGE
Lieutenant General, U.S.A. (Retired)

CONTENTS

AUTHOR'S PREFACE

THIS BOOK is not a complete history of the Air Transport Command. The full telling of that story could not be managed in a single volume; some idea of its scope may be gained from the fact that the official, military "History of The Air Transport Command, Army Air Forces" comprises some fifty manuscript volumes — and even so, there are gaps in it. The author's interest in writing this book is in describing how something as nearly new as anything can be under our sun came into existence, something which is changing our world, and which increasingly will closely affect us all, in war or in peace. The Air Transport Command was the principal single agent in its creation, and it is with this story that the author is familiar. Hence the method chosen is to trace and describe the new, hopeful, frightening thing that transport aviation has become through telling the general story of the Command. A more detailed narrative would merely obscure the more important thesis.

Any alumnus of A.T.C. who reads this account will notice immediately how much has been left out. He will undoubtedly feel that I have made wrong selections, including those of events, achievements, incidents, persons, less interesting or less worthy than others he well remembers. To give only a pair of related instances: I have said almost nothing of the remarkable struggle in early 1942 to open the North Atlantic Route to the United Kingdom and equip it to handle the passage of the 8th Air Force, nor have I mentioned two greatly loved former T.W.A. men, Brigadier Generals Lawrence W. Fritz and A. D.

Smith, whose names are so strongly associated with the North and Central Atlantic Routes.

I can only ask for tolerance: the choices were so infinite. No one man's selection could satisfy the rest. There is material for more than fifty books. This one tells only part of the story — how the emergencies of the war led us to the threshold of the true Air Age, and what that means to us now.

This book is also a sad case of battening off the works of other people. The historical staff of the Air Transport Command, which worked under the author's supervision, in Washington and scattered all over the earth, comprised some fifty full-time officers, enlisted men and women, and civilians. About two hundred and fifty more officers and enlisted men served as part-time Base Historians, "additional duty." The full-time staff and the great majority of the part-timers worked splendidly. The fruits of all their observations, researches, and writings have been the author's to plunder. It is a shame not to give credit in each case by name, but to list them all would be endless, to select a few, invidious.

The debt goes beyond the historical staff, to innumerable officers, mostly very busy men, delightful friends, and excellent soldiers, who again and again took time out to explain the facts of life to a nosy historian. Among these he is especially indebted to the remarkable group of men who were the "Theater Officers" in A.T.C. Headquarters.

Specific thanks must be given to Dr. John D. Carter (as Captain Carter one of the wartime staff's strongest members), the author's successor as Chief of the Historical Division, who was most generous with his own time and that of his staff when it came to compiling material for this book; to Major Bernard Peters, U.S.A.F., the Command's Public Information Officer, for help, advice, and for digging up many obscure items of information; and to Lieutenant R. G. Wilson, U.S.N., Naval Air Transport Service Assistant Public Information Officer, for providing a mass of helpful information on that Service.

The writing of this book was made possible by a John Simon Guggenheim Memorial Foundation Post-Service Fellowship, the second time that that wonderful foundation has given this writer the freedom to undertake a major enterprise. Finally, it would be gross ingratitude and an unforgivable oversight to fail to mention the writer's indebtedness to his wife, who was, in the first place, a real asset in his military career. She herself served as a civilian in A.T.C., and since has heard this book discussed *ad nauseam*, had most passages in it read aloud to her twice and some more often, given constant and excellent advice, and done a large part of the typing.

O. La F.

Santa Fe, New Mexico
    1948

THE EAGLE
IN THE EGG

THE OPPORTUNITY OF NEED

ON THE FOURTEENTH OF DECEMBER, 1941, a group of men gathered in Washington to make plans to meet an appalling situation. They represented the Army Air Corps and its infant transport arm, the Air Corps Ferrying Command, the Navy (which two days earlier had established its Naval Air Transport Service), the Office of Production Management, The Civil Aeronautics Board and Authority, the Air Transport Association which spoke for the airlines, Pan American Airways, and Transcontinental and Western Airways.

The fundamental problem before them was logistics — the creation of supply. America and her allies were weak in men, ships, aircraft, and munitions of all kinds. Yet worse, it was going to be extremely difficult to get what they had to where it would do any good. East and West their two enemies occupied, comparatively speaking, compact positions with interior lines of communications. For Germany and Japan the fighting fronts, actual or potential, formed arcs around themselves as centers. We faced the outsides of those arcs, with oceans and continents to cross before we got to them. One of the most important of our allies, China, was all but completely cut off from us already. More than thirteen thousand miles, a sea voyage of forty to fifty days, could bring our supplies to ports near the unpenetrated wall of the Himalayas. The one road into China would soon be cut. It looked as if China's case were hopeless.

In the Middle East, the British faced the enemy on the borders of Egypt. The British forces could be supplied only by going all the way around Africa, by crossing that wild continent at its greatest width, or by sailing the whole expanse of the Pacific and Indian Oceans. India and Australia, lands on the other side of the world, were essential defenses against the Japanese, while northwards we looked to Alaska, thinly held, vulnerable, accessible chiefly by equally vulnerable water routes. Foremost in the thoughts of every American were the Philippines, so far and so dear, where our own lay waiting an overwhelming attack.

Russia, too, was all but cut off. To get supplies to her required the running of the hazardous, bloody gauntlet of the Arctic Ocean above Norway, crossing the great wastes of Siberia, or following a long, twisting route to the Persian Gulf and up the whole length of Persia to the Russian border.

The nearest, most convenient place from which we could hope to attack and do damage to either enemy was the island of Britain, 2100 miles from the New World outpost of Newfoundland.

From all of these far places, these fiendishly scattered and remote fronts, came a constant, urgent, even desperate cry for supplies — men — supplies.

The men who had gathered to consult knew that aircraft could bridge the spaces, overleap the deserts and mountains, conquer time. Their first and immediate step was to concentrate all transport aircraft capable of carrying a payload across an ocean and put them to work. America, the pioneer of aviation, counted its resources. They were ridiculous. Eleven crudely converted B–24A's (Liberator bombers) in the hands of the Ferrying Command, a Boeing Clipper which the War Department had purchased from Pan American and eight more still in the airline's possession (provided one managed to get back from Hongkong), two Martin flying boats, also belonging to Pan American, and T.W.A.'s five Boeing Stratoliners. None of these was really adequate to the task. The Clippers were slow and greatly limited in their use since they were seaplanes, as were the Martins. The Stratoliners and ex-bombers had never been intended for lifting bulky, heavy cargoes. But this was what we had.

We were still in the period when, if one were in San Francisco, one might make a point of going to the Golden Gate Bridge on a Wednesday to see the Pan American Clipper fly past. We had a fine network of domestic airlines, but with the exception of the five Stratoliners mentioned, they were equipped exclusively with medium or lesser transports, chiefly Douglas DC–3's and Lockheed Lodestars, competent aircraft for short and medium hauls, but not capable of carrying any significant load over the distances which now had to be bridged. We possessed no such thing as an aircraft designed from the wheels up to carry cargo. We thought we owned a great bird, but when we examined it, we found it was only an egg from which some day wings might emerge.

The poor few heavy transports we owned were put to work. One after another was dispatched, many loaded with munitions for a point known in code as "Plum" and "X" — the Philippines. They were routed via Florida, British Guiana, Brazil, the Gold Coast of Africa, Khartoum, Cairo, Iran, India, and Java. They were routed this way, but properly speaking there was no route. Lack of equipment, aircraft supplies, communications, and all the countless things which go to make up an air route slowed their progress painfully. Day after day the "Daily Diary" of the Ferrying Command traced them:

20 December 1941: PAA N–18612 arrived Trinidad, Destination "X."
31 December 1941: PAA N–18612 arrived Karachi . . .
10–11 January 1942: All 4-engine ship captains en route to "X" urged to utmost speed consistent with safety.

The progress of each individual plane was important enough for immediate reporting to General H. H. Arnold. Not one had reached Java by the time MacArthur retreated to Bataan. Some got to the Dutch East Indies in time to load their munitions on submarines, others never got beyond India, three of the B–24's reached Australia.

Some sixty heavy bombers, B–17's and LB–30's [1] had been

[1] LB–30 is the common American designation for Liberators (B–24's) as produced for use by the British, with some differences from the models ordinarily used by us. These were ready for delivery to the British and were taken over by us after Pearl Harbor.

assembled as the second echelon of the bombardment wing being built up in the Philippines. After Pearl Harbor they were moved from California to MacDill Field in Florida, under instructions to proceed from there along the same route that the transports were following. Senior officers in Florida saw that neither the planes nor the crews were qualified to make such dangerous flights. The Ferrying Command took over, sending a group from its little handful of specialists who knew how to fly oceans and unexplored continents. A school was opened. After weeks, the bombers began to take off across the Caribbean. When finally, on January 31, the Ferrying Command's Daily Diary reported, "Two ships delivered to 'X,' " "X" was no longer the Philippines, but the points in Java from which it might be hoped that bombers could give some support to the men on Bataan.

It is a pathetic tale. In our admiration of our own might as it finally developed, we forget how feeble we were in the beginning of 1942 and how simply black the picture was. In nothing were we feebler than in the long-range air transport which could have provided the answer to many of the worst of our problems.

Three and a half years later the fighting with Germany had ended, the attack upon Japan was reaching its peak. Twenty-six scheduled flights of the Air Transport Command crossed the Atlantic Ocean daily each way, thirty-eight set out daily across the Pacific. From India, 71,000 tons of cargo were flown to China in one month. At the peak of effort on both fronts, in April, 1944, 2500 military aircraft were flown to the forces overseas. The Command's network of routes embraced the world. In preparation for the final moves against Japan, the Command brought 160,000 passengers from Europe across the Atlantic to the United States between May 1 and September 15; thereafter, the need for haste having ended with the occupation of Japan, its commitment dropped to 10,000 passengers per month. During the same period and for the same purpose, it handled the return of nearly 6000 aircraft to the United States accompanied by 86,000 Air Force personnel. At its greatest strength it disposed of over 1000 four-engine transports and 2000 heavy two-engine transports, not counting minor and miscellaneous types.

It was practicable and reasonable for the Air Transport Command, with assistance from Troop Carrier units, on eleven days' notice, to fly the first wave of Occupation troops into Japan, including two fully equipped divisions. Along with them went such articles as jeeps, tractors, bulldozers, small aircraft, the heavy trucks known to the Army as "six by sixes," and 2300 barrels of gas and oil. This was accomplished in eleven days without major reduction of the Command's worldwide schedules.

Nor did the Air Transport Command have any monopoly. To its equipment, capacity, and rate of accomplishment must be added the flights of the Naval Air Transport Service, with 226 four-engine, 205 two-engine aircraft, flying more than 70,000 miles of routes, and the wide services of the R.A.F. Air Transport Command. In three and a half years the oceans, formerly crossed by single planes piloted by men whose daring won the world's admiration, had become one solid hum of air traffic. Routes, complete, well-equipped routes, reached every part of the world outside of Russia's orbit, backed by a weather-reporting system of a completeness far beyond any airlines operators' wildest dreams in 1940.

Something new had been created. Desperate need had made it possible. From the military point of view, strategic air transport had come into being, an entirely new thing. From the civil point of view, mass long-range air transport had been achieved, transportation in terms of thousands of tons and thousands of passengers. As a by-product, the routes had been created: military necessity, which overrides considerations of economy and cost, had presented the world, till then crossed by a few faint air trails, with a complete air highway system.

The development was by no means only in size. Technologically the world had shot ahead in aviation. The usual practice when working out and testing new methods is to do so on a reduced scale. This practice was reversed. The experiments leading to the techniques of mass long-range aviation were carried out on a scale far larger than their anticipated post-war use. For instance: Under ordinary circumstances, if there were foreseen a possible need for using twin-engine aircraft to carry payloads of several tons at altitudes of 20,000 feet or higher, one or two planes would be set aside for experimental use until the many problems involved could be learned and solved. In the war, several hundred DC–3's and C–46's were kept doing just that for all they were worth, over the Himalayas. The result was a mass of knowledge about performance and efficient air lift under extremely unfavorable conditions which ordinarily it would have taken a decade or more to gather.

The blind landing systems which alone have made it possible to maintain the Berlin air lift through the winter were evolved by the Air Transport Command during the war. In 1941 it would have been inconceivable that a couple of million people could be thus maintained.

The sound of aircraft has dwindled. Our armed forces are economizing. The airlines can operate only if they make a profit. Air travel and air freight remain expensive and select. Still, we count twenty trans-ocean departures a day where we used to count one a week. Air travel, domestic and foreign, has become a commonplace in our thoughts. The military air age has been put under wraps, the civil air age has hardly begun, but the change which has taken place could not have occurred in three and a half years of peace. The imperatives of war forced twenty years, at least, into three. The egg hatched, and in it was an eagle.

The account of how this came about is not, unhappily, merely a story of great achievements. Now to our horror we see the war-clouds again, low upon the horizon. We do not know if we can dispel them or not. Transport aviation materially changed the course of the last war. If we have another, it will alter its whole nature just as importantly as will the long-range bombers and the new, dreadful weapons. The tale of what has been done to date, and how it was done, is among other things a peephole into the future which concerns us all.

II

PLANNERS AND FLYERS

WE WERE NOT CAUGHT entirely unprepared. It was America's great good fortune that in the years immediately before Pearl Harbor the key positions of our Air Staff were filled by a remarkable group of men, of whom General H. H. Arnold is the archetype. They were airmen, and much more than that. They knew aviation through and through, they fully foresaw its possibilities, they were courageous thinkers and daring planners. Many of them risked their military careers in supporting the great prophet, Billy Mitchell, some had been kept long in obscurity because of the force with which they fought for real air power against the ground-minded brass hats of the nineteen-twenties and early nineteen-thirties. As America began to rearm they came into their own. They gave us the nucleus of the air force which they later developed so astonishingly, and among other things, in the broad scope of their planning and action, they gave us the beginnings of the air transport system we were to need so desperately.

They must share the credit, and can well afford to do so. In the earliest stages the British led us in the strategic use of air transport. Little or nothing could have been done, in the wild struggle into which we were plunged, without the skill, dash, and patriotism of our airlines.

Airmen in those days had a special quality. I do not know whether it will persist as flying becomes commonplace. Military and civil aviation still were pioneer enterprises. The "old men" of aviation — the flyers of the First World War, the airline founders — were under fifty years of age, the first flyers

of Kittyhawk were still alive. The progress of their craft had
been such that they had never lost the habit of doing things
which had until recently been known to be impossible. Anyone who associated with them noted that — generals, lesser
officers, producers, airline executives, and flyers — they were in
some sort frontiersmen. They were ready for new conquests
and strange developments, not in the far future, but tomorrow.
Part of the unending conflict between the airmen and our General Staff in earlier times came, I think, from this quality. The
two groups of minds were entirely differently conditioned, regardless of understanding or lack of understanding of aviation
as such.

The American airlines long anticipated that they would play
an important part in the event of war. Through their central
organization, the Air Transport Association, they kept in touch
with the War Department, working and reworking their plans.
As I have said, their equipment consisted of twin-engine passenger aircraft, typified by the Douglas DC–3. These aircraft
could have been effectively mobilized for troop movements
within the Northern Hemisphere; they could have handled
limited amounts of cargo. In the war as it developed, the airlines as they then existed did make possible fast travel of personnel and relatively small and light, but important, items of
cargo, but they could offer little to alleviate the situation we
confronted overseas. At the time of the Japanese threat to
Dutch Harbor these preparations bore their greatest fruit.

The fact that the joint Air Transport Association-Air Corps
plans were, on the whole, of little use must not be allowed to
detract from the credit due to their makers. This was an unusual example of foresightedness on the part of both the
civilians and the military. It was also an unusual example of
deep patriotism permeating an entire industry.

Our transoceanic flying, mainly a monopoly of Pan American, was logistically insignificant. At its high point the line
possessed thirteen flying boats. Its principal routes were of
limited value. To Europe it flew only to Lisbon, a neutral
enclave in Axis-held or dominated territory. Across the Pacific
its main routes were subject to immediate cutting in the event

of a Japanese attack. Still, Pan American's clippers, crews, and ground crews were a valuable nucleus.

Equally important, Pan American had extended its operations over much of Latin America through a series of locally established lines, and it also owned forty-nine per cent of China National Aviation Corporation, the balance being owned by the Chinese government. It provided the skilled men and procured the equipment for that extraordinary organization. Above all, the company possessed priceless experience in organizing and operating dependable services in a variety of undeveloped countries.

Our civil aviation, like our military, possessed only the *potential* ability to meet the requirements of a world war. That potential, given time, could become a priceless asset.

It was the British who developed the prototypes of strategic air routes over which supplies could be delivered far from the homeland. This delivery includes that peculiar form of air transportation which has, illogically, become known as "ferrying," that is, the delivery of the aircraft itself under its own power. In anticipation of war in the Middle East and the closing of the Mediterranean, as early as 1938 the British opened a crude sort of route from Lagos West Africa across Africa south of the Sahara desert, to join the Cape-to-Cairo route at Wadi Seidna airport near Khartoum or at El Obeid a little further west. By 1940, Imperial Airways maintained a scheduled service over this route, although on a very small scale. By delivering aircraft and supplies by boat to Lagos, then flying them to Egypt, a great saving could be made over the long voyage around the Cape of Good Hope. The capacity of this line was limited. It was used principally for the ferrying, the self-delivery, of aircraft.

After the fall of France, Britain moved to ferry larger aircraft across the North Atlantic, a daring undertaking, but infinitely quicker than shipping them. At first the flying was done under civilian control, the famous "Atfero" (Atlantic Ferrying Organization), the crews of which were a fearless and fascinating group of American flyers. The first plane was delivered over the Atlantic on November 11, 1940.

The R.A.F. then established its Ferry Command especially for the flight delivery of aircraft, under Air Chief Marshall Sir Frederick Bowhill. The Ferry Command took over Atfero on August 1, 1941. By then the Command was delivering aircraft in many parts of the Empire, although the North Atlantic was its only major ocean crossing.

These were the foreshadowings and the materials which the Allies had to work with. Among other shortages, there was an acute shortage of pilots competent to do the kind of flying required. The idea that the average civilian flyer can turn forthwith to military flying is as fallacious as the idea that untrained huntsmen can pick up their rifles and form a modern army. The great majority of civilian pilots have had experience in light aircraft only, usually in single-engine types. They are competent to fly cross-country only under "contact" conditions — that is, when they can see and guide themselves by the ground.

T.W.A., as has been noted, was the owner of five Boeing Stratoliners, the only true four-engine transports other than seaplanes then in service. Through operations with these it had acquired unique experience in flying heavy aircraft. Accordingly, under contract with the British, it opened schools for training Atfero pilots, especially the famous Eagle's Nest School at Albuquerque, New Mexico. Thus little by little, to a small degree, the United States became involved in the British beginning of strategic air transportation, and by so doing minutely increased its own preparedness.

After the passage of the Lend-Lease Act in early 1941, with its clear indication of the people's will to give aid to Britain and her allies, our Air Staff as well as higher agencies gave long thought to ways of speeding the movement of aircraft to Britain. Air Staff was also concerned about our own supply lines should we become involved in war east or west. Increasingly the top authorities felt the need of an air service which could take American leaders and representatives, military and civilian, as well as diplomatic communications, direct to the United Kingdom. In view of enemy air activity over and around Great Britain, this was not a service which could be asked of a civilian organization. Plans were laid for a military shuttle.

On April 21 General Arnold, then in London, proposed that the Air Corps take a hand as well in ferrying British aircraft. Planning went forward along both lines, and very rightly with an eye to improving the military position of the United States. The Air Corps quickly grasped the idea that the cross-country ferrying of large numbers of British bombers would give its own pilots experience in which they were sadly lacking.

At that time aircraft were picked up at the factory by civilian pilots under contract to the producers, and flown by them to ports of embarkation, or to Montreal where they were taken over by Atfero. The fees charged for this service were exorbitant, and the pilots, not being under military discipline, took their own sweet time in completing a flight.

After much discussion, on May 28, 1941, the President wrote to the Secretary of War:

> Dear Mr. Secretary:
>
> I wish you would take the full responsibility for delivering planes, other than the PBY's [1], that are to be flown to England, to the point of ultimate take-off.
>
> I am convinced that we can speed up the process of getting these bombers to England and I am anxious to cut through all of the formalities which are not legally prohibitive and to help the British get this job done with dispatch. . . .
>
> For your confidential information I am suggesting that the R.A.F. take the responsibility for the planes at the point of ultimate take-off, but whether this suggestion of mine is approved by the British government or not I want the Army to make sure that the planes are delivered speedily.

Early in the afternoon of May 29, Colonel Robert Olds, then assigned to the Plans Division of Air Staff, was called into his chief's office. He came out about three-thirty, and told his secretary, Mrs. Jennie Smith, "Jennie, we've got a job to do." He had been instructed to set up the Ferry Command, to take charge of ferrying as outlined in the President's letter, and of the proposed shuttle to Britain. That afternoon he secured the assignment to his command of Major Edward H. Alexander. He moved so rapidly that when the adjutant general published

[1] Naval seaplanes.

the order activating the Air Corps Ferrying Command on July 5, the order had to be made retroactive, and already the nucleus of his staff had been formed, the plan of action devised, and the new organization was nearly ready to go.

Colonel Olds was the man for the job. He began flying in the First World War. He had made a number of non-stop, transcontinental records in a B–17, and commanded six of these bombers on a flight to Buenos Aires and return.[2] The next year he took part in another flight to Rio de Janeiro under Major General Delos C. Emmons. He held the Distinguished Flying Cross, and had received the Mackay Trophy and the bronze trophy and medal of the International League of Aviators.

Colonel Olds made a deep impression on those who knew him. A few speak of him with a kind of despairing annoyance, a few found him too strong medicine to take. Most of those who were associated with him speak of him with deep love. He was fiery. As a colonel, he did not hesitate to write extremely sharp communications to much higher-ranking officers, and he got away with it. He knew what he wanted done, and he fought for his ideas. He was devoid of side, never pulled rank, was a delightful companion off duty. He was driven by a demon of energy. During his time with the Ferrying Command he was tormented by recurrent arthritis, but he was reluctant to give up playing squash. He might talk and plan with his subordinates late into the night, or enjoy himself to the full with friends; he would be at his desk the first thing in the morning, raring to go. He made each individual officer feel that he was trusted and would be backed up to the limit — so long as that officer fulfilled his assignment. If he fell down on the job, Colonel Olds had a short way with him,

[2] It is no reflection on the men who made these flights to note that they were wildly known as "good-will flights," and were in fact one of the stupidest things ever dreamed up by a bumbling State Department. They were generally held in Latin America to be a demonstration of our mailed fist combined with aerial espionage, and I well remember the rejoicing when, on an earlier "good-will flight" one of our bombers crashed.

but unless he did that, his commander backed him against the highest authority.

Colonel Olds was promoted to Brigadier General in January, 1942. On March 26, because of his health, he was relieved of his command. Shortly thereafter he received the Distinguished Service Cross, and was promoted to Major General. He then took command of the Second Air Force. The terrific strains he had put upon himself took their toll; he was invalided again, and died at Tucson, Arizona, on April 28, 1943, a man for his country to remember.

By June 8, the original staff of the Command was complete. In addition to Major Alexander and Mrs. Smith (who remained an important figure in Command headquarters throughout the war), Lieutenant Colonels S. S. Hanks and Harold Hartney, Majors William H. Tunner and Thomas L. Mosely, and First Lieutenant Louis T. Reichers completed the group. Representatives of the Maintenance Command, the R.A.F., and the British Air Commission were assigned. Later in the month First Lieutenants A. Felix Dupont and Richard C. Lowman and Mr. George Brewer were added. After some difficulties, Mr. Brewer was later commissioned major.

All of these men rose to higher grades before the war was over. Some of them played outstanding parts in the history of the Command. Their contributions will be recounted in the appropriate places. Praise is due to all of them, and to the small staff of civilians and enlisted men who worked with them, for they were but a handful to do a big job, and they did it well.

The new Command was given one large room, later partitioned, in the basement of the Munitions Building. The place was hot, dark, and ill-ventilated. What ventilation it got lost some of its virtue due to the fact that the windows gave on the back door of the cafeteria, and garbage was piled beneath them. Here in the oppression of June in Washington the men and women, Americans and Englishmen, toiled to work out the ferrying system. Routes from the aircraft factories in California and throughout the country to the British acceptance points were decided upon, as well as to New York and New Orleans for aircraft going by boat to the United Kingdom and to Russia. A Western Division of the Command, at first hardly more than a name on paper, later, under new designations, a major unit, was established in California. Action was started to build airfields in Maine, resulting in the completion in early 1942 of Presque Isle and Houlton Fields, which became famous in the war. Meantime, arrangements for the North Atlantic shuttle continued.

The stated mission of the Ferrying Command — to run a low-frequency airline and perform domestic ferrying — was limited. Under limited men it would have been carried out to the letter, with a minimum value to the country when war came. These men were not limited, nor were their opposite numbers on Air Staff. Before a single plane had taken off under its order, the Command was already entering upon greater undertakings.

No one knew better than Air Staff that the United States was woefully short in pilot and crew experience. Regular Army and Reserve pilots lacked cross-country and long range practice. I have already noted how small was the supply of men qualified for flight in heavy aircraft — four-engine transports and bombers. The British as well were still short of men for Atfero.

The Command busied itself at once with securing an improved and stepped-up Army training program at certain fields. It worked out a plan to encourage the civilian ferry pilots, as they were replaced by military, to join Atfero. In conjunction with the R.A.F. it worked out means for getting an increased flow of men for Atfero from the T.W.A. training schools, and arranged for Army pilots to get four-engine training at them. In connection with this last, the eternal difficulties arising from a completely separate Army and Navy showed themselves, when the Navy objected to the use of airline pilots holding Naval Reserve commissions as instructors, but this was ironed out.

Once ferrying operation had become completely military, it was planned to rotate combat flyers through the Command, until the greatest possible number would have had the experience of cross-country flying in a variety of types of aircraft. The smaller number which would fly the Atlantic for the shuttle would, of course, receive even more valuable experience.

The matter of training was by no means the only matter outside of their literal mission with which Colonel Olds and his group concerned themselves. Short-range aircraft, fighters and light bombers, were carried overseas by ships. This was a slow procedure, and worse, it involved an appalling loss of aircraft through submarine action. In late 1942 the Ferrying Division of what had then become the Air Transport Command reported that losses in aircraft flown across the Atlantic were 3.7 per cent as against over 33 per cent for those carried by ship. We can be confident that conditions were no better in 1941. A plan was tentatively developed for a route via the Far North, from the vicinity of Hudson's Bay across Greenland and thence to Iceland. This route, if feasible, would not only eliminate long over-water flights, but would detour around the chronic bad weather which hung between Newfoundland and Great Britain. To further this project, the Command provided a B–24 for a survey headed by Captain Elliott Roosevelt. It was instrumental in securing the establishment of meteorological and communications posts at various Arctic points, and before the winter closed down work began on bases for its use at the sites Captain Roosevelt had spotted. It also borrowed Lieutenant Commander Charles H. Hubbard, an Arctic expert, from the Navy, and later arranged to have him commissioned in the Air Corps and permanently assigned. Command headquarters also looked to the westward. The Navy seemed fairly confident of what would happen if it ever got the opportunity to tangle with the Japanese fleet, but the vulnerability of the Wake-Midway-Guam route was painfully apparent. Through the summer of 1941 the Air Corps Ferrying Command's mission was purely domestic. That did not stop Colonel Olds and his staff at all. They did not hesitate to bite off what looked like more than they could chew — and chew it. They were avowedly headed for overseas ferrying.

In part because of their interest, Ferrying Command funds were allocated to the development of an alternate route which, after Pearl Harbor, became the key route to Australia. It made a fish-hook-shaped detour, south from Hawaii to Canton and Christmas Islands, then west in a great loop through Fiji and New Caledonia. The original plan called for a continuation through Townsville, on the northeast coast of Australia, from which the Philippines were accessible via Port Moresby. Construction at Canton and Christmas was undertaken by the Army, further westward by Australia and New Zealand under Lend-Lease. In co-ordination with this plan, the Navy developed bases at Palmyra and Johnston Islands. Work began in October, 1941, and proceeded under forced draught. The importance of this undertaking hardly needs stressing.[3]

In this period there was a further development of the first importance, not attributable to the Ferrying Command, but in which it took a deep interest. Whether we ourselves entered the war against the Axis, or limited ourselves to equipping the British to do the fighting, it was essential that the water route to Africa be replaced, or at least supplemented, by an air route, especially for the ferrying of aircraft. This meant a well-equipped route from Florida to where the bulge of Brazil reaches towards the dark continent. The value of such a line to us in terms of continental defense was also obvious. Further, the vital line across Africa itself needed to be built up into something of real capacity. The War Department, accordingly, called in Pan American, the agency most experienced in such work.

Changes in contracts and in the firm's organization occurred, which are of little interest. As finally worked out by September of 1941, Pan American established three subsidiaries. The

[3] *In Air Transport at War*, Harper & Brothers, 1946, p. 41, Mr. Reginald M. Cleveland says: "When the problem of giving aid to General MacArthur's forces in Australia arose, the Pacific was conquered by the use of islands on which the preparatory work had been planned and developed by the foresightedness of Pan American Airways. . . ." The development of the alternate Pacific route as outlined above is a matter of clear, official record. Mr. Cleveland appears to be thinking of a Pan American branch line which touched at some of these islands en route to New Zealand. As Pan American used seaplanes, and operated, I believe, at a frequency of one flight a week, and did not go to Australia, its arrangements were of little value to the Army.

Airport Development Program, generally referred to as A.D.P., would build airfields and establish the necessary communications and other aids in Brazil. Pan American-Africa would build up the African route from Accra on the Gold Coast to Cairo, and would run the transport service over it. Pan American Air Ferries would deliver aircraft, including those for Pan Am-Africa, to Africa. Ferrying activities were limited by Brazil's neutrality as that country would not permit the passage of combat aircraft destined for a belligerent. Control of Pan Am–Africa and the Air Ferries passed to the Ferrying Command the day after the attack on Pearl Harbor.

The transport potentialities of the route to Africa were recognized, but not much developed.[4] Aside from what Pan American might haul in one or two of its own seaplanes, supplies for the Middle East would come by boat to Accra or to the British installations at Lagos and Takoradi, to be flown across the continent. Except in the element of such ferrying as Brazil's neutrality would permit, the development of the South Atlantic Route and its prolongation across Africa to Cairo was *at that time* little more than a great enlargement of the strategic line originally established by the British. In practice, thirty-two transports for Pan American and British use were flown across before Pearl Harbor.

While the Command interested itself in these far-flung preparations, it proceeded with its operational mission. After some delays caused by difficulties over questions of transfer of title, ferrying by military crews began in July.[5] By December 7, 1941, the Command had delivered 1330 aircraft to domestic destinations (as used in the Command, "domestic" included Canada, while "foreign" included Alaska, Panama, and Hawaii) and had made its first five foreign deliveries, to Cairo. The latter were a special development, which will be described later.

[4] The route via Brazil to the African Coast will be referred to as the South Atlantic Route. With its further extensions across Africa and on to Asia, it will be referred to as the Southeastern Route.

[5] Despite exhaustive research by myself and numerous other people, we have never been able to establish the date on which the first ferried delivery was made. July 7 is generally accepted.

Involved in the ferrying record was a new procedure, description of which calls for an explanation of certain terms and practices. Aviation is romantic; it is also highly technical. Military aviation imposes upon the practices and techniques of the craft and science its own special practices, and above all, its terms. Some of the latter are necessary and precise, some jargon, some sheer gobbeldy-gook. In writing this story I am trying to avoid the worst of the lingo, but it is impossible to avoid the necessary terms, while the practices, of course, must be treated. Explanations, therefore, will have to occur from time to time.

Aircraft are divided, first, into "types." A type is a basic design, such as a B–24 (Liberator), B–17 (Flying Fortress), C–54 (Douglas DC–4).[6] Types are divided into "models." A model is a variation of the type sufficiently stable for the new version to be manufactured on a production line basis. Thus it was found early in the war that B–17's lacked protective firepower in several directions. More guns were added. This was a permanent change, and was incorporated in production, producing a new model, the B–17A.

Within one model, there are differences of "modification." A modification is a change made to suit a special purpose, which cannot be incorporated in the process of manufacture, as it is to be applied only to a limited number of the planes manufactured. Aircraft to be based in India, for instance, must be equipped with an elaborate filtering system against abrasive

[6] The whole question of nomenclature is a mess. Thus, the Army lacks a single type-designation for the invaluable Douglas DC–3, which appears as a C–47, C–53, and with several other numbers. Therefore when it wants to refer to the type as a whole, it is forced to violate its own practice and use the manufacturer's term, "DC–3." To the Navy this type is an R–4D, to the British a Dakotah, and it is sometimes referred to in advertising as a "Sky-train," one of the less happy products of the ad-man's brain. Generally, however, a single type has but four names: the manufacturer's, the Army's letter-and-number, the Navy's letter-number-letter, and the British name, which may or may not be the same as the manufacturer's. The letter P– was originally placed in front of the type-numbers of fighter aircraft, because they were known as "pursuits." Thus, to make things easier for everyone, a fighter is designated by P– and a photo plane by F–.

dust and special self-sealing fuel-tank linings which will not be corroded by the "aromatic" gasoline which is manufactured in the Far East. Aircraft to operate in the Arctic must have a special heating system, adaptations of the hydraulic system to handle non-freezing fluids, windshield defrosters, and a multitude of other modifications.

Such modifications may be a major operation. Aircraft of a given model, modified for special uses, may differ from each other more than do the different models of that type. The distinction is not one of degree, but of method.

At the time that the Ferrying Command took over, the problem of modification had become serious. Making the changes at the factory meant the movement of heavy items of equipment from where they were made to the factory, with corresponding delays, burden on the railroads, and increased costs. Frequently, where a new modification was to be made on only a few aircraft, it meant that experts had to be sent from, let us say, the factory producing a special type of carburetor heater to the aircraft factory, to show the local engineers how to do something they might never be called upon to do again. The system was wasteful of time, men, money, and transportation capacity.

The solution was to establish "modification centers," strategically located in relation to groups of manufacturers, and fly the aircraft to them. Thus all aircraft of whatever type which required the special carburetor heater would land near where it was made, and have that item, along with various others, installed by experts.

This, in turn, meant that the ferrying routes became complicated. It was not sufficient to fly the planes by the shortest route from the factory to Wayne County Airport in Michigan for the installation of overseas equipment and then to Montreal. A plane might have to go from California to Montreal via Tucson, Fort Worth, and Memphis. This also raised the problem of the efficient use of pilots. Modification might take several days or even longer, and the crews could not be allowed to sit idle while that went on.

The solution hinged upon military control of the crews. By

a remarkable system of reporting, made possible in part by the
communications network of the Civil Aeronautics Authority,
continuous track was kept of the location of each plane and
pilot. When his plane had landed, the pilot was instructed
either to return to his base, pick up a plane at the point where
he had landed if one was ready to go, or proceed to another
point to pick one up. In this arrangement, as was to be the
case so often, the willing co-operation of the airlines was a
prime factor. Ferry pilots had the first priority on the airliners. At that time this priority was not established by government order, but was enforced voluntarily by the airlines
themselves.

The close tracking of planes and men also ended the purely
unnecessary delays which had been common when the planes
were ferried by civilians. An RON (remain overnight) message
from a point off the direct route, or beyond which the flyer
should easily have passed, needed to be supported by a good
reason. There was no room for detours to visit the home folks
or the girl friend, no layovers for the swell party that would be
thrown the following night.

As the Command's activities grew, control of domestic operations was taken over by Major Tunner, while Major Moseley
controlled foreign operations. Major Tunner's work, which
eventually earned him a major general's stars, was not so
glamorous as his opposite number's, but it was complex, in-
cessant, vital. Both of these men, confronted with operations
new in military experience, and to a considerable extent new
in all experience, carried them out with a common sense and
boldness worthy of their commander.

Ferrying involves certain elements of risk. The ferry pilot is
constantly taking up aircraft he has never seen before, often
enough of types with which he has had but brief experience.
The planes have been factory-tested, but they have not had the
thorough workout which ensures that they are free of "bugs";
yet he must set out with them, not on trial runs in the vicinity
of his base, but on the more complete commitment of an extended flight across country. There are bound to be accidents.
Remarkably enough, there were relatively few crashes in the

early days of the Ferrying Command, and even fewer attributable to pilot error. Yet, before July was over, the first fatalities occurred, when the power plant of a Hudson bomber failed, causing a crash which killed First Lieutenant R. F. Rush and Second Lieutenant Ned L. Warner. They were the first of many who gave their lives in the ferry and transport service.

I mentioned the delivery of five aircraft to Cairo, the first which the Command flew overseas. In October, 1941, it was arranged that the Command should ferry sixteen Liberators to the Middle East in order to provide the British with a heavy bombardment unit, and that four of the ferry crews should remain to instruct the R.A.F. men in their use. After some negotiation, permission was obtained from Brazil for the planes to cross her territory fully armed, provided they carried American insignia.

The Ferrying Command accepted the assignment with enthusiasm. It ran into a fantasia of difficulties. Though the mission was established on October 17, it was not until November 21 that the first Liberator, piloted by First Lieutenant Elbert D. Reynolds, took off from Bolling Field. The Command, from lack of experience, failed to anticipate certain problems, but on the whole no one could be blamed for the delay. The project involved too many new elements, for each of which solutions had literally to be invented.

On November 25, Reynolds made a forced landing, being on the last gallons of fuel, at El Obeid in the Sudan. The landing was made at night, his radio was out of order, and there were no runway lights. The local people placed two automobiles to throw light on the runway, then they added some lanterns, placed in a confusing manner. Reynolds came down slightly off the runway, one wheel touched an invisible pile of dirt, and the result was a total wreck. By great good fortune, no one was hurt.

Five more Liberators left the United States before Pearl Harbor and reached Cairo safely. The remainder were taken over by us when we got into the war. The project was hardly a success, but it was most instructive. Its story re-emphasizes how far we had to go before we reached the peak of efficacy which we now tend to take for granted.

The second half of the Ferrying Command's stated mission was the opening of the shuttle service to the United Kingdom. For this Colonel Olds secured the temporary assignment of Lieutenant Colonel Caleb V. Haynes (later Brigadier General), a flyer almost as famous as himself, and of outstanding experience in long-distance flights with heavy bombers. He was equipped with a B–24A which had been roughly converted into a transport by taking out most of its armament and installing flooring and seats of a kind in the bomb bay.

As the nucleus of "Atlantic Division" of the Command, Colonel Haynes was joined by the then Major Curtis E. LeMay, who later commanded the 21st Bomber Command, and Master Sergeant Adolph Cattarius, a flight engineer of great experience and ability.

Prestwick, not far from Glasgow in Scotland, was selected as the British terminus. The weather there was fairly good as British weather goes (the United Kingdom is definitely not an airman's paradise), and the approach to it was as far as possible from German air bases. The first flight took off from Bolling Field at Washington on July 1. Colonel Haynes was pilot, his co-pilot was Captain James H. Rothrock, who later piloted Captain Roosevelt on his Arctic survey. The navigator was First Lieutenant John B. Montgomery, the engineers were Master Sergeant Cattarius and Technical Sergeant Charles M. Kincheloe (both of whom were field officers by the time the war ended). The radio operators were Technical Sergeant Joseph H. Walsh and an R.A.F. operator whose name, lamentably, has not been recorded.

The plane flew first to Montreal, thence, with eight passengers, to Gander Lake in Newfoundland. It took off from Gander at 3.05 P.M., Eastern Standard Time. Some eight hours later, after a not very eventful flight, it approached the British coast. The overcast was solid and the ceiling low. Colonel Haynes circled over the town for two and a half hours, then went out to sea so that he could let down safely, and came in at an altitude of 800 feet. The Prestwick control tower ordered him back up to 3000 feet, at which altitude he flew blind. When he was over the field, the control tower gave him his location, told him the ceiling was 600 feet, and said, "You're on your own now."

He went out to sea again for three minutes, then let down, turned about, and came in over the town of Prestwick at the nerveracking altitude of 550 feet, proceeding thence to the airfield for a safe landing.

On that trip, as on all of them, the passengers were intensely uncomfortable. The cold at high levels over the North Atlantic was bitter, and the heaters were inadequate and had a habit of getting out of order. Smoking was allowed only on the flight deck, to which the passengers were admitted one at a time when things were quiet.

On the return flight, the weather over Newfoundland was so bad that Colonel Haynes continued non-stop to Montreal, and from there to Washington without further incident.

At the time, this round trip was covered with complete secrecy. The crew later received the Distinguished Flying Cross, but the citation was secret. An event of historical importance went unnoted, and has now been forgotten and buried under the great deeds of the combat flyers. In the track of Colonel Haynes' crudely converted B–24 were to come the transports and the bombers by the thousands. On that July day began the change by which today we think without surprise or wonder of the airliners, not seaplanes but land planes, crossing the oceans with the regularity of buses.

On the second flight, the B–24, which carried only a single tail gun, was intercepted by a roving Dornier bomber, but escaped by diving into the overcast. Later, a flight piloted by Lieutenant William N. Vickers, Jr., a reserve officer, let down through the overcast to come out over a convoy. Vickers immediately found himself the target of intense anti-aircraft fire, and hastily climbed back above the clouds. It was Vickers, too, who encountered such violent weather near Philadelphia that he thought he was done for. So extreme was the turbulence that the experience was reported to General Arnold as evidence of the toughness of Liberators.

In September occurred the most remarkable of all the flights made by what the British named "the Arnold Line." Mr. Averell Harriman was going to Moscow with an Anglo-American commission. He himself went by boat, but it was decided to fly some of the participants, and also thought advisable to have aircraft under American control available while the visitors were in Russia. Two of the Ferrying Command's B–24's, piloted by Major Alva L. Harvey and First Lieutenant Louis T. Reichers, having completed routine trips from Washington to Prestwick, were held there for the mission.

Ambassador Constantin Oumansky, returning from the United States to Russia, was to be one of the passengers, and acted somewhat as liaison man with the Russian authorities. After careful study, it was decided that the two planes should fly around Norway to Archangel and then south to Moscow, rather than trying to go straight in, over German-held territory. The possibility of German interception, even on a high, night flight, was one factor in this decision; equally important was the fact that the Russians could not guarantee that planes coming in from the direction of the enemy would not be attacked. It may be noted in general that Russian identification of aircraft was poor throughout the war, and that they proved themselves over and over to be excessively quick in attacking friendly planes, whether with their own aircraft or with ground fire.

An excellent and simple code was worked out, chiefly of groups of numbers, by which the American radio operators could communicate with Russian stations and aircraft. The whole enterprise was, of course, kept extremely secret. When Oumansky gave the pilots their final instructions from Russia, he entertained them rather by leading them mysteriously out on an open stretch of lawn, looking all about him dramatically, and talking in a low whisper.

Harvey took off from Prestwick on September 23, at 9.20 P.M., Greenwich Time. Reichers followed ten minutes later. Near the Shetland Islands they were picked up by British patrol planes, but were recognized — after a few moments of worry — when they fired the colors of the day. They continued in the cold, dark night, rounding Norway two hundred miles off the coast and crossing the Barents Sea far above the Arctic circle.

They came over Archangel by daylight. It was overcast, and there was snow and sleet, so they decided to go on non-stop to Moscow. Now there developed a new cause for worry. Although the radios were working perfectly (they were able to communicate with Edinburgh), they could get no answer of any kind from any Russian station. As the Russians were to them a mysterious and unpredictable people, this silence was most disturbing. Oumansky was more upset than anyone else, in fact he was genuinely frightened. It appears to have occurred to him that his government might have decided that the "accidental" crash of an American plane would be a tidy way of liquidating him.

Harvey came over Moscow. Still he could get no word of any kind from the ground. He picked out an airfield and landed, without any instructions or apparent recognition of his presence. Once he was on the ground, Russian officers came to meet him, and shortly he and his crew were facing the inevitable Russian welcome of caviar and other fine foods and lavish pourings of vodka. Reichers similarly picked out a field, and was received in the same manner. They had successfully made non-stop flights of 3150 miles under difficult, even dangerous conditions. Their achievement should rate among the great flights of history.[7]

Reichers remained eleven days, Harvey eighteen. They were irritated by the constant surveillance under which the Russians kept them and by the restrictions placed upon their movements, while their aircraft were studied minutely and at leisure.

Olds had seen the great opportunity that the Moscow flights offered, and instructed his men accordingly. When Harriman released him, Reichers took off on the second, and equally noteworthy, part of his journey. The Russians, he reported, gave him remarkably good weather information, and he particularly praised their weather map, which he attached to his report. Even to a layman, the map is miraculously clear and complete.

[7] An excellent description of this flight has been written by Quentin Reynolds, who was a passenger on it, in *Only the Stars are Neutral*.

His course was to Baku and then to Habbaniyeh in Iraq. He found that the Russians were in error about the height of the Caucasus Mountains, which had peaks considerably higher than their data showed. From Iraq he went to Cairo, and then south, exploring the area over which Pan American was to create the new route.

So far all had gone smoothly, but he had a little difficulty when he came to the field at the town of El Fasher on the edge of the Sudan. It was Ramadan, and the radio operators were Mohammedans. They had feasted all the night before, and were spending the fast-day in sleep, so that he was unable to communicate with them. He made his landing, then reported to the commanding officer, advising him that he had to refuel. Nothing the size of a B–24 had ever been in that area. Reichers required 2500 gallons of gas. The commanding officer, he reported, almost wept. His gasoline was in imperial four-gallon tins, widely scattered and buried in the ground for safety in case of attack. What Reichers wanted represented the freight of a hundred camels plying steadily between El Fasher and Khartoum for a month. The five hundred tins required were dug up, and the fuel poured into the plane.

His next stop was at Takoradi on the Atlantic Coast. There he found that no weather information could be had, for lack of communication. The R.A.F. officer in charge remarked that even a flight to Freetown was an adventure. They were of the impression that the weather across the Atlantic was generally good at that time of year, so on that basis he set off across the Atlantic for Brazil. He reached the mainland at Natal, where he found one runway torn up. As using the other one would involve landing in a high, cross wind, he went on to Fortaleza, where he effected a landing on a rough field. His next stop was Belem, where he found Pan American established. From there he continued uneventfully to Washington, bringing invaluable information about little-known, important areas.

Major Harvey's return flight was even more remarkable. Unfortunately, while Reichers writes a vivid report and also talks well, Harvey's reports are extremely dry and concise, so that little color can be had from them. Colonel Olds, acting on his own initiative, had ordered Harvey to continue around the world via India. He wanted to know more about the routes in that direction. It was not until the major was entering the Pacific that Air Corps Headquarters discovered what the Ferrying Command was up to, and by then it was too late to call Harvey back.

His route took him from Habbaniyeh to Karachi at the western edge of India, and then to Calcutta. He found that the runway at Dum Dum airfield near Calcutta was only 2400 feet long — theoretically an impossible length for landing a B-24 — but with great skill he made his landing. He then found that his wheels were sinking in, the surface not being up to his plane's weight. Noting the concrete block on which airplanes are turned about while testing their compasses, he taxied to that and parked there. This is almost the only incident he mentions in his report. He went on to Rangoon, Singapore, Darwin, Port Moresby, Wake Island, Hickam Field near Honolulu, and March Field in California. He remarked that he and his crew were tired after their long transoceanic flights, so he remained there overnight before returning to Bolling Field via Fort Worth.

Operations over the North Atlantic had to be suspended on October 18, as winter weather made the crossing virtually impossible in the then undeveloped state of the route. By that time the Command was making some progress in securing the communications, weather reports, and other aids, as well as the construction of bases across the Far North, which would eventually make year-round crossing routine. It is a pity that American public opinion had not advanced to a point at which the Ferrying Command could have been established a year earlier. Then in the first winter of our sorrows the United Kingdom might have been readily accessible by air, and the war shortened immeasurably.

Twenty-two round trips had been flown in three months and a half, or about one every five days. By present standards that is indeed small potatoes. Before the beginning of hostilities in Europe there had been no such thing as non-stop flights between the New World and Great Britain, other than a few

famous, individual feats of daring. Pan American, in consulta-
tion with Lindbergh, had been hestitantly poking at the idea
of a route via Greenland, a project scouted by many. After
1940 the R.A.F. and allied British Overseas Air Corporation
had blazed the trail. Nothing of the volume, frequency, and
near-scheduling of the "Arnold Line" had ever been seen before. Nor had anyone ever before attempted to establish a
regular service over a major ocean with land planes. Most firsts
are small, and so was this one, nonetheless it was a first of great
significance.

While the Command was reaching to the north, it also
reached to the south. On August 21 Colonel Haynes with
Major LeMay as co-pilot flew the first of the Command's planes
to go to Cairo by the southeastern route. His exploratory
flight, which also carried passengers and mail, was followed by
Reichers' return trip. Regular service began on November 14
and continued until December 7, after which flights were controlled by urgent, sudden needs and regular scheduling became impossible.

This was also a small, important beginning. There is the
quality of mental daring in the concept of an established service extending over more than nine thousand miles, across parts
of two continents, a great sea, an ocean, and the whole of
another continent to the farther side of Africa.

When the enemy finally struck, little though we had, it was
yet infinitely more than we should have had six months earlier.
The absolutely essential route across the South Pacific was almost ready — it went into use early in January. A large body
of cross-country flying experience had been built up. Domestically, at least, we had learned the techniques of ferrying. We
had learned a lot about flying the North and South Atlantic
and Africa, knew what we needed to get routes established, and
were on our way towards building them. In October, Pan
American–Africa had started regular flights between Accra and
Cairo, so that a transport airline across Africa was developing
rapidly. Pan American Air Ferries and the Army shuttle pilots
had built up familiarity with the whole Southeastern Route.

We were woefully short of men with adequate experience

for the over-seas operations our situation required. Our lack of competent aircraft was desperate. We had a world of knowledge yet to learn. Nonetheless, we had opened up horizons which were to lead to a new factor in war. It is the fashion at present to praise the men of little rank and to belittle the high staff, the "brass." In this matter let us do justice to the brass. It was the planners of Air Staff, the genius of General Arnold himself, the drive and foresight of the commander of the Ferrying Command, which packed those last six months with life-saving new beginnings.

III

OPEN WAR

As soon as the United States was at war, the men in what was then the Combat Air Force (and those in Air Staff agreed) thought that there was now little more need for the Ferrying Command other than as operator of a sort of courier service with a handful of transports. The combat flyers would ferry the planes they were to fight. Our urgent need cut off deliveries to the British — as we have seen, even the undelivered balance of the sixteen Liberators was turned back for our use. The flyers temporarily assigned to the Command, with the valuable experience they had built up in the course of their ferrying, would be returned to combat duty. On December 9 all ferry pilots then en route (twenty-six pilots and ten navigators) were ordered to land their planes at the nearest airfield and to proceed by the most expeditious means to the West Coast.

On the following day the Combat Air Force awoke to the fact that while it had obtained a number of pilots, it had stopped the flow of planes. The Ferrying Command was hastily restored to full vigor.

On December 12, in addition, Colonel Olds was given supervision of the execution of all War Department contracts with the airlines, a move which centered all transport operations except those of the Air Service Command under one head. On December 13 a new contract was made with Pan American to extend Pan Am–Africa's and Pan Am Air Ferries' operation to Teheran in anticipation of possible future extension to Russia. A further contract arranged for the ten seaplanes in Pan American's possession to fly a truly remarkable route, via Brazil across Africa and India to Singapore. On December 24 a contract was signed with T.W.A. for that line to start overseas service with its Stratoliners, henceforth designated C–75's.

The Ferrying Command had moved a little too rapidly with Pan American, and by its new contract left the Navy out in the cold. That service had a greater use for flying boats, which at best the Ferrying Command regarded as makeshift equipment for its purposes. Accordingly all but three of the clippers were turned over to the Navy, leaving the Ferrying Command in control of four (including the one previously bought by the War Department).

On December 13, also, the President delegated to the Secretary of War his power to take over the airlines. This power was never fully used, because of an important decision of policy on the part of Air Staff. This decision had two parts. The first was that, insofar as it was possible, the normal commercial activities of the lines should be maintained, a priorities system enabling the various agencies of war to make the fullest use of a going, efficient system of transportation. The second was that, rather than call up all reserve officers in these companies, draft others, commandeer planes, and incorporate all into the armed services, they should be called upon to fly, as lines, under contract and with aircraft supplied by the government. This was by far the best way to get the advantage of existing, smoothly functioning organizations with ample experience. The natural instinct of panic is to act drastically and to take over everything. Essentially, the policy outlined was generally settled in the conference of December 14, 1941, mentioned at the beginning of this book. It is apparent that under the disastrous circumstances of that time, the high officials of the Army and Navy kept notably cool.

The arrangements made with Pan American and T.W.A. had many of the elements of those made with other airlines throughout the war. They were sensible, and eminently fair to the lines. The government bought the aircraft, then returned them to the companies to fly under contract — later, of course, supplementing or replacing them with new and better

planes built for the government. This was a sound arrangement, making it possible to take military risks with the planes,
or transfer them to military operation if desired. The early
contracts specified where the operators were to fly. Later ones,
following a model largely developed by Colonel James H.
Douglas, Jr., specified the type of equipment to be flown and
the quantity, but left it open for the Army to shift the actual
flying to wherever the situation required. This was a nice
compromise, retaining the absolute control and flexibility
which were essential to military operations, while taking the
greatest advantages of what the airlines had to offer.

The first of the Clippers took off from New York on December 18 with a load of P–40 spare parts for General Chennault
and the Flying Tigers. It reached Calcutta early in January,
according to General Chennault "in the nick of time." Two
others headed farther east with .50 caliber ammunition which
was eventually delivered by submarine to General MacArthur.
Meantime the Air Ferries delivered four PBY's to the Netherlands East Indies. It must be remembered that these flights
involved taking seaplanes across the whole width of Africa, and
that the crews were operating largely in territory which was
completely unknown to them. At the time, of course, there
was no mention of these missions, they seem to have been forgotten since. They deserve to be famous.

After these first rush flights to the Far East, the Clippers
were established on a shuttle between New York, Miami, Natal
in Brazil, and Lagos on the Gold Coast or Fishermen's Lake in
Liberia, thus establishing the first transport service across the
South Atlantic, to tie in with the trans-African operation.

Use of the C–75's was delayed by the elaborate job of modification that had to be done on them to make them militarily
serviceable. Their deluxe equipment, including the "pressur-
ized" cabin, was taken out, and their interiors re-equipped to
handle some passengers and a fair load of cargo. Early in February they supplemented Pan American's activities with a regular service from New York through to Cairo. When the coming of spring made it possible to reopen the North Atlantic
route, beginning in April three of the C–75's were transferred
to that route.

While these two lines and Northeast Airlines shuttling to Greenland and Labrador were beginning the re-establishment of regular transport services, the Command's own B–24's were engaged in special missions which will be described later. As nearly as can be told from the rather chaotic records of those times, aircraft flown by military crews returned to scheduled service about the first of June, when five new and superior B–24D's were put on the South Atlantic shuttle between Natal and Accra.

On January 7, 1942, the first aircraft, a B–17, left Hickam Field on Oahu to fly by the new route to Australia. For a time, the Ferrying Command ran a few of its B–24's between the United States and Australia in a sporadic, almost accidental manner. It depended upon the Navy, largely, to return its ferry pilots when they had delivered aircraft down under. In December, Consolidated Aircraft had come up with a remarkable plan for drastically remodelling a Liberator so as to make it into a moderately efficient transport. That company also had accumulated a good deal of experience in flying the Pacific in the course of delivering aircraft to the Dutch East Indies. It now proceeded to carry out the proposed modifications on several of the LB–30's, the British-type Liberators, which had originally been destined for Egypt. The company formed a subsidiary called Consairways, which began regular service to Australia for the Ferrying Command in the beginning of April.

The Ferrying Command was not the only organization that was going in for air transportation; control of that function was greatly divided. The Navy, which came in a trifle late on appreciation of air transportation, made its own contracts. Priorities, after being briefly administered by the Ferrying Command in December, 1941, were turned over to G–4 of the War Department General Staff, which meant essentially that they were administered by the Services of Supply. The S.O.S. also cast distinctly longing eyes at the transports themselves. The Air Service Command possesed the 50th Tranport Wing (I cannot explain why the only such Wing in existence was numbered 50), which consisted of a small fleet of strictly military transports, and all domestic contract flying was under its control. The Ferrying Command was occupied with the develop-

ment of foreign transportation and with both foreign and
domestic ferrying. Its principal customer had become our own
Air Forces, and for a time delivery to other nations virtually
ceased.

Such divided control was bad doctrine, as events were to
show emphatically. The men at the top, as well as the men in
the aircraft and on the bases, had no time for doctrine. They
were too busy making airplanes fly usefully and batting down
new emergencies as they cropped us. They went by trial and
error, inevitably, until sound practice was evolved. So far as I
know, the first formal statement of the underlying doctrine,
evolved from a study of the evolution of tested practices, was
put forth by the Historical Section of the Air Transport Command well on in 1944. The men who established the theory
had no time to formulate it.

Nonetheless, inadequate, full of makeshifts and bad practices
as the system was at the beginning of 1942, it had begun to
exist. Combat aircraft were moving overseas, although in a
trickle, key men and a few supplies went east and west by air,
the three great routes, across the Pacific, across the North Atlantic, and southeast to the Orient were open. In the minds of
a few men at the top, notably of General Arnold, there was
already the vision of a steady flow of airborne supplies.[1] One
could not say that the Air Forces' preparation were bearing
fruit, but they were blossoming hopefully.

[1] Lieutenant General Harold L. George, of whom much will be said in
the course of this story, told the writer with some emphasis that General
Arnold was the first to foresee the possibilities of strategic air transportation.

IV

BOMBERS FOR THE INDIES

AT THE END OF 1941, the first thing in all minds was to get help to General MacArthur, hopeless though the undertaking seemed. Sixty-three heavy bombers, a few LB–30's supposedly ready to take off, the rest B–17's newly received from the factory or due to be received shortly, were assembling at Sacramento to join the bomber force in the Philippines.[1] When it became apparent that they could not reach the islands via the Pacific, it was decided to send them the long way round, by the Ferrying Command's Southeastern Route. This movement was given the name of "X Mission." The code word for the Philippines was Plum, but in order to avoid excessive use of a code word, with resulting increased danger of its compromise, it was common practice to use an informal code word for a special project such as this.

The attempt to send combat aircraft, flown by their own crews, over that long, incompletely prepared, little-known, hazardous route was of prime importance to the future of the Ferrying Command.

The planes began crossing the continent on December 19, going via Fort Worth and Jacksonville to MacDill Field near Tampa. There the Third Air Force would be responsible for

---

[1] Various records show 80 planes involved altogether; 7 LB–30's and 65 B–17's; 63 planes in all, and finally, 58 planes. I believe that 63 is the correct figure. The differences lie partly in inclusion of a few aircraft which departed over the Pacific early in December, and presumably stopped at Oahu, and of aircraft staged at MacDill Field destined for other fronts.

dispatching them. After a good look at the first flights, the
local authorities wired A.A.F. Headquarters that the aircraft
and crews were by no means ready to go. No maps or briefing
information were available. The planes were off in weight and
balance. The crews were green and inadequately "blended,"
that is to say, the crew members had not become a team.

General Arnold called in the Ferrying Command. Colonel
Olds sent Lieutenant Reichers of the Moscow flight and Major
Roderick Towers, who was later called back to other duties.
In addition to making the remarkable Moscow-Cairo-Brazil
flight, Reichers had been the engineering officer who untangled
the endless technical snarls involved in the Sixteen Liberator
Project. He is a slender man of medium height, a lively nar-
rator, enterprising, and with a good dash of pepper in his system. With his thorough knowledge of aircraft engineering,
ability and experience as a pilot, first hand knowledge of much
of the route to be flown, and his drive, he was the perfect man
for the job.

Reichers and Towers found a lamentable situation. The
crews were newly trained. Their training was after the manner
of that time, chiefly in daylight flying under the ideal conditions of Texas, the Southwest, and California. They were young,
and like so many young flyers, at once brash and fearful. The
pilots, at the time they arrived at MacDill Field, had only from
fifteen to twenty hours flying time in four-engine aircraft. They
lacked experience in bad weather flying, and in night landings
and take-offs. They had heard terrible stories of the inter-
tropical front across the Caribbean and the unpredictable
storms of South America. Beyond South America lay the mere,
unknown vastnesses reaching to the Orient.

They had very little experience of instrument flying. This is
one of the essentials of safety. Flying may be divided into two
types, contact and instrument. In pure contact flying the flyer
depends upon his view of the ground or water beneath him
and of the horizon to tell him where he is and what position
his plane is in. In practice, pure contact flying is practically
never attempted; if no other instruments, the pilot uses his
compass to check his direction and his altimeter to give him his
altitude.

Experienced flyers fly instruments even when they could fly contact. It is safer. The pilot looks out of the window to admire the view, to assure himself that he is where he ought to be, and to avoid collisions. He depends upon his instruments to tell him everything he really needs to know, with the exception of his exact position and his drift (corresponding to the leeway of a sailing vessel), which are given him by his navigator. When the stars and horizon do not show at night, or when one is passing through a cloud, the human senses are not competent to tell a man, for instance, whether he is flying right side up or upside down. If he tries to fly under such conditions by means of his senses, he is said to be flying by the seat of his pants. His intruments will keep him straight. At the stick of a plane in broad daylight, when the horizon is unclear and the clouds are in motion, you may have the curious sensation of seeing by your instruments that you are swinging off your course and one wing is dropping, although you can feel nothing yourself. Instinct impels a man to look out the window and trust his eyes. It takes some training to make him really believe that the panel in front of him is more trustworthy. In bad weather, under overcast, under a host of conditions, only by this means can he bring his plane through safely. These men were expecting to set out on a fantastically long flight, untrained in instrument flying.

The crews were not blended. As Reichers said later, the pilots did not trust the navigators, the navigators and crew chiefs doubted their pilots' competence, the co-pilots and pilots were relative strangers, the gunners were unsure of everybody. These men could not depart as they were. They had to be schooled.

They did not know where they were going, but they knew it was to be a long journey with combat at the end of it. They may have guessed the Philippines, or the direction in which they were going may have suggested other fronts. Probably when they talked among themselves they made the same wild guesses and naïve deductions that their fellows made under like circumstances all through this and every other war. Wherever it was to be, it would be a long way from home, and there would be no supplies. They had been equipped in California.

En route, wherever they could they talked fast and drew more equipment. Extra pistols, spare generators, extra sets of tools, sextants, bedding, grub, ammunition, first-aid kits, clothing. In the tails of the aircraft, extra self-sealing fuel cells were stuffed, a heavy weight placed where it could do the most harm. Some of the Liberators landed at MacDill Field so overloaded and out of balance that they had to use their elevators when taxiing in order to keep their noses down. On an average, the bombers carried overloads of 3000 pounds. Add the fuel needed for long hops across oceans, and even with perfect weather and contact conditions these planes were doomed.

Telegrams went to Ferrying Command Headquarters. At Bolling Field there was the only portable aircraft scales then in existence. It was loaded into a B–19 and flown down. To the force on the ground were added Captain James C. Jensen and Lieutenant William E. Ragsdale (later shot down over Java), pilots, and Lieutenant Robert J. Arnoldus, navigator. These men had the North and South Atlantic flights behind them. They could not only teach the greenhorns, they could give them comfort. I myself remember how distinctly encouraged a new bomber crew was, facing its first ocean flight over the Pacific, when it learned that I, their wingless passenger, had crossed the Atlantic six times. It made things seem easier. The Ferrying Command group were top-notch airmen. They could talk to the youngsters, flyer to flyer: "There's nothing to it if you do as I tell you. When I came across last October . . ."

Reichers unloaded the planes and reloaded them, weighing them with care, and checking their balance until he had them in shape to fly. The group prepared maps and briefing materials from their personal knowledge, and what had been assembled up to that time by the Command and by Pan American. They opened a school in night landings and take-offs, instrument flying, and flying through the kinds of weather that lay along the route. In the course of this instruction they blended the crews.

The first plane was dispatched on December 29, 1941. The last took off on February 27 of the following year. Of the sixty-three planes of X Mission, six crashed along the routes, four of which were total wrecks. One loss was unnecessary. Over Reicher's protest a B–17 which was not in proper balance was despatched with a weather front only a few miles ahead of it. Reichers told the pilot to go under the front at 1000 feet. The pilot disregarded the instruction and tried to get through at 12,000 feet. The plane broke up in the air, but the crew bailed out safely.

The delays ended the chances of any of these planes reaching the Philippines. Supplies along the route were inadequate, repairs difficult to secure. Progress was slow. It was difficult to control crews which, in transit, were under no one's direct command. The Ferrying Command dispatched its own "control officers" along the route, with Major Alexander going to the key point of Bangalore in India, but their authority was uncertain. These officers reported that some of the flyers, wearied by their arduous flight over ocean and desert, and overnight stops at what were still grimly uncomfortable tropical stations, lingered among the flesh pots of Egypt, and that it was difficult to make them hurry their departure.

Some reached the Far East in time to take part in the struggle to hold the Indies, some reached Java only to retreat to Australia, others became the nucleus for the 9th Air Force in India, or joined the battle for the Middle East.[2]

An unexpected weakness had been exposed. Air Staff was already laying plans for the strategic bombing of Germany. The Air Corps knew that not all its bombers would fly in the excellent Pacific weather. Not all could cross the peaceful ocean under leisurely conditions which allowed waiting for perfect days, by the stepping stones of Wake and Midway Islands. Nonetheless, the new crop of pilots seems almost to have been trained for Sunday flying, despite the example of the R.A.F. (whom the Navy was first to emulate) of giving its trainees their final polish in the foul weather of Northern Scotland.

Among other things, X Mission demonstrated that the pas-

[2] I regret that the English have foisted this term upon us, as they did "ferrying." We grew up calling this area the Near East, which makes sense. "Middle" implies more of the same on either side, which is not the case with Egypt–Libya.

sage from the Zone of the Interior to any of our major over-seas destinations called for a different kind of flying skill from that required in combat. The essence of effective supply is the maintenance of *flow*. Flow cannot be maintained if the planes are grounded whenever the weather is imperfect. With the long ocean crossings, requiring twelve hours or so of non-stop flying, it is not always possible to forecast the weather at the far end accurately; after the pilot has passed "the point of no return" — the point at which his fuel will not take him back to his starting point — he may run into fronts or storms. This was particularly true in the early days, before our weather-observing system reached its later point of high perfection. Once he had joined his unit, it was generally true, although there were numerous exceptions, that the combat pilot would not be sent on a mission unless the weather was favorable.

The combat pilot is conditioned to taking risks. We earnestly pray that he and his crew and his ship will come back every time undamaged. Still, his primary mission is to drop those bombs on the target; only then does safe return come first. We expect his plane to take a beating. If he has short-ened the life of his engines by forcing them to a very high pitch of performance, and thereby also has exhausted his fuel supply or reduced it dangerously low, the probable necessity for so doing is recognized. He is not, cannot be, taught to be cautious, conservative, and economical.

Efficient ferrying calls for opposite virtues, it calls for the practices which will set the aircraft down at its destination on time and in condition for battle. In rushing to build a starvel-ing air force up to something approaching adequacy before the war, and in the even greater rush to build it up and get it into action in a losing war, it was impossible to take the time to train men two ways at once. The speed with which they were trained, however, resulted in the end in loss of time. The weaknesses of our training were later remedied, partly as a result of the experience of the Ferrying and Air Transport Commands. X Mission first demonstrated these weaknesses, and also the inherent difference between two types of flying, and hence the need for specialists.

Out of this developed what later became one of the most important of the Air Transport Command's functions, the "control of tactical ferrying." Aircraft and crews for combat use are referred to as tactical, hence the movement of aircraft to their foreign destinations with their own crews on board became known as "tactical ferrying." A little later in the war it was a common practice for skilled ferrying crews to deliver the aircraft while the tactical crews went over as passengers on transports. This was a wasteful procedure. The better solution, forced upon us at the beginning by sheer necessity, as we had neither the transports nor the ferry pilots, and later developed on a large scale, was to supply the tactical flyers with guidance, control, and such aids to flying as could be placed along the routes, in order to enable them safely to accomplish a mission for which they had not been specifically trained.

In the opening months of 1942 we moved these sixty-three bombers, one by one, to the Orient. Headquarters followed their individual progress with painful attention. It was considered highly creditable to the Command that only four were wrecked. In the autumn of 1944 I watched one hundred and ten B–17's land in one afternoon at Valley Air Base on the Isle of Anglesey. They were coming in at several other bases in the United Kingdom that same afternoon. If even one had been lost en route, that would have been a matter for serious attention clear up to Command Headquarters in Washington. This was October 23, five days after the date on which, in 1941, the North Atlantic had been declared unflyable. As I watched, and remembered the ranks of aircraft I had seen along the Southeastern Route, the endless running up of engines which made the night hideous at Accra, I thought of Jensen, Ragsdale, Arnoldus, and Reichers, and wondered if they had had any idea of what they were starting.

V

THE BARNSTORMERS

IT WAS SAID in the last chapter that an essential of effective supply is flow. Flow requires two basic factors: adequate production and adequate means of transportation. In the first four months of 1942, the United States had neither. Lieutenant General Harold L. George, who as Colonel George succeeded Olds in the Ferrying Command, said once that production was then such a trickle that you stood at the end of the line with a basket, waiting for an article to be produced. Whatever it was, the combat air units in the battle areas were out of it. As soon as it fell into the basket, you hunted up a plane and flew it out. This was the period which veteran pilots of the Command described as "barnstorming."

Two of the Command's B–24's were in Cairo on December 7, one having been retained temporarily by Major General George H. Brett, then Chief of the Air Corps, for his use, the other having just arrived. General Brett took his plane, piloted by Captain Paul F. Davis, to India, up into China, to Singapore, and then to Java. Along with the other of the Ferrying Command's planes on the spot, this ship ran a flying taxi service, moving leaders about during those frantic days, and evacuating assorted personnel at the end from Java to Australia. Its career ended when it was strafed on the ground at Broome, Australia, on March 3.

The surprise attack which caught Captain Davis' B–24 also destroyed another, and in a more tragic manner. This plane had taken off from Bolling Field on December 20 for Australia. After the usual in-and-out services around Java, it reached Darwin January 7, then joined its mates in shuttling back and forth from the southern edge of Australia to assorted points in the East Indies. Like them, it depended upon cloud cover for safety in the air, as it carried only a portion of the usual armament. It landed on fields in Java, only to have to take off immediately to avoid being caught on the ground by raiders. The men went short of sleep, the plane fantastic lengths of time without regular inspection or maintenance. Piloted now by Lieutenant Edson E. Kester, this B–24 took on a load of evacuees at Broome, and had just taken off when the Japanese attacked. Two Zekes jumped it. Among other deficiencies, this B–24 had not been provided with self-sealing tanks. It burst into flames on receiving the first burst of fire, and plunged into the sea. One sergeant survived, having been thrown clear when the plane broke up on hitting the water.

The B–24, piloted by Lieutenant Ben I. Funk, which had landed at Cairo on December 6, was held back by Brigadier General Elmer E. Adler of the Air Section of the U.S. North Africa Mission, until on December 22 the Ferrying Command succeeded in prying it loose and sending it on with a load of 3000 pounds of .50-calibre ammunition to Darwin. They reached their destination before the month was out, and engaged in the kind of services described. On January 23, this plane took off from Darwin with a load of .30-calibre ammunition to be delivered to Del Monte, Mindanao, in the Philippines. There it was to pick up enlisted specialists for evacuation. Lieutenant Theodore J. Boselli was the navigator. Upon him much depended. The available accounts tell only that the Command's B–24 was accompanied by "an LB–30." I have been unable to learn who flew it, or to whom it belonged.

They departed at 4.30 P.M., flying a circuitous route to avoid passing near Japanese-held bases until darkness covered them as they approached the island of Ceram, east of New Guinea. They had been protected by cloud cover until then, thereafter it was clear, but darkness gave them relative safety. Boselli guided them accurately to the field, which was an improvised, grass-covered one, and they landed half an hour after midnight. They took on twenty-five passengers and returned to Darwin, again having darkness as far as Ceram and some clouds there-after. They set down at Darwin at eleven in the morning, un-loaded three of their passengers, then flew on through two violent tropical fronts to Malang in Java. By the time they landed there, the crew must have been exhausted.

Captain Funk and his plane continued, covering the terri-tory between Rangoon and Melbourne, flying General Wavell to Java, and evacuating men and women from Java until the last possible moment.

After the destruction of the other two Ferrying Command aircraft on March 3, the remaining Ferrying Command crews were ordered home. Funk's aircraft remained in Australia. Shortly after he left it, it made another flight to Mindanao. Running out of gas on the return trip, it was ditched in the sea beside an island north of Australia, apparently without fatalities.[1] This was the kind of flying which, of necessity, only the military pilots could undertake, while the airlines under their contracts were straining every effort to initiate the steady transport schedules farther from the scene of action upon which the real solution of the supply problem depended.

Even assuming adequate training and equipment, not all bombers flying overseas could be handled by tactical crews. Aircraft wear out under the hard use of battle conditions, many are shot up. There had to be more aircraft en route and at the fronts than there were crews to fly them, if the crews were to remain continuously active. To meet this need the Ferrying Command began training a special corps of men for overseas ferrying, starting with an original nucleus of thirty-two, for which reason the undertaking was known as "Project 32." This enterprise paid sudden dividends. In May, 1942, the probabil-ity of a major Japanese attack upon Midway Island became known. We were still woefully short of long-range aircraft in the Hawaiian Islands. Beginning on May 22, the Project-32 men were set to flying bombers to Hawaii as fast as they could

[1] In this condensed account I have depended heavily on the excellent description by Major Ben H. Pearse, "Old Bag of Bolts," originally pub-lished in *Air Force* and republished in *Air Force Diary,* James H. Strau-bel, editor, Simon and Schuster, 1947.

be brought to the West Coast. Between then and June 7 they delivered thirty-two B–17's and twenty-six B–26's to Hickam Field on Oahu. Delivering fifty-eight planes in sixteen days, even over the two thousand miles of water between California and Oahu, seems like small potatoes now. At the time it was an achievement which earned the Command a special commendation, and large or small, it was an important element in our victory at Midway. The flight takes about twelve hours; with the shuttles Pan American was running for the Navy and Consairways for the Ferrying Command, the men could return to California the following day. The number of ferry crews available was small — not all the Project-32 men were on hand — so that for them it meant that when they had returned, they were sent out again with the minimum of rest consistent with safety, and sometimes not that.

In the first week in June, military crews flying new, superior B–24D's were placed on the South Atlantic shuttle between Natal and Accra, on regular schedule. A steadily increasing supply of ferry pilots was on hand. In the Pacific the fronts had stabilized. The Command's planes no longer flew frantic, erratic missions. There were yet to be many occasions when, locally, schedules went overboard, there were to be many special and curious undertakings, but the barnstormers had come home.

VI

MEN AND TONNAGE

IN THE FIRST MONTHS of the war, reorganization was going on all through the Army, from its top level division into the three principal branches — Ground Forces, Air Forces, and Services of Supply (later Service Forces) — on down. The Air Corps Ferrying Command, like almost every other major unit, had to build and reorganize itself, and conduct operations, all at the same time.

On December 30, 1941, Colonel Olds established a Domestic and a Foreign Division. Characteristically, he acted first and sought authority later, so that the new arrangement was in effect for some time before it became official. The Foreign Division had charge of transport and ferrying operations from the borders of the United States outwards, except operations to Canada. The Domestic Division's activities were in theory confined to ferrying within the United States and Canada, but the problem of moving pilots around effectively, especially to and from points where there was no commercial air service, soon put it into the transport business in a small way with such miscellaneous aircraft as it could wangle. These tranport activities developed eventually into the "Snafu Airline," a competent, informal organization which many remember with affection.

The Domestic Division was commanded by Lieutenant Colonel William H. Tunner, as he had now become. This was the beginning of the mission which was to lead him to general rank. Major General Tunner played so important a part in the Command's history that it is fitting to stop and take a look at

him. An unusually handsome man, cold in his manner except
with a few intimates, somewhat arrogant, brilliant, competent.
He was the kind of officer whom a junior officer is well advised
to salute when approaching his desk.[1] His loyalty to the organization he commanded was notable, and so was his ability to
maintain the morale of his men. The men of his Division held
themselves to be somewhat apart from and above the rest of
the Command; even after he had been transferred to India and
many of them were scattered into other parts of the organization, they remained Tunner's men. He defended them against
all comers, and was every whit as ready as General Olds to
stand up against higher echelons when the welfare of his command was threatened. Air Transport Command Headquarters
came to look upon him with a mixture of exasperation, admiration, and reliance. They wished he would mend his ways, be
less independent, more willing to conform. Action to realize
this wish was baffled by the frequency with which the non-
conformist proved to be in the right.

Tunner faced a fantastic problem. Aircraft production was
beginning to take on real volume. Foreign ferrying was well
enough, but the big activity in that period was the enormous
domestic movement. Trainers were coming off the lines in
ever larger and larger quantities for the wildly expanding training fields, fighters and bombers for squadrons in the late phases
of their training and getting ready to move towards combat,
others to ports of embarkation and to Montreal for our allies,
and hopefully, soon enough transports for the Ferrying Command itself and what was to become Troop Carrier Command.

No longer could experienced or relatively experienced combat pilots be assigned to ferrying duty. They could not be
spared. The Command's established source of supply was cut

[1] It is curious to note how many high officers ignored this custom when
their minds were on other business. I twice had the privilege of reporting
to General Arnold, and each time went to his office set to dish out my
best salute, but the situation prevented it. The first time, he found
several of us exchanging short-snorter signatures, and promptly joined in.
As for my own Commanding General, General George, every time I
went to his office either he had a cigar in his hand or was otherwise so
engaged that a salute would have been discourteous.

off after Pearl Harbor, and the demands upon the Domestic Division steadily increased.

The Ferrying Command turned to the reservoir of civilian pilots not already flying for the airlines or in other flying essential to defense. In January General Olds moved to recruit women pilots, knowing that here was a potentially valuable source the use of which would not interfere with the recruitment of combat flyers. General Arnold, who was not then enthusiastic about the use of women, stopped the move in response to a protest from Miss Jacqueline Cochran, the famous pilot. Miss Cochran was then about to go to England in connection with the development of ferrying there by women, and felt that no similar activity should be started in the United States unless she were on the scene.[2]

The system for making use of male civilians who, as has already been pointed out, were generally competent to do only rather simple forms of flying, was worked out principally by Colonel Tunner. Fairly stiff minimum standards of skill, experience, and age were worked out. Some knowledge of instrument flying was required. Pilots who met these standards were employed, not at the high-blown salaries paid to the men who flew for the contract carriers, but at a scale comparable to the pay of the officers who flew beside them. Contracts were for six months, renewable for another six months. The civilians then entered into what was in effect in-service training. They began by delivering the most elementary aircraft — primary trainers and liaison planes — which are flown only under contact conditions and in relatively short hops. Between flights they went to school. Steadily they worked their way up until they were performing long-range flights across the continent in the largest types of aircraft.

The men who showed adequate proficiency were then commissioned. Those who could not make the grade were dropped when their contracts expired. The majority of these men were young and all were healthy. The fact that, if dropped by the Command, they were likely shortly to receive the famous greet-

[2] Miss Cochran's forthright letter to General Arnold is on file in the archives of the Air Transport Command.

ings may have stimulated some who otherwise might not have been overeager. Most, however, were not the kind of men who wait for a draft. They wanted in, and they wanted to fly. Service with the Ferrying Command might take them anywhere in the world. Shortage of applicants was not the problem.

Tunner modified his standards for acceptance from time to time in the light of experience. Other branches of the Air Forces thought them too high, and tried to have them modified. With the support of Command headquarters he did not conform. Eventually, his standards were taken over completely as the standards for all "service pilots" — that is, men qualified for flying but not for combat.

By this method over thirteen hundred well-trained pilots were developed and commissioned in the course of 1942, and some seven hundred the following year, through a process of training which also executed a large share of the ferrying. The system was perfected and refined later. Operational Training Units for certain special skills and for crew-blending were set up. Six classes were established, Class I consisting of men qualified to handle single-engine trainers, cargo, and utility (liaison and other such small types) aircraft, Class V those who were qualified on four-engine bombers and transports. The sixth class was Class P, pilots who were competent to fly single-engine pursuits; the special designation was given because skill in this type of flying did not advance a pilot towards handling heavier aircraft.[3] Pilots were also required to secure the rating "i," which meant that they had met the Command's standards in instrument flying. The finished product, Class Vi, could fly anything and was ready for overseas ferrying, or for overseas transport flying side by side with the men drawn from the airlines.

[3] The full list of Classes is:
   I, single-engine trainers, cargo, and utility aircraft.
  II, twin-engine trainers and utility.
 III, twin-engine cargo and medium transports.
 IV, twin-engine medium bombers, heavy transports, attack, and pursuit
     types.
  V, four-engine bombers and transports.
  P, single-engine pursuits (fighters).

When graduates of the military training schools began to be received, it was found necessary to put them through the same course. It is interesting to note that throughout the war the Ferrying Division (as the Domestic Division became) looked with skepticism upon the proficiency of men who had newly received their wings at the Air Corps schools. Later, it was found necessary to put returned combat pilots through a somewhat similar course, much to their disgust. The Air Forces, in turn, drew off a proportion of the highly finished Class V men for such duties as forming a nucleus for long-range B–29 operations.

I have described this system in some detail, because it is an important contribution to the strange art of preparing after war has started. That it could be put into effect at the very beginning of 1942 and continue, not as a makeshift, but as a valuable technique, throughout the war is a tribute to the Domestic Division's commanding officer.

As domestic ferrying was systematized, the Command got on with its foreign operations. The first aircraft delivered to Australia by the Command took off on January 12. In the end of January, General Arnold decided that a route to Alaska along the line of the projected Alcan highway was necessary, both for the defense of Alaska and, should Russia declare war upon Japan, to enable us to swing our bombers into Siberia. We did not then know the Russians as we later learned to. A contract for transport service over the route was made with Northwest Airlines, who got going so fast that their survey plane entered Canada on March 2, before permission had been obtained from the Canadians. They were held up for a day, until General Olds straightened the matter out. By the end of the month Northwest had carried 170 tons of cargo and 258 passengers over the new route, and was operating on schedule.

Ferrying and transport activity over the South Atlantic to Egypt and beyond were building up. The Command had control officers and details of other personnel distributed along the route. General Olds' last activity as commander of the Ferrying Command, in the latter part of March, was a visit to Brazil which had an important bearing upon her decision, shortly thereafter, to permit our armed forces to establish bases within the republic. On his return from that mission occurred his relief from his current assignment and his promotion.

As has already been mentioned, he was succeeded on April 1, 1942, by Colonel Harold Lee George. As the new commander became a general before the end of the month, it is simpler to refer to him as General George from the start. His appointment is an indication of the importance the Commanding General of the Army Air Forces ascribed to the Command. An airman through and through, General George was an important member of the "Billy Mitchell group" who risked their careers to win a true air force for their country. In July of 1941 he was appointed to the key position of Assistant Chief of Air Staff for Plans, and it was in large part under him that the strategic bombardment plan against Germany was worked out. This was a thick book, which lived in a very strong safe until the Eighth Air Force was ready to execute it line by line.

General George is a planner par excellence. More than any of the older officers with whom I had an opportunity to talk, his imagination overleaps all barriers, as if his whole method of thinking were a form of flight. He talks vividly, with a New England gift of pithy, homely expressions and a marked, very pleasant Massachusetts accent. He is small, wiry, good-looking, with a liveliness of face and eye not typically Yankee. In his clothing he is something of a dandy. I do not think that administration is his forte, and I suspect that he needs to be held down occasionally by less inspired subordinates. He is capable of almost incredible hours of hard work — during the war, seven-thirty in the morning to anywhere from six in the evening to midnight was routine — and possesses the art of relaxing quickly when opportunity offers, into humor and good fellowship. He has kept remarkably young physically and mentally, including in the frank and rather naïve pleasure he took in finding himself, as commanding general of the Air Transport Command, a famous man in that famous air force which he and his companions had labored so long and so hopelessly to build.

Even more than his predecessor, General George was conscious of the strategic possibilities of airborne supply. He himself would say that this came of his close relationship with General Arnold. Under his command, emphasis on the development of air transportation increased, and the move towards regular, scheduled service was strengthened.

By the end of April the great routes were all in operation, the Alaskan, Pacific, and North and South Atlantic. The Southeastern Route extended the South Atlantic to Cairo, to the delivery points to the Russians in Persia, and on into India. The latter extension was to meet the needs of the First Ferrying Group, which had been assembled from Ferrying Command personnel and sent to Assam to initiate the famous service over the Himalayas to China. This group was not under the Command, but was assigned to the 10th Air Force.

An important development in improving the whole military air transport picture was the Presidential order under which all but two hundred of the DC–3's in the possession of the airlines were taken over by the military. These could be retained in military service as passenger aircraft or, as was done with most of them, converted into fairly efficient transports, designated by the Army as C–53's. This move alleviated an acute shortage of medium-range transports. The remaining two hundred were what the military calculated would permit the airlines to maintain approximately their present rate of services on all but a few routes which it was more advantageous to close down, simply by more efficient operation. As General Harold H. Harris, himself a Pan American–Grace Airlines man in civilian life, once said, they "squeezed the water out of the airlines." The achievement of the commercial operators in rising to this situation, and showing that in fact they could maintain their traffic, is a magnificent one.[4]

Colonel Haynes took off on the first flight to the United

[4] *Air Transport at War,* cited previously, opens with a dramatic description of President Roosevelt being persuaded, "early in 1943," to tear up an order which empowered the armed services to take over the airlines complete. This authority already existed under the order of December 13, 1941. I do not know what the President may *not* have done in the ensuing months; what he did do was issue the order just described.

Kingdom on July 1, 1941, a few days after that the first plane was ferried domestically. By a year later, the Command had made 13,595 domestic and 632 foreign ferried deliveries — probably more than half of the latter being under its supervision but not by ferry crews. It possessed (as nearly as can be deduced from cloudy and conflicting records) in the neighborhood of one hundred and twenty twin-engine aircraft, principally C–53's. For its transoceanic operations it had four clippers flown by Pan American, the five C–75's being flown by T.W.A., five LB–30's flown by Consairways in the Pacific, five B–24D's with its own crews in the South Atlantic service, and five more B–24's stationed at Bolling Field on call for special missions. Twenty-four heavy aircraft in the Army's transport fleet — the number is pathetic.

Yet it was getting results. Across the North Atlantic it had flown 1588 passengers and 425 tons of goods and mail, across the South Atlantic 3284 passengers and 790 tons. Six hundred and forty-nine passengers and 110 tons had been carried over the Pacific, 691 passengers and 575 tons on the Alaskan route. It already had the capacity to meet an emergency on the other side of the world with the rapid delivery of fairly solid quantities.

As an organization, it was shaking down and acquiring form. From January to the end of June it increased in numbers of officers and men from 1650 to 11,000, not counting the civilians who worked for it in flying or on the ground. Further increases were expected. The Regular Army proportion dwindled accordingly, as it did in every outfit. For this one, a number of top-ranking airlines executives were recruited and commissioned. They were just the talent General George needed to have under him in view of the great changes and developments that were due. As the professional military men and the airlines men educated each other and became blended, they gave the Command efficiency, enterprise, and a unique character.

VII

ONE BASKET

I HAVE SPOKEN BEFORE of the fallacy of divided control of strategic airborne supply. This is fundamental military doctrine, applying to all means of transportation, and to ferrying as well. In respect to ferrying, it was dramatically demonstrated in early 1942 with the opening of the "Bolero movement," which was the delivery of the first elements of the 8th Air Force to Britain.

The route had been developed and opened up by the Ferrying Command. As the initial tactical units made ready to travel over it, it became apparent to Lieutenant Colonel (later Brigadier General) Milton W. Arnold, a young regular army officer who had pioneered the route and had general supervision over it for the Command, that there would be serious trouble if the 8th Air Force retained control over its aircraft while they were in transit. The control of ferrying was a specialized business, and over the crude North Atlantic Route as it then existed especially it called for experts, fully familiar with all the problems and difficulties, and for a single, unified treatment all along the route.

When Colonel Arnold tried to convince the general in charge, he met immediate and violent rejection of any such idea. The general asked him who the hell he thought he was and how he had become such an authority on the abilities of his (the general's) troops. The units went over under 8th Air Force control, there were confusions, delays, and losses of planes, and finally an entire flight of six planes was forced to make crash landings on the Greenland Ice Cap.

The course of events resulted in Colonel Arnold, with the support of General George and Colonel Smith, his Chief of Staff, being allowed to state his case to a joint meeting of the various agencies concerned. He recommended that operational control of the movement be given to the Ferrying Command. The presiding officer, a lieutenant general, took the recommendation badly. Later General Arnold wrote: "His reaction could not have been more violent than if I had suggested that he immediately join the German Air Force. He stated that Army regulations were built about the inviolate prerogatives of the individual commander, consequently the precedent could not be destroyed. I told him I was not interested in Army regulations or how we have done it in the past in the Indian wars, but we must, for safety and efficiency, consolidate the routes."

His own superiors supported the colonel, and convinced General H. H. Arnold that this approach was the only sound one. From that time on, regardless of whose aircraft were crossing the oceans over the Command's routes, they were under the Command's operational control.[1]

The ferrying problem, thus, was straightened out early, but air transport continued to be divided. This resulted in the development of manifold weaknesses.

If the two principal services, the domestic one run by the Air Service Command and the foreign one run by the Ferrying Command, are considered — as occurred — as private enterprises of the Army Air Forces, and the Air Forces determine where they shall run and what they shall carry, it is inevitable that the overseas and domestic air organizations will get more than their share, the ground forces less than they need. Meantime the Navy, with its own private airline, will use its capacity in the same manner. The needs of organizations, rather than of the war, will be served.

Domestic and foreign transportation cannot be profitably

[1] This account is based on "Establishing the Bolero Ferry Route" by Samuel Milner, in *Military Affairs,* pp. 213–222, Winter, 1947, and on a letter from General Milton W. Arnold to Mr. Milner, April 8, 1948. As Technical Sergeant, Mr. Milner was a valuable member of the A.T.C. Historical Staff during the war.

separated. A number of articles are required urgently by various units in various foreign theaters. These articles are manufactured at points in the United States far from each other. If Air Service Command has the final say on domestic air transportation, it will determine which of these requirements shall be met by its limited air capacity, as far as delivering the articles to the ports of aerial embarkation is concerned. Its decision as to priority and as to the time and point of delivery may or may not have been co-ordinated with the foreign transport organization. Regardless of directives from the Joint Chiefs of Staff or other high echelons, real collaboration is always hampered by the weaknesses of human nature manifested in organizational rivalries and jealousies, and by differences of procedure.

Air Service Command was a sort of Air Force Quartermaster and Ordnance Corps, handling supplies, maintenance, and repairs peculiar to the Air Forces. Each of the overseas Air Forces contained its own Air Service Command, of which the central, domestic organization was the parent. Understandably, A.S.C. was inclined to give heed particularly to the requests of its overseas opposite numbers. The Ferrying Command, on the other hand, would often have a different appreciation of relative urgencies, and might well substitute for some of the cargoes flown to its departure points by A.S.C. for rush delivery, others, received by rail, and requested by other agencies — including supplies needed for the maintenance of its own activities. The result was haphazard and inefficient.

It is my own impression, fairly well grounded, I think, that A.S.C. tended strongly to the view that the Air Forces' air transportation was intended primarily for Air Force use, while increasingly as the Ferrying Command developed its philosophy and realized its own potentialities, it moved away from this concept towards the concept of itself as an agency for the service of the whole war effort. These differences of philosophy had historical cause: from the very beginning the Ferrying Command served international clients in its ferrying, and its pre-war transport lines were for the use of much higher levels of government than just the Air Corps. Air Service Command's history was just the opposite.

Divided control of the actual aircraft, furthermore, meant both competition in procurement and a serious loss of flexibility. Aircraft — or railroad cars or trucks or ships — are easily shifted about as may be required, within a single command. As between two major commands, the matter is much more difficult. The War Department could, of course, *order* the Air Forces to jolly well transfer twenty DC–3's from domestic service to India, and Headquarters, Army Air Forces could similarly direct A.S.C. to do so, but this would be an unusual procedure. If a man is good enough to command one of these major units, he is presumably too good to be ordered in that fashion except in an unusual situation. Ordinarily, he is *requested*. The Commanding General of Air Service Command would feel that he was having his teeth pulled out if he had to turn over a lot of equipment to what was, in effect, his rival — and *vice versa*. Whoever was on the losing end would, and did, stall, or comply ungraciously. The DC–3's provided would most certainly not be the pick of those in his possession.

These factors were well recognized in regard to strategic surface transportation, which for the Army was virtually entirely in the hands of the Army Transportation Corps of the Services of Supply, and existed to serve the Army as a whole. There was a good deal of logic in the attempts which occurred up to early June, 1942, by Lieutenant General Brehon Somervelle, who commanded the S.O.S., and was no small operator, to add air transportation to his list. These attempts ran head on into the other principle, established after so many years of struggle, that aviation must be under the control of airmen. Transfer of the transport aircraft to Somervelle's organization would have created more dualisms than it would have eliminated.

In the spring of 1942, long-range military air transportation was a plum that many people desired. The chief rivals were the Air Service and Ferrying Comands. The former had long been in the transport business in a small way through the Air Transport Wing. As the organization charged with assembling, storing, repairing, and forwarding air supplies, it felt that it should legitimately control the aircraft increasing proportions of these supplies should go. Normally, too, it furnished the "housekeeping" troops which manned the bases through which the traffic flowed, although already its rival tended overseas to man its bases entirely with its own personnel, or used bases manned by civilians under contract to it. As the former Maintenance Command, A.S.C. had looked with equanimity on the highly specialized shuttles to Prestwick and Cairo; what was developing as air transportation headed towards the big time was something else again.[2]

General George and his staff saw their Command as intended to serve the whole Army, at the least. Already, in practice it had also carried passengers and goods for the State Department, the War Production Board, and other agencies — even for the Navy. They believed that all air transportation other than tactical should be in a unit devoted solely to that activity, and there was no doubt whatever in their minds as to what unit that should be. Not only should A.S.C. not expand, it should give over the domestic services it was then running.

Army Air Forces had one of its big reorganizations on March 26, 1942. As part of this, a compromise was worked out. The Air Service Command was given the Western Hemisphere, the Ferrying Command the Eastern. The result was waste, duplication, and hard feelings. The old argument about where Iceland belonged came up. A.S.C. flew to Iceland. Ferrying Command flights to the United Kingdom originated in the United States and stopped at bases staffed in whole or in part by its own personnel in Labrador, Greenland, and Iceland en route. Was it a violation for them to drop off passengers and cargo at those stations? Similar situations existed in both directions. Even if a sort of Chinese wall had been set up, with A.S.C.'s

---

[2] Air Corps Maintenance Command became two organizations, Air Service Command, and Air Matériel Command. The latter performed actual procurement, initiated new production, tested and approved new models and devices, and made all contracts, including those for the Ferrying and later Air Transport Commands with the airliners. The Army Air Forces reorganized themselves many times during the war, and these two units merged, separated, and changed names monotonously, in a manner of no interest to this narrative.

aircraft shuttling only inside it, A.C.F.C.'s outside of it, and everything transhipped at meeting points, the latter's aircraft would have had to return continuously to home bases within the United States for overhaul and maintenance. Should they then, wastefully, return and depart empty?

The Ferrying Command did nothing whatever to abate its services between the edge of the United States and points such as Greenland, Brazil, Hawaii, and Alaska. Air Service Command put United and Western Airlines to flying on the Alaskan route, and it slipped in some flights clear across to the United Kingdom. In some areas, as Miami to Natal, A.C.F.C. had going contract operations and A.S.C. simply could not find the aircraft with which to muscle in. Everybody was dissatisfied, and no one more so than General Arnold. After two months' trial of the compromise, he appointed a board to work out a true solution. The board never did present its findings. General Arnold took action by himself.

In this he was undoubtedly affected by a remarkable letter from Mr. J Welch Pogue, the chairman of the Civil Aeronautices Board. Mr. Pogue described the many services which the airlines were then rendering to the armed forces, not only in actual flying, but in training, repair, modification, and overhaul. Already heavy demands had been made upon them for personnel, and conflicting, unco-ordinated requirements of the Army and Navy threatened to bring about a collapse. Further, various organizations were flying on parallel routes. There was no assurance that the most important things were getting preference for transportation. It was likely that aircraft of one organization would fly light or only partly loaded in one direction and return loaded to capacity, while that of another would reverse the process — in short, two aircraft were being neatly made to do the work of one.

The best solution, he pointed out, was to take both Naval and Army air transportation, merge them, and establish them as a separate agency directly under the President. It was hopeless to expect the Navy to consent to such a measure. General Arnold, however, could at least clean his own house.

Mr. Pogue's letter is a brilliant expression of sound doctrine.

The recommendation that air transportation be extracted entirely from the rest of the armed services, of course, was dictated by the then sovereign independence of the Army and Navy, which has now been somewhat reduced. General Arnold received the letter on June 15. On the twentieth he published General Order Number 8, which changed the name of the Air Corps Ferrying Command to Air Transport Command, effective at once, and placed it in charge of all ferrying for the Army, all air transportation for the War Department except that carried out by Troop Carrier agencies, whose rôle is explained below, and the control, operation, and maintenance of bases and routes outside the United States, effective July 1.

With this the air-transport equipment and personnel of the Air Service Command were transferred to the Air Transport Command. Equally important, at least as far as the Air Forces were concerned, the newly reconstituted organization was confirmed in command and operation of the bases, and hence the routes, over which it operated outside the United States. In practice, it had already begun to exercise similar authority over its principal domestic bases. This was a reversal of policy. In 1941, the A.C.F.C. had rejected a similar proposal. As its operations then were, it seemed better to follow the usual procedure of tactical units, which concern themselves principally with flight operations and look to the organizations specializing in ground activities to take care of the airfields and serve their planes. By now it had become clear that the Command required somewhat different procedures and techniques from those used in tactical operations, and further, with cargoes and passengers to be handled, it added to the usual functions various new ones with which the airlines were more familiar than the Army. Hence there was established the unusual arrangement of an operational organization doing its own housekeeping. Following these changes, the Services of Supply turned over their administration of domestic air priorities, and with that bowed out of the aviation picture.

What had happened was more than a mere enlargement of the Ferrying Command. It was the establishment of a powerful concentration of related functions in a single body, and for the first time brought the whole process of moving supplies by air, which had grown up experimentally and haphazardly, into line with proven doctrines. The function thereby ceased to be an interesting airmen's experiment and became a solid part of the Army's logistical equipment.

To meet its new responsibilities, the Air Transport Command organized itself into the Ferrying Division and, to start with, six Foreign Wings, the Caribbean, South Atlantic, and Africa–Middle East, covering the Southeastern Route, the North Atlantic running to the United Kingdom, the Alaskan, and the South Pacific. Originally, it intended to make the Ferrying Division also a Wing, equal to the others, but Command Headquarters reckoned without Colonel Tunner. Olds had established the term "Division" when he divided the old Command into two parts. In military usage the word has two meanings: a field unit consisting ordinarily of 10,000 or more men, generally commanded by a major general, and a principal unit of activity within a headquarters staff, such as the Intelligence Division or Operations Division. As the whole Command contained barely 1600 men when the two Divisions were established, and their chiefs operated as members of the Headquarters staff, it was almost certainly in the latter sense that Olds used the word.

An Air Force wing corresponds to a brigade, one echelon lower than a division, and normally is commanded by a brigadier general. By July, however, Tunner's organization had increased greatly and now, responsible for foreign as well as domestic ferrying, was due to increase yet more. He vigorously protested the "reduction in echelon," largely on grounds of its effect upon the morale of his people, and he made his protests stick.

General Order Number 8 was only an Air Forces order. When it stated that the Air Transport Command was charged with air transportation "for all War Department agencies" the statement might be regarded as self-serving, although it was to some extent supported by a War Department letter of June 6, which generalized that the Ferrying Command was a War Department agency. An Air Force order was in no way binding upon the commanding general of a theater, or in fact upon anyone outside of that portion of the Air Forces which was directly under General Arnold's command.

Unaffected by these developments was the Troop Carrier Command and the overseas Troop Carrier units which stemmed from it. The function of Troop Carrier Command was to organize, equip, and train twin-engine transport units to be assigned to the overseas Air Forces. These formed the *tactical* air transport which served both its own Air Force and its theater. As we all know, their duties included dropping supplies and paratroopers over and behind the front lines, towing gliders for similar use, and a host of dangerous, glorious services. Most properly, this kind of transport medium was placed under the command of the user.

The R.A.F. did, as a matter of fact, carry air transport unification one step further. What corresponded to our Troop Carrier aircraft were the property of the R.A.F. Air Transport Command, they and their crews were turned over to local commanders on a sort of indefinite, revocable loan. The feeling in the A.A.F., as it evolved its doctrines, was that this was undesirable. The two organizations were engaged in importantly different types of flying; they required different training, some differences of equipment, and different operational techniques. It was preferable to keep the two groups separate, and let each perfect its specialty.

So long as the Air Transport Command derived its authority solely from General Order Number 8, there existed another unmended split, at the point where the fundamental doctrine of maintenance of flow of supply clashes with the equally fundamental doctrine of command control, as it was evolved in the United States Army during the First World War.

The essence of the doctrine of command control is that, when a man adjudged competent therefor is assigned to a task, and given the equipment and the men with which to accomplish it, what the Army asks of him is that he does accomplish it. So long as he remains within regulations, how he goes about it is his own affair. If he fails, then there is intervention and heads roll. As a corollary, it follows that within his area of activity a commander controls all units and equipment.

There are obvious limits to the application of this doctrine. In many instances uniform practices have to be established. The lower the level of the unit involved, the more the commander is required to conform and the narrower the area of independence. Nonetheless it does apply all down the line, and its practice produces excellent results. Its success, obviously, depends upon the selection of the right men for the right jobs. It was under this doctrine that General Tunner insisted on doing things in the Ferrying Division in a manner different from that of the rest of the Command, and under it, also, that General George refrained from ordering him to conform.

In the First World War General Pershing succeeded in developing this doctrine, insofar as it applied to commanders of foreign theaters, to a high degree, with the result that at present American commanders of overseas theaters and lesser areas have an unusual independence. This gives full scope to the talents of a MacArthur or an Eisenhower, but in some lesser men it creates the delusion that they are little kings, and that every man or thing which arrives within their territory is theirs, to do with as they choose.

The Commanding General, Army Air Forces, ordinarily directly commanded only those parts of the Air Forces which were within the continental United States. From them, the components of the overseas Air Forces moved overseas, where they came directly under the command of the theater commander. Thus Air Service Command trained and organized the personnel to move to the theater, where if, for instance, they landed in the United Kingdom with the 8th Air Force, they became the 8th Air Service Command, an integral part of that Air Force, which in turn was under General Eisenhower. From the point of view of General Headquarters in Washington, all of these elements are *tactical*. Their assignment to one or another theater is dictated by the grand strategy, but once they arrive, they are at the disposal of the theater commander, for him to employ in accordance with his local plans and situations. From the theater commander's point of view, of course, some of his moves are strategic, others tactical, for in a sense the division between strategy and tactics moves downward with the echelon. To the highest Headquarters, it may be said, these elements have become tactical partly because they are now committed, and except under unusual circumstances cannot any longer be manipulated from the top.

To too many theater and area commanders at times the larger needs of the war as a whole became obscure. The Army Transportation Corps had its trouble with commanders who tried to retain for their own disposition ships which had brought them cargoes. They failed to realize that in holding back a ship, they endangered the continued flow of the things which enabled them to exist. The Air Transport Command and its predecessor had similar experiences. I have already told how General Adler, at Cairo, held back a B–24 which was urgently needed for the relief of the Philippines. His action in holding back that aircraft, and General Brett's more reasonable action in taking the other B–24 then in Cairo to carry him on his own important missions, removed from their proper operation the only two aircraft which might possibly have actually reached General MacArthur. From then on it proved difficult for generals overseas to keep their hooks off the converted bombers and their experienced crews. When ferry pilots brought in combat aircraft, they wanted to keep the pilots. Sometimes they could be made to see that if they did, they would cut off the flow of aircraft; occasionally it took flat orders to make them let go.

This situation became aggravated when the transport routes passed through one theater on the way to another, or penetrated deeply into a theater. The newly constituted Air Transport Command ran its own bases. Here were aircraft passing through, carrying supplies to a recipient further on, when the commander of the nearer area also greatly needed those supplies. Here were units running bases which claimed not to be under his command, and which followed practices unlike those which he had established. Furthermore, he could greatly ease some of his local logistical problems if he could divert, even temporarily, one or two of the increasingly large number of transports which went shuttling through his domain.

Ridiculous and amazing things occurred. One island commander, a cavalry colonel, insisted on taking the ground crews off their duties at the airfield in order to keep them up on their close-order drill and to use them on a project for clearing brush, with the result that transports and ferried ships landed to find no one to fuel or serve them. In North Africa the local Air Service Command, finding that A.T.C. was flying in for its own operations certain supplies of which the Theater's Air Forces were short, kept an enlisted man busy painting out all destination labels as containers were moved to the warehouses it controlled. All supplies were then pooled and issued as the local authorities chose, which was generally not to A.T.C. As the point at which this was done was soon to become an important point for transshipment of supplies to our forces in China and India and to the Chinese, it can be imagined what continuation of this practice would have meant.

In November, 1943, the Command set up a special service known as "Fireball," with through planes from the United States to Assam to deliver greatly needed supplies for the very important air supply-line over the Himalayas to China. The first Fireball plane left the United States on November 17, but not until well into December did any of these planes reach Assam. In normal routing, they stopped at Agra in India to refuel. Agra was a principal base of the 10th Air Service Command. The authorities there simply put armed guards on the aircraft, unloaded them, and pooled the supplies with those of the 10th Air Force. This virtual piracy was accomplished, literally, at the pistol point. I am not given to the use of exclamation points, but I think one is justified here. !

Some of these events, as can be seen, occurred well after the period I am describing. They reflected the narrowness of men's thinking and the tenacity of what might be called "the Pershing concept of command control" with its belief in absolute power over all things within the commander's realm.

Perhaps the most fantastic experience of all was that of Captain Henry Wilder (as he then was) who was sent by A.T.C. Headquarters to make a tour of the Command's bases within a certain Base Command. Through the area involved were passing a very important part of A.T.C.'s ferried aircraft. The Base Commander, a colonel, forced Captain Wilder to destroy his notes, his reason being that no official communication whatsoever could leave his area except through him. Captain Wilder's story resulted in an inspection, which in turn resulted in the colonel's transfer to a mental hospital.

Strategic transportation of any kind must be controlled entirely by the agency which designs the strategy. It must move immune from local interference. It must give to each local commander only that portion of its capacity which is determined by the grand plan. The Commanding General of the Army Air Forces had said that the Air Transport Command was thus and so and should be treated thus and so. His writ did not run in India, on Canton Island, in Greenland. A.T.C. was in need of protection.

Two War Department circulars, one issued September 21, 1942, the second February 26, 1943, provided the needed authorities. After the second circular there could be no doubt but that the Air Transport Command was something unusual in American military history, a major subordinate command based in the Zone of the Interior, operating and establishing its personnel and bases in all theaters under its own, direct command. Depredations upon it might be made, but they were now plainly unlawful. So unusual is such a situation that, not only in the field, but in A.T.C. Headquarters staff officers who dealt with other staffs, even with Air Staff itself, found themselves constantly forced to explain at length the nature of the Command. Later the 20th Air Force, which flew the B–29's, was given similar status, as it was conceived as a high-level strategic striking force which must remain under the highest central control.

The Air Transport Command was now truly the War Department's agency. In fact, although it was a lower echelon of a major subdivision of the Army, it was an agency of the whole government as oriented towards waging war, excepting always the area reserved for the sovereign Navy. As practices became more highly evolved, the Command communicated directly with War Department G–3, the Operations Division of the General Staff, and its relations with Joint Chiefs of Staff became steadily closer. Within the limits imposed by the iron curtain which hung between the Army and the Navy, it met Mr. Pogue's recommendations.

The Command's new status was very fine. Unless it had a counterbalance, so independent an organization might become insensitive to the needs of those it served. A further, closely related step had to be taken. As it was all part of a single process, it may rightly be described here, even though it was not completed for a year or more. The further step was the setting up of the group of procedures which became known as priorities, traffic, and allocations. Administration of these matters became so important that the Air Transport command added to its establishment an entirely new major staff office, Assistant Chief of Staff for Priorities and Traffic, commonly referred to as "P and T." During most of the war this office was headed by Colonel Ray W. Ireland, in civilian life traffic manager for United Airlines. Its higher personnel was a group of able men, many drawn from the airlines, and almost all from civilian life.

As noted, the Command received from S.O.S. the control of priorities upon the airlines, which included all the domestic airlines in their normal operations, and the very small operation of Pan American to Lisbon — which gained in strength when the Command, receiving more suitable aircraft, turned the clippers back to the line. As it now owned all military air transports in strategic service, it obviously controlled the priorities upon them. A decision by Headquarters or, in practice, by lower authority down to the officer in charge of loading, could determine what went by air immediately, what waited its turn.

According to the aircraft that could be scraped together, the state of development of the various routes, and the judgment of numerous authorities — above all of A.T.C. itself — as to relative need, larger or smaller numbers of aircraft, which is to say, greater or lesser "lift," were assigned to the various routes. Early in the game, especially in the case of the Southeastern Route, the same line served several different theaters or major commands: the Southeastern reached to South Atlantic, Central Africa, and Middle East Theaters, Persian Gulf Command, and China-Burma-India Theater.

The proper loading and dispatching of freight and passengers then became a complex matter, to deliver goods at all these points in just proportion and avoid having aircraft traveling over long distances to the farthest ones with nearly empty holds.

Even when theater and other local commanders had learned to keep their fingers off the Command's transports, these other factors gave rise to inefficiency. Among other things they created extremely complicated problems of loading when an aircraft was to deliver to several recipients without having to have its entire load shifted so as to ensure continued balance after it had delivered to the first recipient. There remained also the very human problem, especially at those points where cargoes were unloaded from planes coming in from the United States and reloaded on others bound to farther points, of a sort of high-minded theft of sorely needed articles for local use. The A.T.C.'s own personnel were by no means innocent of this practice. Even after the extremes of raiding which I have already described had been eliminated, this abuse persisted, as stealing between outfits always has. The lack of a sound allocations system made such "borrowing" much easier.

The system devised to remedy these ills was ingenious; it was principally the work of the Priorities and Traffic Division. The routes were considered in their capacity to carry cargo, the "lift," which existed upon each of them. From this point of view they were divided into "channels," each channel being the route considered as reaching only to a single recipient, or the lift allocated to that recipient.

The establishment of channels was a technical preliminary. Near the end of each month, Priorities and Traffic advised G–3 of the General Staff the lift or capacity that would be available in all quarters for the second month following, and of the amount of traffic the various routes could handle. Against this information, G–3 balanced the asserted needs of the various overseas commanders as communicated directly to it, in the light of its own appraisal of these needs (it would be indeed an unusual commander who asked for too little), and above all in the light of the grand strategic plan. It then advised both A.T.C. and the commanders what tonnage was allocated to each recipient for the month after next. In the lower head-quarters, P. and T. and Operations together translated this in terms of channel capacity and the assignment of aircraft to the routes.

Of the tonnage allocated to a given recipient, fifteen per cent, called "the reserve band," was held back for cargoes and passen-gers moving on priorities issued by very high domestic author-ities such as the War and State Departments, and for the Com-mand's own requirements. Later this portion was reduced to the neighborhood of five per cent. The remainder was entire-ly at the disposal of the overseas commander, who was, after all, the best judge of what he wanted in a hurry. It was he who assigned the priorities on goods to be delivered to him by air.

It will be seen that this system fits into both the doctrine of command control, and the doctrine of single, central control of the transport medium. Not the aircraft themselves, but their capacity was put at the disposal of the man responsible for the job at the end of the line, and it was entirely up to him to use it wisely.

Some of the theaters and commands got into trouble through lack of understanding of the system. Having ordered quan-tities of matériel on the usual Number Three Priority and the lowest, Number Four, a new need would arise which would cause them to superimpose Twos, and much more rarely, Ones. The special nature of a Number One Priority was generally recognized, and it was not often abused.[3] Under the channel

[3] During the war a great deal of bunk was published in ignorance, concerning the assignment of priorities to passengers. There was a wide-spread belief that priorities went by rank, which was not true. I have known valuable enlisted men to receive higher priorities than minor gen-erals. The prime criterion was urgency. A general officer's time is sup-posed to be valuable, and there was a reasonable enough tendency to give them Number Two priorities, in order to avoid having them wasting their time waiting their turns at junction points. Number One was sometimes referred to as a "White House" priority, because it was pretty much routine, for obvious reasons, to give that rating to emissaries of the President.

system, if the commanding general at Cairo set up a large shipment on Number Two Priority, this did not mean that the
flow of Three shipments to, say, India was interrupted. It
meant that the flow of Three supplies for Cairo was held back.
Had the precedence of cargoes according to priority not been
confined strictly within each channel, it would have been possible for commanders to rob each other of capacity by assigning inflated priorities. One of the functions of the reserve band
was to take care of situations which required sudden shipments
when allocations had been used up.

When a commander superimposed priorities too freely, backlogs of lower-priority cargoes piled up. At times these backlogs
became so large that it was actually quicker to ship goods by
boat than to hold them until they could be moved by air. To
eliminate this trouble, the Air Transport Command sent out
selected officers from P. and T., who were assigned to the
theater Priorities Boards. Their expert knowledge ended the
abuses of misunderstanding. This measure, one might say, completed the circle of General Staff-theaters-Air Transport Command. With this final touch the system operated smoothly
and effectively. True strategic air transport had come into
existence.[4]

The ideal situation would be for the operational agency to
be able to shift the greater part of its lift to any portion of the
globe at the behest of the General Staff, in case a sudden, critical situation had to be met. In practice this was not possible.
Routes are limited in the amount of traffic they can handle by
the adequacy of their communications systems, the number of
aircraft that can be accommodated on a given base at one time,
the supplies and fuel stockpiled along them, and various other

[4] Late in the war, a joint A.T.C.–N.A.T.S. committee suggested a further improvement. They claimed that G–3 and the corresponding Naval
authority were not able to judge the correctness of the "asserted needs"
of overseas commanders closely enough. Usually these assertions were too
large, but sometimes the central authority erred in disallowing requests
which should have been granted. They recommended that representatives
of the General Staff be stationed at the various overseas headquarters, to
report to Washington, from first-hand knowledge, their estimate of what
portion of the theater commanders' request should be granted.

factors. Limitations of runways may also prevent the use of the larger types of aircraft. These factors restrict flexibility considerably.

Even more important was the variety of the aircraft themselves. Of necessity, the Air Transport Command placed twin-engine transports on those portions of routes on which the bases could be relatively close together, which was mostly over land, reserving the heavy transports in the main for the flights over large bodies of water. Thus the service to Alaska was conducted entirely with twin-engine transports until late in the war, whereas across the Pacific only four-engine equipment would serve. In a great emergency the Pacific lift could be swung into Alaska, provided adequate runways were available, but the reverse could not be done. The bulk of the aircraft flying between the United States and Brazil, and again from the Gold Coast of Africa all the way across to India and China, were twin-engine, imposing similar limitations on flexibility. Decreasing the lift along one route, then, and increasing it along another, meant many headaches. Fortunately the general strategic pattern established at the beginning of the war held throughout. Not until after the defeat of Germany was it necessary to contemplate shifting a large lift capacity from one side of the world to the other. Had it not been so, there would have been many more gray hairs than were actually developed in P. and T.

In an emergency, aircraft can be flown into and out of fields which would ordinarily be regarded as impossible. This was demonstrated many times by Ferrying Command and A.T.C. and above all, magnificently, by Troop Carrier pilots. The prime requisite for a strategic air-transport system flexible enough to meet the sudden situations of modern war, wherever they may arise, is the possession of a fleet of military transports capable of crossing any ocean.

It is an interesting commentary on men's minds that it took at least eighteen months after the beginning of hostilities for the practices and the organization for air transportation described in this chapter to come into being, whereas in ferrying their major elements existed from the start. Where the special case of the movement of a major tactical unit brought up the conflicting doctrine of command control, the one experience of the Bolero movement settled the conflict once and for all. Ferrying simply got started right.

From the beginning ferrying was handled by a single agency. Every overseas commander cried constantly for aircraft, but the central authority decided who got them. Essential control was always where it belonged; the Ferrying Command operated as the agent of the top authority from the outset. When intermediate commanders did attempt to divert ferried aircraft destined for a more distant recipient, they were opposing, not the Command nor the Army Air Forces, but the War Department. In this case correct practices were established so naturally that the practitioners were hardly aware of them.

VIII

THE BIG GAMBLE

THE FORMATIVE PERIOD of which the key date is that of the establishment of the Air Transport Command was marked by new contracts with the airlines. It was at this time that contracts for flying specific routes were replaced by the broader ones under which the lines agreed to serve wherever they were asked to. More and more contracts were added as time went on, until before the fighting ended there was no line worth mentioning which was not included in the war. Pan American, Northeast, Northwest, Consairways, American, Braniff, Eastern, Pan American-Grace, T.W.A., United, and Western went into foreign operations. In domestic flying many of these, as well as All American, Chicago and Southern, Colonial, Continental, Delta, Inland, Mid-Continent, National, Penn Central, and Southwest were under contract until domestic air transportation was made purely military. The broad wording of the contracts made the lines truly an arm of the Air Forces. It was, as I have mentioned, the policy to avoid asking the contract carriers to go into active combat areas, but that policy was not always followed, nor is combat the only danger airmen must face.

Putting the hitherto domestic airlines into overseas operations was not entirely to Pan American's liking. In Latin America there were some small, independent lines of a somewhat barn-storming nature, many using outmoded equipment such as Ford tri-motor planes; apart from these, as has been told, Pan American had a virtual monopoly of experience in foreign operations. Its Clipper captains were a select group of famous men. The developments of 1941 and very early 1942 had tended to strengthen the company's position as the one civilian instrument both for crossing the oceans and for building airways and maintaining services in strange lands. The company had built up a definite mystique about running airlines overseas, as if this were something which only a gifted few could undertake. It had also become the one American company with which many foreign nations were acquainted and with which they were accustomed to dealing. It had extensive diplomatic experience, and at times was better able than the State Department to conclude delicate negotiations regarding aviation with certain nations.

The Command's policy broke through the mystique and the monopoly, until at the end of the war not one, but eleven lines were well experienced in the field and eager to continue on a commercial basis. In co-operation with the Civil Aeronautics Authority, towards the end of hostilities and thereafter it was A.T.C.'s policy, where military requirements permitted, to have the contract lines fly those routes over which they hoped to run their peacetime, commercial services, in order to allow them to become familiar with the routes. The impact of all this upon the original firm was obviously heavy. It must have been an important factor in leading it to make its famous "single chosen instrument" proposal. The freeing of so many lines from domestic limitations and the attendant extensive training given them in operating with four-engine aircraft was a contribution of the first importance to the advancement of the air age.

At the time when the Ferrying Command emerged as the Air Transport Command, it was all very well to make contracts or issue letters of intent, but the contracts were valueless without aircraft, just as, in the transport field, the Command itself was shackled. The Army Air Forces were engaged in a great gamble. *Not one of the aircraft types with which they planned to develop a great transport system had yet come off a production line.*

The Air Forces as a whole, including the Air Transport Command, agreed with the War Production Board in discounting the well-established Douglas DC–3. It was, they believed, too slow, too limited in range, too small, and too low in its ratio of ton-mileage to gasoline consumed.[1] In an understandable, but erroneous, emphasis on combat aircraft in preference to anything else, for a brief, dark time before the war, production of these invaluable craft was stopped entirely. It must be remembered that from the point of view of manufacture, all major aircraft are in competition, not only for materials, but for the many, complicated, expensive accessories such as altimeters and gyro-compasses, the bewildering array of gauges and indicators which makes up the ordinary instrument panel. Everything was short before the war. Until they grasped the idea that one heavy transport shuttling between San Francisco and Brisbane might mean a dozen B–24's in action that would otherwise be grounded for lack of parts, combat airmen naturally wanted transport production stopped.

On two occasions in 1942 the War Production Board urged that DC–3 production again be stopped, and Air Staff concurred. Each time the day was saved by Troop Carrier Command, which insisted on having a large supply of proven aircraft, planes which it *knew* could stand up under varied conditions, give steady performance, and take off from and land on primitive, front-line air strips. It might be that some of the new models soon to be available could do everything the C–47, the military cargo model of the DC–3, could do and fly rings around it into the bargain — on paper. That was all very well, but until there were hundreds of them on hand and their performance had been proven, the paratroopers and airborne troops and the front-line supplies would travel in C–47's.

As told in Chapter VI, on July 1, 1942, the Air Transport Command possessed just twenty-four long-range transports, of which none was satisfactory. The C–75's, the Boeing Stratoliners, were slow, carried too little payload — only 4300 pounds as against an LB–30's 9650 or a Clipper's 12,200 over a range of 2400 miles — and when fully loaded and carrying its full supply of fuel for a long flight, could not gain sufficient altitude.

[1] The ton-mile, that is one ton flown for one mile, is the standard unit for measuring work done, and by far the truest measure of achievement.

The Clippers had great carrying capacity, but they were excessively slow — cruising at 140 miles per hour — and being seaplanes were limited as to their use. The most nearly satisfactory were the converted bombers, which had range, speed, and lift, but even these were makeshifts. All types were regarded as temporary equipment with which to make do until the real transports came along.

In the nineteen-thirties Douglas built a four-engine aircraft capable of carrying fifty passengers. After a year of testing he realized that he had been over-ambitious. The plane was unsafe. He sold it to the Japanese, who probably figured that they could load a lot more than fifty of their people on it. It crashed in 1939, eliminating numerous Nips.[2] Douglas went back to his drawing board and redesigned the plane with a lesser capacity. The first of this model, the now famous DC–4, the Army's C–54, was expected to be ready some time in July.

Also before the war, Curtiss-Wright had built a single, hand-tooled model of a large, fast, powerful twin-engine transport, which was purchased by the British and successfully flown in commercial operation. With the knowledge gained from the performance of this model, improvements were made, and Curtiss went ahead with small-scale production at their St. Louis plant. The company was following the standard procedure of developing a few aircraft for thorough testing before moving into wholesale manufacture of the type. At the instance of the Air Forces, the planes in construction were extensively remodelled for combat use, bucket seats along the walls replacing passenger seats, the floors made heavy and strong, sound-proofing and other unnecessary sources of weight removed, and jump equipment installed. (The C–47 is a similarly altered model of the DC–3.) The first of these aircraft, the Curtiss Commandos or C–46's, were likewise expected in July.

From its extensive experience in modifying B–24's for transport use, Consolidated Aircraft worked out a new model, to

---

[2] In a state of apparent confusion, Drew Pearson in 1945 described this deal as virtual betrayal of his country by Douglas in selling the Japanese the prototype of a new, powerful bomber.

be built for that purpose from the start. As the company was already working to capacity manufacturing B–24's and PBY's ("Catalina" seaplanes for the Navy), it was a significant victory for the proponents of air transportation when the company was given permission to devote a part of its facilities to the new transport. These were expected to start coming off the line in September. Externally, and from the flyer's point of view, they were the same as the B–24's, and could be regarded as an already partially tested model. This plane was known as the C–87 or, uninspiredly, the Liberator Express.

Lockheed, producer of the P–38 and of the Lodestar, a neat, fast little transport, was at work on the famous Constellation, or C–69, a four-engine airliner which promised to be faster, easier to manoeuvre, and to have more lift than anything then being made. It was expected that C–69's would be available in early 1943, and that they would become the principal type in the Army's whole fleet.

In addition to these four types, the Air Forces were planning on a number of twin-engine planes built of plywood and other non-critical materials. There is no need to bother the reader with a description of these.

If a civil airline should want to start operating with an unproved model, the Civil Aeronautics Board would not permit it to do so. Normally an airline will not commit itself to a given type until it has been thoroughly and elaborately tested, sometimes by a year or more of flying. The first of a type accepted by the Army or the Navy has "X" (for "experimental") prefixed to its symbol. A few of these will be so accepted, for thorough flight-testing. Usually the Army suggests changes and improvements. When the testers are satisfied with, for example, the XB–29, some more are purchased, and designated YB–29's. These get a further workout, as much as possible under the same conditions as those under which they will be used in war. Then, and only then, is the manufacturer told to get his production line going. Many a hopeful type never gets beyond the "X" stage.

Of the coming transports, only Consolidated's C–87 could be regarded as in any way tested. This was the type in which Air

Staff and the Air Transport Command was least interested. As I have already told, they were in favor of having production of the DC–3's stopped. Air Staff knew its business. The staff of the Air Transport Command was an impressive galaxy of airline and military talent. I have often wondered what possessed these men, with all their wisdom and experience, to go overboard so completely on a string of aircraft about which nobody knew anything. This was no matter of the "military mind"; the former top airlines executives in uniform committed themselves just as deeply, and the civilian War Production Board went farthest of all.

Nothing ever came of the minor twin-engine types, except for one unfortunate and curious-looking number which used to hang disconsolately around the Washington Airport. This plane had every desirable characteristic, it was far in advance of those we used during the war, only, unfortunately, with a full load of gasoline its payload was fifty pounds.

In effect, the C–69 was also shelved. Once the C–54 had proven itself, and the very first two or three C–69's built showed, under testing, that more work was needed upon them, it was thought better to have Lockheed concentrate on more and better P–38's and other combat aircraft. At the end of the war the Air Transport Command had half a dozen Constellations, but none had been taken into its regular operations.

The first C–46's turned out to be full of bugs. At the urging of the Army, Curtiss had transferred production from their St. Louis plant, which was designed for small-scale, careful manufacture of new types, to its main production line before the model was ready or the engineers trained. The first seventy-five produced were so unsafe that they had to be sent back to the factory for major modifications. At one time Colonel (later General) Lawrence G. Fritz, formerly of T.W.A., then Assistant Chief of Staff for Operations in A.T.C., wanted all C–46's grounded until they could be remodelled. Modification piled on modification until they numbered one hundred and fifty. The plane was faster, bigger, more efficient than the DC–3. Pilots either hated or loved it — most hated it. It got a bad name, and the name stuck. In Africa men called it "fourteen hundred rivets flying in loose formation." Curtiss-Wright's life was made miserable.

The C–46A was a little better than the C–46, the C–46B still better, and along about the time that the C–46D was coming up in early 1944, the type was at the stage when under normal circumstances it would have been accepted as a "Y" model. The whole situation was grossly unfair to Curtiss. That corporation was pushed into premature production by the men who could not wait to get rid of those old-fashioned DC–3's. As a result the plane got a bad name which it could not hope to live down. Yet both the Army and the Navy accomplished things with it that could not have been done with any other, and it was the plane par excellence for the hardest service of all, over the Hump to China. In 1945 Curtiss produced the C–46G, which is a honey. By then the Army had stopped buying C–46's.

Early in 1943 the Air Transport Command's planners figured on getting 641 C–46's in that year, and on eliminating DC–3's entirely. At the peak of operations, just after V–J day, it had 621 DC–3's and 462 C–46's. By April, 1946, as its activities settled to the peacetime scale, it was using 397 of the older type and only 5 C–46's. Had the Command not been able to receive a steadily increasing supply of the Douglas transports throughout the first full year under its new name and enlarged mission, its twin-engine operations would have been impossible. The skepticism of Troop Carrier Command had saved our bacon. And it was with the same, reliable old DC–3's that the Berlin air lift was opened and maintained for months.

By the grace of God, the C–54's and C–87's lived up to expectations. With them, the C–47's, and for all their faults, the C–46's, the great air movements of supply and troops became possible.

In a sense all of our military transports were makeshifts. With the exception of the C–87, they were all originally designed to carry passengers. Following the general trend of aircraft design of the period, the wings were low, sprouting from almost the bottom of the fuselage, which meant that the whole body of the plane had to be set high above the ground so that the propellers could turn. Doors were in the sides of the air-craft, and as they were single-tailed, it was impossible to cut a door in the rear end. All loading had to be done by some means of hoisting, and the side doors limited the size of the articles that could be put on board. These disadvantages meant thousands of dollars in hoisting machinery and a waste of mil-lions of man-hours.

They could have had a more serious consequence. When A.T.C. and the Naval Air Transport Service began operating into Okinawa, the field they used was constantly under attack. It was essential, therefore, that their aircraft, big, fat trans-ports which made very tempting targets, get in, unload their supplies, load the wounded on board, and set out without delay. In practice they achieved the remarkable "turnaround time" of forty-five minutes. Doing so depended on a "fork lift," which may be crudely described as a mobile freight ele-vator. Of these A.T.C. had flown in one, N.A.T.S. for some reason, none. That single, overworked fork lift might be con-sidered the key to the entire operation. Had anything hap-pened to it, so that unloading had to be performed by hand, transports would unquestionably have been lost. As it was, if a Navy R5D was on the deck at the same time that an Army C–54 had come in,[3] one of them had to wait until the other was through with the lift, thus doubling its chances of being potted.

The C–87 was originally designed as a bomber. It happened that Consolidated not only built an unusually rugged aero-plane, with long range and great lifting power, but that they gave it high wings and a twin tail. The high wings meant that the fuselage set low to the ground, eliminating hoisting. A door was cut in the tail between the two sets of rudders and stabil-izers, so that very long objects could be loaded on board. Apart from being a rather fatiguing plane to fly, the C–87's chief fault lay in the fact that its fuselage, bomber-style, was too small in diameter. The plane was actually capable of lifting more cargo than there was room to put on board.

[3] There are times when communication between the services can be carried on only through interpreters.

new wildernesses for the fighting men. They worked in every
variety of climate, under every imaginable discomfort, with
little in the way of equipment and with vast ingenuity, cloaked
by secrecy then, forgotten later, lonely, weary, exposed to all
the world's ills from those of the Arctic to those of the Equa-
torial jungles, and always game. They were exasperated by the
unreality of some of the directions they received from Headquarters; they sometimes exasperated desperately busy men in
Headquarters, trying to juggle the four corners of the world,
by their irregularities. The books did not apply, so they threw
them away. It could happen that, as they progressed from trial
to error to knowledge, what began as a courageous violation
of a regulation ended as standard operating procedure, or-
dained by regulation.

The Command grew steadily. In January it had counted
1650 men, in July, a little more than a year after those eight
officers had been assembled, 13,676, by the end of 1942, 47,000.
The very rate of expansion was, and remained almost to the
end, a fertile source of problems.

The development of its routes also increased. In the summer of 1942, the Southeastern Route bulked largest in the
story, serving as it did as the supply line for the Middle East,
Russia, India, and China. One of General Old's last important
decisions before he relinquished his command had an important effect upon the usefulness of this route. This was when,
after a survey made in December, 1941, by Lieutenant Colonel
Philip G. Kemp of the Ferrying Command, he determined
that it would be well worth while to undertake the supposedly
impossible task of creating an air base on Ascension Island,
that lonely dot in the South Atlantic. The work was done by
the 38th Engineers, famous for many achievements, but for
none greater than this. Ascension is a depressingly hostile, bar-
ren mountain, bare of vegetation except on its cloud-wrapped
top, virtually waterless, finely free of level ground. The lower
part of its looks rather as if a large mountain from the edge
of the Mojave Desert had been picked up and stuck in the
middle of the ocean. The 38th Engineers landed on Ascension
Island on March 30, 1942. On July 10, Captain William N.

Vickers set his converted B–24 down on the runway, on the 13th work was officially finished.

Ascension Island is not an easy spot for navigators to find. There is not a check-point for a thousand miles, nothing but empty water, or empty-looking water from which a German submarine might emerge, its anti-aircraft guns blazing. Perhaps stimulated by the dire consequences of failure, navigators were very successful in finding it. Placement of a base there meant a great increase in the value of the route. Light bombers, such as the A–20's which were greatly in demand by the Russians, could now make the crossing. It became much safer for heavier planes. A shorter hop and refuelling point, lessening the heavy load of gas, not only meant safer flying for ferried aircraft but increased payloads for transports. For a time it was one of the world's busiest stations. The island is virtually abandoned now. The wideawake terns, which constitute its principal population and for which the field was named, are seldom disturbed.

Greater ease and capacity across the oceans was not the only concern. Overland, where DC–3's would serve, it was possible to develop more lift than the trans-oceanic services could then supply, the difference being made up by surface vessels whose cargoes were picked up at the edge of Africa and flown on from there. With the route to Cairo getting into good shape, short-range aircraft such as the P–40's of the early war could be dispatched after being brought to the coast by boat.

At the moment that the Ferrying Command became the Air Transport Command, General Rommel was at the edge of Cairo. The British Imperial troops were holding desperately. Rommel had paused to set his forces for the final attack, which was expected hourly. On the night of the second of July an R.A.F. officer visited Colonel Macauley, the Command's liaison officer at Heliopolis Field outside Cairo, and told him that the British had run out of anti-tank shell fuses, which meant that they would be almost helpless when the German attack was launched. A shipload of fuses was then being unloaded at Lagos, 3100 miles away. Could the Command fly some of it in?

Macauley radioed the base at Accra, where Colonels Byerly and Kemp (the latter the same who surveyed Ascension Island) represented A.T.C. with Messrs. Kraigher and Khristopherson of Pan American as their opposite numbers. (These gentlemen ended the war as colonels in A.T.C.) The message reached the officers between one-thirty and two o'clock in the morning. They called the Pan American men out of bed, and all set to immediately. As fast as the Pan Am–African planes came in at Accra, they were unloaded and refuelled. The urgent situation was explained to the pilots. Most of them were looking forward to a well-earned sleep, and fuses, which explode so easily, are the kind of cargo pilots prefer not to fly, but there was no hesitation on the part of any of them. The first plane took off at four in the morning, landing at Lagos at six, to be followed during the day by six others.

At a few minutes before four in the afternoon of July 4, the pilot of the first DC–3 was calling Heliopolis tower for permission to land. Colonel Macauley telephoned the R.A.F. officer.

"The first load of fuses is coming in now. Do you want us to fly them to the front?"

"I say, old man, that really isn't funny. This is no time for spoofing."

The American convinced him that he was telling the truth. By that time a second transport was over the field. As the front lines were near, and there were no suitable runways, it was decided to unload the planes at Heliopolis and run the fuses out in lorries. In the course of the following hours, fifteen tons of fuses were brought in. They were delivered to the front, the gunners armed their shells and loaded their anti-tank guns, almost as the Germans moved to the attack. Rommel was thrown back, in no small part because of the fast action of the Command's soldier-civilian team.[1]

[1] In the early days, records were often poorly kept. So many events piled on top of earlier ones that memories faded. This movement of fuses has been widely confused with another, of tank shells, which occurred shortly thereafter. In that movement, two rush cargoes of shells were flown from Ohio to Egypt by the *R.A.F.* Air Transport Command in LB–30's. The American A.T.C. followed up with several plane-loads

The fuse delivery was a good example, on a moderate scale, of the emergency value of an established, going military airline. At that stage of a battle, tactical transports, the Troop Carrier type, would have their combat rôles assigned and be assembled accordingly, if not actually committed. To have used them to fetch the fuses would have meant taking them out of the tactical picture for several days, and would also have meant a fatal loss of time in getting them to Lagos. They would, further, not have been familiar with the route. The A.T.C. men tore up the timetables, but they worked within the pattern of familiar operations. On a strategic supply line, air lift was ready. Ordinarily it was, one might say, dispersed, only a portion of the aircraft travelling over the line on one day, in keeping with the schedules, but it could readily be concentrated.

There was seldom a time when the Air Transport Command was taking on only one new expansion. It generally managed to keep three hands busy. In September, 1942, United Airlines began contract flights alongside Consairways to Australia, using the new C–54's. That service was materially increased. Preparations were going forward for a large ferry service and possibly a transport service to Russia via Alaska, and important steps were being taken towards a complete revamping of the Pacific route.

Reaching in the opposite direction, the Air Transport Command took off another large bite. I have mentioned that the Ferrying Command furnished the First Ferrying Group for transport operations from India to China under the 10th Air Force, and later delivered additional aircraft and supplies to the group. The Command followed the group's activities with interest, increasingly so as the doctrine of single control of such activities became more clearly grasped.

delivered at leisure. A year or so later authorities in Headquarters, A.T.C. quite innocently deceived the *March of Time* into dramatizing a movement of fuses from the U.S. to Cairo which never occurred. The distorted tale is now firmly fixed in our Air Force's folklore, denying the R.A.F. deserved credit for a very fast piece of work. They got the shells to Cairo within four days after Cairo wired the request. For the account of the delivery of fuses I am indebted to Colonels Byerly and Kemp.

The attempt to supply China by air was undertaken at the direction of President Roosevelt. It was clear in February, 1942, that the Burma Road would almost surely be cut off. It was hoped that the British Imperial troops, plus Stilwell and what Chinese-American forces he then had, could hold the upper end of Burma with the strategic town of Myitkyina.[2] From Myitkyina a natural route led to China, passing west of the high part of the Himalayas. Its practicability is shown by the fact that P–40's were ferried to the Flying Tigers this way. China National Aviation Corporation's DC–3's and DC–2's had flown it, as had one of the Ferrying Command's B–24's.

Work on Myitkyina's air field was rushed, but the Japanese overran it early in May, before it was completed. The Ferrying Group, on arriving in India, found itself faced with the appalling task of carrying cargoes from the steaming Assam Valley, over a series of subordinate mountain ranges to the main ridge of the Himalayas, the famous "Hump," at a comparatively low section reaching only to 18,000 feet, with a 16,000-foot pass. Once the Hump was crossed, there was a fairly rapid let-down to the hand-made Chinese airfield at Kunming. The route had everything the matter with it; it was the most unflyable one over which it was ever proposed to establish regular, comparatively massive, scheduled service.

Although production of DC–3's in the first three quarters of 1942 increased steadily, there were never enough to go round, and competition for them was severe. The new production was in the model known as C–47's, intended for military use, capable of handling relatively heavy cargoes, built without any unnecessary conveniences. The Troop Carrier Commands had first call on these. Other units got mostly C–53's, passenger aircraft taken from the airlines and modified for cargo carrying, but less rugged and capable of less lift. A small number of DC–3's, mostly in the latter model, were delivered to C.N.A.C. and the First Ferrying Group.

The operation started as a trickle. In April and May, the

[2] Pronounced, I believe, "Mich'inaw." In a moment of intense weariness, an A.T.C. staff officer remarked, "A word to the wise is sufficient, but two y's to the word is a superfluity of naughtiness."

first two months of the traffic, the group delivered 196 tons,
C.N.A.C. 112. In June, with the coming of the monsoons,
the military delivered 29.6 tons, C.N.A.C. none. Slowly volume picked up until in November, when flying weather was
good, the group flew 819 tons into China, the airline 316.

The civilian organization's apparently poor showing was not
due to inability on its part, but to a change of policy of significance to developing air transport in general. In August,
highly placed observers proposed that, since the airline had
such long experience, it should be placed in charge of the
Hump operation, the aircraft turned over to it, and that the
military should operate under the airline's general direction.

General Stilwell, who was more interested than any other
American in getting supplies over the Hump, answered in
emphatic terms. He said that it would be unfair and bad practice to put civilians, who were not subject to military discipline,
over Army pilots who were liable to greater dangers for much
less pay. Adequately regular operations by the civilian airline could not be assured unless it was placed under military
control — the reverse situation. Also, without such control, it
was impossible to keep the line from being forced by Chinese
officials to waste priceless capacity flying in goods for profitable
resale, and it was similarly impossible to keep the planes from
being diverted to highly paid missions inside China. In his
opinion the only way to secure adequate use of the available
lift into China was to keep the operation as purely military as
possible, and to place C.N.A.C. under a firm contract to the
United States Army. Chiang Kai-shek's consent to this plan
was shortly won, and C.N.A.C. put under contract. Thereafter
the line sat at the second table so far as receiving new aircraft
was concerned.

This occurrence must not be interpreted as detracting from
the honor due to a group of pilots, among the most skilled and
adventurous in the world, who flew splendidly over the world's
worst route throughout the war. Difficulties are bound to
occur when a firm still thinking in terms of commercial operation is affiliated with the military, and in this case there was
the special, powerful element of the unconquerable selfishness
of many Chinese officials.

The military themselves were hampered by a problem which brings us back to basic doctrine. The First Ferrying Group had been incorporated in the 10th Air Force, although with a special, separate mission established by the President and re-emphasized by General Marshall and General Arnold. The top staff of the 10th Air Force thought in old terms. These were its planes and men, a transport capacity which was woefully needed in many directions. Spare parts and supplies, also greatly needed all around, were coming in from the United States. The 10th Air Service Command pooled all of these, since they were all consigned to the one Air Force, with the result that the group went short. The Air Force itself frequently diverted the planes to missions supporting its primary concern, which was the defence of India.

In view of the very limited tonnage which it was then thought could be carried over the Hump, it was necessary to select those articles which would have the greatest effect in small quantities. These were air-corps supplies and gasoline to keep General Chennault's 14th Air Force in operation. Thus the maintenance of strategic supplies to one Air Force was made the responsibility of the commanding general of another, who was preoccupied with his own grave problems, including tactical supply. In human nature it was inevitable that the effectiveness of the group should be reduced by diversions.

Add to these factors the dangers of the forbidding route, the loss of planes in flight, enemy interception, foul living conditions, sickness, heat, lack of personnel, and the absence of all those amenities with which a benevolent nation is supposed to shower its troops oversea, and one wonders with admiration why the men did not give up. Far from it, they struggled to their utmost.

The Air Transport Command was fully cognizant of what was happening. What it did not realize, from lack of direct contact with the flyers, was the inherent difficulties of the operation in itself. In October, 1942, it submitted a memorandum to General Arnold, which was in effect a statement of general doctrine in respect to a specific situation. The memorandum stated that the India-China service was failing for "lack of singleness of purpose" on the part of those in charge of it. Further, those in charge were not familiar with this type of operation. In every way the efficiency of the undertaking would be increased if it were placed under the existing air transport organization, with its single line of command, special experience, and wide resources. Granted a certain number of additional aircraft, including some of the new C–87's, the Command undertook to deliver 2500 tons in February, with continuing increases thereafter to what it believed was a conservative estimate of 5000 tons a month. The estimates were excessive, and later returned to plague the Command.

General Arnold passed the proposal to the General Staff, which approved it. To command the new activity, A.T.C. secured from General Stilwell the services of Colonel Edward H. Alexander, who as Major Alexander had been the Ferrying Command's Executive Officer. On the 1st of December, 1942, he activated the India-China Wing of the Air Transport Command at Chabua, Assam. With this the Command inherited an operation which had killed men, wrecked planes, and cost one general officer his stars.

The problem of relations between the Army and C.N.A.C. was only an example of the larger one between the Army and the contract carriers generally, which were worked out and stabilized during this period. The question of what these relations should have been was debated all through the war, and will be debated for many years to come. A great cause of irritation to many of the military was the very high pay, utterly beyond comparison with their own, which contract pilots and crews received for performing the same duties (but usually outside of combat areas) as were performed by captains, lieutenants, and enlisted men. It may be said in general that in many parts of the world during the war civilians worked side by side with troops, especially on construction, and the very high wages, sometimes strikingly better living conditions, and relative freedom of the civilians were a source of real resentment.

In regard to the contract carriers, opinions run all the way from belief that the necessary number of airlines personnel should have been taken directly into the Army and the operation been purely military all through, to the belief that the commercial carriers should have run the whole show, and the Army's rôle been reduced to asking for the services it needed. In the considered opinion of such men as General George, in the event of another war we should place the airlines in much the same relationship to the military transport arm as that which was worked out in the course of the last one. With the reservation that the discrepancy in pay should be eliminated if possible, the writer concurs.

In flight operations, the Command's control over its aircraft issued to the contract carrier's crews had to be direct, not indirect as in an ordinary charter relationship. There was no room in a war for duality of control or for arguments over instructions and orders. Deep down, A.T.C.'s relationship with the carriers had to be governed by the doctrine which underlay the military unification. Hence the very broad contracts under which the Command turned aircraft over to the lines, which they maintained and stood ready to fly anywhere.

The situation of Pan American–Africa conflicted with these requirements. Here was a complete airline, from top executives to grease monkeys, operating side by side with the military organization. The airline had been there first, it had its own ways of doing, its officers seem sometimes to have been impatient with military control. As happened in various parts of the world, the airline men were definitely not impressed by the Army way of doing things, and frequently enough with good reason. Pan Am-Africa procured many of its own supplies, ran its own communications. It was so well entrenched that at times the Air Forces men who were ultimately responsible for the success of air transport operations in Africa felt as if they were guests rather than employers.

If discussion of proper relations with the carriers in general are frequent and prolonged, among old-timers on the African route arguments as to Pan American-Africa are endless and bitter. Few take a middle point of view. The early A.T.C. officers, regular army men, reserves, airlines men, civilians, individually, either take the position that the organization should

have been left alone, or that it should have been liquidated
months before it was. One group says that it was competent,
devoted, selfless, entirely patriotic. The other grants the competence and that at the time of certain emergencies the civilians
rose well to them, but says that at all times the organization
was more interested in building Pan American a new empire
than in winning the war, that "it was always Pam Am first and
the Army second." It is another of those insoluble debates.
We know that the Pan American subsidiaries in Africa did a
splendid job in building and establishing the route, and we
know further that divided control, an organization with dual
loyalty to its parent company and to its employer, are militarily
unacceptable. The rest is controversy.

For the general reasons given, it was decided to militarize
the Central African Route in the latter part of 1942. The contracts with Pan American-Africa were terminated in a series
of phases, until by December 15 that organization ceased to
exist. All the indications are that this was a desirable step,
essential to tying this section of the route completely into the
military network.

In the course of militarization, the Air Transport Command
made an unfortunate mistake. The Command wanted, of
course, to recruit the greatest number possible of the Pan Am-
Africa personnel, especially the flight and supervisory personnel who were eligible for commissions. Further, although
it knew that the airlines would continue flying for it as they
were then doing, it greatly underestimated the future use it
would make of Pan American, if not of the rest. In order to
persuade the maximum number of men to join the Command,
and especially to stay on in Africa, it used some pressure.

Some of these men had been overseas a year or more, most
of them stationed in highly uncongenial parts of Africa, and
they wanted to get home. Not all of them liked the idea of
giving up the relative freedom and lush salaries of their civilian status in exchange for a uniform and military discipline.
The Command's Africa–Middle East Wing, which was entrust-
ed with the recruitment, advertised that it was unlikely that
contract carrier operations would increase, that there would

be no draft-exempt aviation jobs awaiting them when they got home. They could take their choice between accepting commissions in Africa, or going home to be drafted and find out where the Army would place them. Faced with these alternatives, the majority of those who had hung back accepted military service.

It turned out that there shortly was plenty more work for Pan American to do. It was not long before the determined few who had held out and insisted on returning to the parent company were passing through Africa again in the uniform of a civilian pilot, with civilian pay and the added delight of being based within the Unted States. Some of these were inclined to take an attitude of "well, you suckers," towards their former companions who had stayed on, and many of the latter, weary with the long, monotonous, disagreeable service in a disagreeable land were all too ready to say the same thing to themselves.

The militarization of the route from the Gold Coast to India did nothing to make Pan American love A.T.C. any the better. As has been pointed out, the Command was already equipping domestic airlines with heavy aircraft and putting them into foreign operations, destroying Pan American's monopoly of experience. The Southeastern Route was a valuable plum. To be the exclusive transport operator on it, and to run it as a contract job, under the firm's name and with the firm's employees manning the bases, meant a priceless advantage in postwar competition. By the time militarization was complete, the Allies were solidly lodged in North Africa. The opportunity to be the first and principal flyer across what was obviously destined to be one of the great routes of the world had been destroyed almost before it came into existence. The airline was not happy.

The secret of the landings for the invasion of North Africa had been well kept. Not more than half a dozen men in Command Headquarters knew anything of it. Two others, who were to lead in the first transport and ferried flights, also knew. Outside of these, no one in the whole Command had any suspicion of what was in preparation.

There was not much time left when General George told
Colonel Harold R. Harris, formerly of Panagra Airlines, now
his Assistant Chief of Staff for Plans, what was coming up.
Harris took Lieutenant (later Lieutenant Colonel) Tom
Murphy, a Western Airlines man, into his office with him.
Murphy was the Plans Division's specialist on Africa, and had
been deeply occupied in planning alternate routes to the Orient
should Egypt fall. The two men worked nearly twenty-four
hours straight, subsisting largely on black coffee. As they could
not let any draughtsman in on what they were planning, they
drew their own maps in a crude but accurate and usable form.
The plans with which they emerged were not only workable,
but proved to be an accurate forecast of the various stages from
the first flights in support of the invasion to the establishment
of permanent routes once West Africa and North Africa had
been secured.

The Command's initial missions for the first phases of the invasion were the opening of a shuttle service across the Sahara
to Oran, and the delivery of a group of A–20's, light attack
bombers.

A flight of six C–87's was set up for the transport mission.
Major Edward N. Coates, a Ferrying Command veteran with
extensive African experience, was put in command. His second in command was Major James S. Sammons, another old-
timer. Coates knew what was up. Sammons did not know, but
as he said later, "As things went along we began to guess."
The planes, taken as they came new from the factory, were
assembled at La Guardia Field, New York, overhauled, and
marked with large American flags. Thence they proceeded to
Morrison Field, the Command's main base in Florida, with
little time to spare.

Here they ran into an obstacle. Already at the main points
of departure from the United States, standard procedures had
been developed for final preparation of crews and aircraft going overseas.[3] Coates and his men had been readied on short
notice, and from the point of view of the local commander,

[3] Referred to, of course, by that horrible device for avoiding saying
what you mean: "processing."

they and their aircraft needed overhauling. Coates could not explain why an exception should be made. Under security rules, outgoing crews were supposed to stay on the base and keep away from telephones. Coates managed to get permission to telephone Headquarters, and in veiled language explained the situation. The commander quickly received instructions from indisputable authority to let the flight proceed.

They travelled without incident across Brazil and the South Atlantic, and thence to Kano, a very ancient, very dirty walled city on the southern fringe of the repellant, arid country below the true desert of the Sahara. Before them lay an 1800-mile, non-stop flight over territory about which very little was known, with the equally little-known Atlas Mountains to cross at the end of it. Nor did they know whether the French West Africa military would fire on them if they passed over any of their posts, or even send up fighters to knock them out of the sky. The governor of that colony was Pierre Boissin, who remained a loyal Vichyite until he saw that the cause was lost, after which there was nothing he would not do for the Allies.

The four flights of the A–20 group began coming in to Kano on November 16. The news of the invasion broke. On November 24 came the long-awaited message from General Doolittle asking for immediate opening of the transport line and for first delivery of several tons of radio equipment. Coates took off on the initial flight.

The desert, like the sea, was a navigator's problem. From the air it looked like an equally undesirable thing to land on; sea or desert promised likely death. They ticked off the hundreds of miles without incident until they reached the Atlas mountains, which they found to be higher than they were supposed to be, and covered with clouds. After the mountain crossing they were not entirely sure where they were, but hunted along the coast for Oran.

La Senia Field, where they were to land, had just been put into crudely workable condition after the bombing it received during the early invasion. The radio equipment with which incoming aircraft would normally communicate was on board Coates' plane. Visibility was not good. After some circling they finally made contact with a signal corps jeep, which gave them the minimum of guidance to make landing possible.

Their stay in Oran was enlivened by a minor incident. The Air Force had taken over French barracks. The cook, finding the kitchen dirty, tried to de-bug it with high-octane gasoline, then lit his fires. He thus eliminated the kitchen quite thoroughly and abruptly, but fortunately not himself.

Daily flights in each direction between Oran and Kano continued until Governor Boissin surrendered Dakar and with it French West Africa. Along the coast, as forecast in the Harris-Murphy plan, bases could be placed comparatively close together. Twin-engine aircraft were set to flying it, and it became a busy airway both for transport and ferrying. The desert-spanning C–87's went on to other duties.

The ferrying assignment, known as "Kit Project," was the delivery of the 68th Observation Group consisting of thirty-six A–20's to Algiers on demand. The aircraft were to be flown by their own crews. This sounds like a simple task indeed, now that the base on Ascension Island made the South Atlantic crossing more than within such planes' capacity. What is actually involved beautifully illustrates the meaning of "control of tactical ferrying" in the early days.

Lieutenant Colonel Reichers, the same man who took part in the Moscow flights and had so important a part in X Mission, was put in charge of Kit Project. His second in command was Major Marion L. Grevemberg. Captain Theodore D. Boselli, the Command's ace navigator, was in charge of navigation, and Major Edward A. Abbey was the flight surgeon. Two B–24D's and two B–25C's (twin-engine Mitchell bombers, sturdy and of long range for their size) to be ferried to Egypt were set up to convoy the A–20's. The operation began on October 26.

Reichers established his staff at Morrison Field. He found that no arrangements had been made for carrying spare parts or having supplies stocked along the route, so he arranged with Coates to have 7500 pounds of operational spare parts go forward by the C–87's. As the A–20's began coming in to Morrison Field, he found that they were badly loaded and out of balance, so he reloaded them. The group as a whole was too in-experienced to staff itself. Reichers reported: "The ATC staff was required to improvise an operational staff, overhaul and re-equip the combat aircraft, and prepare inadequately trained crews to depart at the earliest moment on a flight of more than 8000 miles . . . ending with a 1700 mile hop over virtually unknown territory . . ." [4]

The group was divided into four flights of nine planes each, each to be led by one of the heavier bombers flown by A.T.C. personnel. The flights were named, rather dramatically, Tiger, Shark, Panther, and Fox. Tiger Flight, led by Reichers in a B–24, departed Morrison Field on November 8. They stopped at Borinquen Field in Puerto Rico, fuelled, and took off again. Beyond there they encountered a front, which had been fore-cast. According to the forecast, it would be mild, and could be topped at nine thousand feet. When they found that they could not top it at eleven thousand, Reichers led them down to four thousand feet to go under it. Near the center they encoun-tered heavy rain, accompanied by mild turbulence, which re-duced visibility to zero. Reichers ordered the formation to disperse for instrument flying.

The standard practice in such cases is for a formation to scatter widely, both because the turbulence knocks the planes about and may cause collisions, and because one thing which his instruments will not tell a pilot is that he is too close to another plane. Reichers had gone over this with the young pilots before departure. Now, however, instead of dispersing, several of them closed in on the B–24, "flying on its instru-ments"; with the result that there were several narrow escapes from collisions.

There was one young pilot in Tiger Flight whom Reichers described as "a protégé" of the Group Commander, who was also in the flight. This boy attached himself to his commander, flying very close to him and depending upon his instruments.

4 Lt. Col. Louis T. Reichers *et al,* "Kit Project Report," in A.T.C. archives. Reichers gives the Sahara-Atlas crossing as 1700 miles; I believe 1800 is correct. Either distance approaches the extreme range of an A–20.

At some point in the rain-blinded turbulence the two planes collided, and both were destroyed.

One A–20 came out of the storm immediately on top of Reichers' aircraft, so close that to save itself it had to peel off in a dive. Entering further turbulence the A–20 was thrown on its back, and a musette bag got tangled with the controls. The crew chief worked desperately to free the controls while the bomber dived at the water at a rate of between three hundred and seventy and four hundred miles per hour. The controls were freed when they were just above the water and the pilot pulled out violently. The plane's wings seemed to point straight up into the air under the violent pressure and there was a loud cracking noise, but the wings held. The radio antennae were torn off, the escape hatch forced open, and both wings were buckled along the leading edge. The pilot managed to get his plane back to Borinquen Field safely.

At the next stop Reichers learned that, although their commanding officer had assured him that all the pilots were trained in instrument flying, only six of the thirty-six pilots had actually had any such training. Their ignorance, and their commanding officer's unawareness of it, cost his life and that of five other men, and put a third plane out of action, nearly destroying it also.

One flight, accompanied by Major Abbey, the surgeon, remained at Borinquen Field overnight. Waked at four in the morning to go on, they found that they could get no breakfast, nor any lunch to take with them. They remained cheerful and game, and took off hungry. The surgeon reported, "Better mental attitude could not be hoped for in veterans, let alone kids." They were, as were so many of the freshly trained pilots of those days, a curious mixture of readiness and unreadiness. The plane flown by 2nd Lieutenant Roy H. Sheehan had its left wing tire blown out when it was coming in to Natal in Brazil — and on Friday the thirteenth. Sheehan made a beautiful landing and brought his bomber to a stop undamaged.

When Tiger Flight was taking off from Natal, one pilot retracted his landing gear too soon, with the result that one of his propellors scraped the runway for nearly three hundred yards. It is amazing that he did not crash then and there. He got into the air, and "did not hear" the control tower ordering him back. His crew chief begged him to return to the base, but in his young eagerness to go on with his outfit, he refused. He made it to Ascension Island, where they found that all three blades of that propellor were bent back over three inches, and that a new engine had to be put in.

At Ascension, also, occurred an incident which charmingly illustrates the youth of these flyers. One of them told Reichers that, having completed a flight of 1400 miles across the ocean, he considered that he was no longer a "junior bird man." The next day this boy managed to get lost on the much shorter flight to Accra, and finally landed at the R.A.F. field at Takoradi.

En route to Ascension Island on November 15, Panther Flight, led by Major Grevemberg, was forced down to five hundred feet to get under bad weather. Still several hundred miles from the island, one of the pilots advised Grevemberg that one of his engines was going out. Over the radio Grevemberg talked to him, giving him instructions in flying his aircraft on one engine and calming him. About half an hour later the engine did cut out, but with the veteran talking him along, the pilot handled his machine correctly and brought it to Ascension.

The rough weather and this incident had delayed Panther Flight so that Fox caught up with it over Wideawake Field. The field's control tower at that moment went out of operation due to a battery failure, a pretty situation with twenty aircraft, one in serious trouble, stacked up over the field. With the lead planes acting somewhat in the capacity of control towers, all of them landed safely.

The group assembled at Accra, still with all but the three planes lost in the Caribbean, and from there proceeded to Kano to join Coates' C–87's. Also on November 24 they received their orders to proceed to Oran. Two flights left Kano the morning of the twenty-fifth. As I have noted already, the distance to be flown was "critical" for A–20's. Over the Atlas Mountains they encountered bad weather and icing conditions.

They ran short of oxygen. Reichers led them to the coast on instruments, and thence to Oran. The field still had no radio equipment, so he brought them in on his own radio.

They expected to find their tents and sleeping bags there, but there was no trace of them. It turned out later that they had been shipped to Scotland. Reichers reported: "Our arrival at Oran was not under very favorable circumstances due to lack of communications, bad weather, shortage of food and lack of sleeping accommodations, resulting in our feeling very unhappy."

The next day nine more of the light bombers, led by Major Grevemberg, came in after encountering similar weather. The remainder, Fox Flight, was delayed to let R.A.F. aircraft through. When it did take off, it was beset by hard luck. Three of the A–20's were forced to turn back with engine trouble. Then, well out in the Sahara, a fourth had trouble with both engines and was finally forced to land on the sand.

The men had been coached what to do in such cases. If Arabs turned up, only one was to leave the plane, the others manning the machine guns until they were sure that their reception would be friendly. They had been provided with gold coins, and with documents in French and Arabic calculated to ensure good treatment. Inevitably, also, they were carrying an assortment of candy bars on board. Arabs soon came to this plane. The documents, the gold, and the candy won the sheik completely. He had a kid slaughtered on which to feast them, and the crew stayed in glory with the tribe. The following day an A.T.C. C–47 landed to pick them up. Then a difficult situation arose. The sheik presented the pilot with one of his daughters, and it took the most elaborate diplomacy before they were able to depart without her.

With that incident Kit Project ended. The A.T.C. men returned to Kano, and then flew on to deliver their aircraft in Cairo.

As is well known, the combat and troop carrier aircraft taking part in the actual invasion of North Africa, with the exception of the fighters, flew from England the whole length of France and Spain, then in over Morocco. This was no slight undertaking. Honor is due, especially, to the twin-engine bombers and transports which made this trip. As soon as the North African coast was clear, the Air Transport Command looked north along the same line. It was an old dream. Faced by the nature of the North Atlantic in winter and the impossibility of persuading the Portuguese to allow either the use of the Azores or Portugal proper, Olds and his staff had hopefully traced a great curve from Brazil to Africa to Britain. In 1942 the North Atlantic Route stayed open until the end of the year, but in January following, the extreme winter weather closed it. Instead, the transports and ferried aircraft went by the great curve to England via Brazil and Morocco.

The link from Morocco to Cornwall was not without its hazards. Weather was not good around the Bay of Biscay. German interception could be expected, and it soon became known that Spanish observation and radar stations were helpfully warning the enemy of planes passing near that coast. It could be considered a nervous sort of a route for unarmed transports. No major transports and remarkably few aircraft of any kind were lost, however, in no small part thanks to the British patrols, and the "Bear Route" as it was called soon carried a heavy traffic.

At the close of 1942 the successor to the Ferrying Command which had so desperately and vainly tried to get half a dozen transports and a handful of bombers to the Philippines, was operating ferry and transport routes which reached to China, Britain, Alaska, and Australia. When need arose it could, and did, bridge the seas between Australia and India, girdling the world. Its contract carrier flying out from the United States increased steadily in volume while more and more military crews joined in the same operations. Its ton mileage for the year exceeded seventeen million, mostly piled up in the last six months. Two hundred and four transports now served it, and above all more and more of the great four-engine aircraft were coming off the production lines. We who were then in the Air Transport Command thought we were members of an impressively big and powerful organization, performing wonders. Looking back, we see that what had happened was little more than the laying of a groundwork, the chick pecking at the shell of its egg.

X

ASIA WESTWARD

THE INITIAL DEVELOPMENT of the Alaskan Route has already been noted. It started with the idea that we might in the not so distant future be basing aircraft in Siberia. By the time that traffic was freely travelling across Alberta and the Yukon Territory to Fairbanks, it was apparent that that hope would not be realized, at least until Russia broke the German death grip. Most soldiers then felt deep admiration for the Russian army; it would have been hard to imagine then that when Russia did declare war upon Japan, the act would be merely irritation, an intervention in our hard-won victory when the opponent was down and the count had reached nine.

Russia was buying P–40's of the late, improved models, P–40K's and P–40L's, B–25's and A–20's from us as fast as we could furnish them, and was anxious to get P–39's. The latter fighter, with the cannon in its nose, appealed to them as being usable against tanks and armored vehicles. To reach Russia, B–25's and A–20's were being flown via the Southeastern Route to Persia. The distance from Washington to Moscow by that route is 11,801 miles, which meant that fifty or more hours of flying time was put on the engines before they reached the zone of combat. Worse, the route took them across the sandy parts of Africa where the engines, especially those of the A–20's, suffered damage from the fine, abrasive sand. As the greater part of the trip had to be made through very hot country, the planes could not be completely modified for the Russian climate and had to be further worked on before they went into action. B–25's look and are tough; on the whole they stood the trip well. A–20's are much more delicate. They became obsolete before the war was over, replaced by the famous hedge-hopping A–26 of the Normandy invasion. On this long circuit what the Army refers to as "the attrition rate" — a euphemism for rate of loss — was high.

The P–40's had to be shipped all the way to Abadan in Persia, or else shipped to Accra and flown on from there. The second alternative was unsatisfactory, even dangerous, as beyond Cairo across Palestine to Peira, or from Khartoum across the Indian Ocean along the southern edge of Arabia the stations were too far apart.

It seemed painfully obvious to the Air Transport Command that this procedure was wasteful of time, men, and machines. From Washington to Moscow via Alaska and Siberia is 9528 miles. (The aircraft did not, of course, depart from Washington, the difference in distances actually was more in favor of the Alaskan Route than the figures show.) The way lay entirely overland except for the narrow crossing of the Behring Sea, all the territory over which it passed lay within the domain of one of the three major allies and therefore stations could be placed as close as desired, so that the shortest range planes could be ferried along it. The climate might be hard on men, but it was much easier on the machines, and similar enough throughout to allow aircraft to leave the United States completely modified for Russian requirements.

The way in which the Command took up the plan of ferrying via the extreme northwest was characteristic. One encounters the same thing in other branches of the Services, in many forms. It reminds one of the adventurer-merchants of the Elizabethan period who first penetrated the realms of what was then "the Duke of Muscovy," to whom the scale of their equipment and resources and the vast extent of their ignorance of the parts of the world they intended to exploit, were no barriers to their undertakings.[1]

In mid-1942 one would think that the Command was stretched about as far as it could go without snapping. We knew nothing about Siberia. We believed that there were land-

[1] Nobody having the faintest idea what Russian sounded like, Queen Elizabeth wrote to the Duke in Latin, Greek, and French, in the hope that he would command at least one of these tongues.

ing fields of some kind at one or two points. If it should prove
that no serviceable air route existed, the Command was ready
to build one, and in any case it was prepared to operate an air
ferry service to Moscow – and a supplemental transport line as
well if desired — or to any other point that Russia might desig-
nate. There was even created, on paper, a nuclear organization
to become eventually the Siberian Wing.

We did not know the Russians. The Command's proposals
were forwarded to Moscow, and rejected in a baffling indecisive,
delaying way. Then Captain Richard C. Kight flew Wendell
Willkie to Moscow in the course of his round-the-world trip.
From Moscow Kight went by a route which, as a route, was
no more than a gleam in a geographer's eye to Kunming, and
from there, pioneering again, north to Siberia and so to Alaska.
He brought us our first information on Siberian fields, which
were sadly in need of improvement, and his voyage from China
later kindled the hope of linking the A.T.C. Hump and Alaskan operations. Kight and his crew made one of the great
flights of history, although it has never been adequately recognized, in good measure because on their return public attention was centered on their distinguished passenger.

More important than Kight's information was the fact that
Willkie and Stalin hit it off, and the Russian attitude towards
America warmed slightly. Admiral Standley, our ambassador,
got to see Stalin himself for the first time in months. He
broached the Siberian ferrying project to him, in a revised
form which would turn the aircraft over to the Russian pilots
on the Siberian coast. Stalin said it was an excellent idea, how
soon could it be put into effect? It was new to him — minor
bureaucrats had never allowed it to be presented.[2]

The Russians played their cards close to their chests. They
had no intention of letting us station troops even on the outer-
most edge of their soil. To put the plan into effect, we had to
allow them to station their ferry pilots and accompanying personnel at Fairbanks. It took months to arrange for the trans-

[2] To the extent that he treats of this matter, Major General John R.
Deane tells a different story in his *Strange Alliance*, Viking Press, 1947.
My account is based on two radio messages from Admiral Standley which
were shown me in A.T.C. Headquarters.

mission of weather information from Siberian stations; the Russians did not want us to know any of their codes, as their attitude developed we were not too ready to give them any important one of ours, and they disliked establishing regular communications across the border.

The picture of the dealings between the two countries in this matter is a curious one. America wanted to win the war; therefore it wanted to get equipment to its great ally in the quickest, most effective manner. Whatever Americans want to do they want to do well, therefore the Air Transport Command was impatient with the stupidity of the long route via Persia. To the Americans the whole thing was clear and open. On the other side, Russia looked the gift horse in the mouth not once, but over and over again. Suspicion and grudging acceptance were their response, hedging the deal this way and that to protect their eternal privacy. Continuous dealings with the Russians throughout the war had the effect upon officers of A.T.C. Headquarters of greatly dimming, if not extinguishing, their early enthusiasm. They still felt that the people were great fighters, but looked with distrust and dislike upon their government.

It was my observation in headquarters of the Air Transport Command that there were certain special interests among the more sincere officers and civilians in late 1942. England was still subject to air attack but the blitz had ended, we had a counter-offensive going strong in North Africa, and the air counter-attack on Germany had been well developed by the R.A.F. with the A.A.F. increasingly contributing. Britain seemed secure, but China and Russia were in terrible plights. Both were fighting when one would have expected them to give up, both were suffering terrific losses and destructions. There was a deep, emotional desire to get all the help we possibly could manage to both of them. While the war lasted, this feeling towards China held steady, but Russia slowly undermined it until, when we learned of that country's wretched declaration of war against Japan, we were merely angry.

Finally the way was clear. An A.T.C. survey party was even allowed to fly to Moscow, piloted by Lieutenant Colonel Harvey, the same who made the flight around the world via Moscow in 1941, borrowed for the occasion. The party was well received and allowed to see as little as possible. The chief reason for allowing it through seems to have been Russia's need for a great deal of equipment, epecially radio beacons, communications, and snowplows for the route, as well as C–47's to use in support of the ferrying.

We had won our essential point, and persuaded the Russians to let us serve them. The first planes began moving out of Great Falls, Montana, early in September. In the course of the month fifty of them, P–40's, A–20's, and C–47's were delivered to Fairbanks. Not all of these were accepted by the Russian representatives, as items of equipment were lacking. Then everything went wrong. Aircraft began arriving at Fairbanks short of essential items. As the season wore on, the planes had to have full winter modification for ferry flight and combat service under conditions of extreme cold. The modifications lagged. There was a report that the Air Service Command officer in charge of them was negligent because of his violent objection to providing aircraft for Communists — the report came from a good source, but I never saw corroboration of it. In the providing of certain special features which were necessary for service in Russia, as many organizations as Air Transport, Matériel, and Air Service Commands and the Quartermaster and Signal Corps were involved, and there was a sorry lack of co-ordination. The unmodified planes piled up below the border. The number of planes reaching Fairbanks fell off instead of increasing; in December seven were delivered: in January, none.

In Washington the Russian representatives would ask politely, "Bot your American efeeciency, surely you can straighten out these problems?" In A.T.C. Headquarters the Alaska Theater Officer took to muttering to himself. For everyone who followed the "Alsib Project" closely, it was a humiliating, infuriating experience — none the less so because so much of the blame attached to other organizations.

There was another source of grief and delay — the almost unbearable conditions under which the men on many of the bases had to work. Quarters suitable to the climate had not been provided, hangars were almost entirely lacking. The men were numbed, bound, pressed down by the intense cold, and the howling, wind-driven snows. Work too delicate to be done with gloves on had to be performed in the open, and a mechanic could keep his gloves off for only ten seconds or so without freezing. The go ahead sign had come too late in the year for the elaborate facilities necessary to maintain a large-scale air operation in the Far North to be shipped in, and the men worked in a cold hell.

In February things began to roll. Seventy-eight aircraft reached the Russians by the northwestern route. In March they received 102, by the end of 1943, 2491 had been delivered at Fairbanks. The route was a going concern over which more than 7000 planes went to Russia before the war ended. Red-starred C–47's provided by us shuttled between Moscow and Fairbanks, linking with our own transport shuttle at that point.

In Fairbanks, our men got on well with the Russian ferry pilots, except for a few whose hatred of "reds" was so deep that they could not be civil. The Russians thought our whiskey pleasant, but weak. We found their vodka devastating. The individual flyers, like their country, played their cards close to their chests. They gave out little information, but one picked up interesting items, such as that they had discovered that, if a fighter pilot ran out of ammunition, he could destroy an enemy plane by coming up under its tail, so that his propeller cut it off. Frequently those who did this survived. They thought we were not serious in war, but rather played at it: thus they were reluctant to give us information or turn over to us, for instance, their formula for hydraulic fluid for extreme low temperatures, because we leaked our secrets. Nor were we seriously fighting, in their opinion. That opinion changed after D-Day. Russian ferry pilots were not specialists, as were ours, but were rotated to ferrying duty after a tour in combat. Their level of skill was well below that of our flyers; our officers said that they still seemed to be flying in the nineteen-twenties, depending greatly upon "flying by the seat of their pants." They were rough with the aircraft, and their accident rate was higher than A.T.C.'s Ferrying Division ever would have stood for.

On the whole, the impression they made upon the Americans in Alaska was not unlike Kight's description of them. They were a likable, intelligent, rough, vigorous, frontier people, with back of these qualities something veiled. The individual, as well as his country, had an iron curtain.

The beginning of real flow of aircraft via Alsib, coinciding with the February, 1943, delivery of 2500 tons to China over the Hump, came when for many reasons the Command could feel that it had the world by the tail and a downhill pull. Estimates of aircraft production for 1943 and 1944 were astronomical. Proposed allocations to A.T.C. were so great as utterly to exceed its existing training capacity. Once again the airlines were called in, to set up in conjunction with the Air Forces the Air Lines War Training Institute, a nation-wide organization capable of turning out thousands of pilots, navigators, radio operators, flight and ground mechanics. It was certainly the most ambitious training scheme ever attempted in aviation; seldom has anything comparable been seen in any field. The Institute worked excellently. It was first cut down, then abolished, as two important changes occurred in the situation. The first of these was that aircraft available proved to be much fewer than had been estimated, partly because of the non-appearance of several new types which never were produced or never got beyond the X stage, partly because of the troubles undergone by the C–46. The second was that, as we moved into the following year, the Command's own training capacity had increased to where it could meet its needs.

In February, 1943, the same month in which the Alaska-Siberia movement began to roll, the Command reached its assigned goal of delivering 2500 tons over the Hump to China. The North Atlantic Route had shut down in January, to remain closed until early April — the last year in which it was thus closed — but the hooklike extension of the Southeastern Route via the Bear Route to England kept the flow of ships and supplies unbroken. Nine hundred combat aircraft had been delivered to the 8th Air Force in the United Kingdom by that time. The Command was running transports to Port Moresby and Guadalcanal in the Pacific, and to Attu. Its fleet grew daily, and it began to feel its strength.

XI

TEN THOUSAND TONS AT TWENTY THOUSAND FEET

THE AIR TRANSPORT COMMAND took over the service from India to China pledged to deliver 2500 tons to that country in February, 1943, and to achieve a lift of 5000 tons a month not long after. The Command did not realize quite what it was up against.

Colonel Edward H. Alexander activated the India-China Wing of the Command on the first of December, 1942, at Chaubua in Assam, and with that the Command's operation started. Colonel Robert M. Love flew a B–17 to India and joined him in Assam in order to get a first-hand view of the situation for reporting to Headquarters. He found that all supplies supposedly earmarked for the transports had been sidetracked by the 10th Air Service Command and pooled with 10th Air Force supplies. The 10th Air Force's commanding general, upon losing a mission which he gave up reluctantly, had made off with six of the assigned DC–3's. These "stolen" planes were not recovered until well on in January, when General Arnold, being on the spot, intervened personally.

These were but minor problems. Out of the fetid, steaming, low valleys of Assam the route climbed over a series of constantly higher mountain ranges, covered with jungle, inhabited by wild tribes — among them head hunters — and infested by the enemy, until it reached the Hump, the main range of the Himalayas. If one flew the direct line to Kunming, the principal Chinese base, the total distance was 520 miles and in

CAVU weather (ceiling and visibility unlimited) one could cross the ridge at 16,000 feet. The straight line called for forty-five minutes over territory securely held by the Japanese. To avoid this, one could detour further to the north, flying a distance of 720 miles and crossing the Hump at the northwestern end of the "low" section where it reached to 16,000 feet. This allowed a CAVU flight plan of 18,000 feet. At any crossing point, when the weather was at all bad, 20,000 feet was the minimum.

The full meaning of these altitudes may better be grasped if one realizes that the lowest flight plan was fifteen hundred feet higher than the pinnacle of Mount Whitney, the highest mountain in the United States, and nearly two thousand feet higher than the top of Pike's Peak. The standard 20,000-foot plan would just fail to clear the tip of Alaska's Mount McKinley.

Once over the Hump, the drop to Kunming and the neighboring bases at 6000 feet was relatively fast. When you got there you hadn't got to much. The runway was hand-laid by the Chinese, of stone, rough and very hard on tires. Accommodations were miserable, amenities virtually none. Occasionally the field flooded. Communications and aids were minimal. Clouds might close in the field, and it was no unusual thing for half a dozen or more planes to be "stacked up" above the clouds, waiting a turn to land.

Kunming itself and all the routes were open to Japanese interception. The bases in Assam were also subject to raids. Occasionally a Jap would try to slip his plane unnoticed into the flight pattern over Kunming and come in as if he were a friendly flyer making a landing — only to pull up when he was near the ground for a neat job of bombing and strafing and a fast getaway. The trick did not work often, but it was worked. To make things pleasanter, roving Japanese ground patrols carried portable beacons which gave off signals matching those of our bases, thus luring aircraft off course. One got so far astray that, after dodging in and out among nameless mountains nearly as high as Mount Everest, it landed finally in Tibet, and the crew came out on yaks.

If a flyer was shot down or crashed over the jungle-clad foothills, and succeeded in bailing out, and if he reached the ground under the tall trees alive, he still had a terrific battle before him to "walk out." The jungle is intense, poisonous, and full of sickness. Not all natives were friendly. Japanese patrols might turn up anywhere. The mountains are steep.

To make this area more appetizing, the India side of it is afflicted by the storms known as monsoons. The Chowdah or little monsoon comes in April, bringing a few weeks of torrential rains. In a personal letter, Colonel Alexander reported of it in 1943: "The weather here has been awful. The icing level starts at 12,000 feet. Today a C–87 went to 29,000 feet on instruments, was unable to climb higher, and could not get on top. It has rained seven and a half inches in the past five days. All aircraft are grounded."

The Chowdah clears up, to be followed by the true monsoon which begins in the middle of May and continues until the middle of October. In this period two hundred inches of rain fall ordinarily. From the end of October to January or February the weather is better, but violent storms with turbulence occur. Then and in February and March winds of seventy-five to a hundred miles an hour are encountered fairly often. From January sixth to eighth, 1945, there occurred a storm in which nine aircraft were destroyed. Winds reached two hundred and forty-eight miles per hour, with updrafts which shot planes up from 6000 to 8000 feet in one minute, and comparable downdrafts. This storm was a record-breaker, but others approached it.

There was radio communication between Kunming and Assam, but virtually no other aids at the start. Even this one help was limited, as static and a phenomenon known as "night fading" often put radios out of operation. If a plane had to come into a China-side field at night, it had to circle for not less than half an hour while portable floodlights and flarepots were set out to show the runway.

Supplies to the Assam area moved from Calcutta part way by a railroad the gauge of which changed several times, requiring trans-shipping. The remainder of the way they could be hauled by road during the dry season, but not during the monsoon. In the wet season they could be brought in only by boats up the Brahmaputra River. This is the slowest of all means of transportation, and equipment was sharply limited.

In the early period the attrition rate for aircraft was calculated at thirteen and a half per cent per month. What gives the picture of this lush desolation far more sharply is the attrition rate for men. Of a hundred men, it was officially calculated, 83.9 would still be efficient at the end of six months, 59.9 at the end of a year, and 27.3 after eighteen months. Thereafter five more men would be lost to useful work each month. General Alexander (he became general in the spring of 1943) constantly pressed his flight surgeons to see to it that pilots were sent home before they cracked up.

In Assam it got so hot that the sun beating on fuel tanks in the wings of the aircraft heated the volatile gasoline close to the vaporizing point. It could happen, especially with C–46's, that after taking off for China the plane climbed so rapidly that atmospheric pressure decreased faster than the gasoline cooled off, with the result that vapor-lock occurred in mid-air. When this happened to both engines at once, the plane was doomed and its crew might be.

It was over this route, under these conditions, that the Command undertook to equal and surpass the tonnage of the Burma road. It sent out additional men and aircraft — C–47's and a dozen four-engined C–87's. It managed finally to disentangle most of its supplies from those of the 10th Air Force. It did not entirely eliminate the special missions in which that body had so freely indulged, for some of the appeals were such that no commander could refuse them — to drop supplies to one or another besieged Allied force — but it cut them down. In November, under the 10th Air Force the military had achieved delivery of 819.7 tons to China, in February the India-China Wing met and exceeded its goal with 2871.5 tons.

Then the bad weather struck. In April, with the Chowdah Monsoon, the tonnage dropped to 1910, and in May it dropped again to 1683.4 This was sad news, yet nowhere else in the world were we carrying so much freight. I well remember that

when the weekly gross tonnage report first came in with the
Hump tonnage included, I went to see the officer who prepared
the report, thinking that he had gone crazy. It was this tonnage, too, which caused the headquarters statisticians to change
from reporting in pounds and pound-miles to tons and ton-
miles.

Early in 1943 the United States was attacked from various
directions for not really trying to give aid to China. Such attractive personalities as Lin Yutang joined in the cry. Officers
of A.T.C. were occasionally tackled at dinner parties and other
social occasions on the matter, and heard some sharp criticisms.
We knew what was being done, and we knew the cost in lives
and equipment, and the incredible difficulty of the undertaking. At that time the Japanese believed that we could never
achieve a lift of more than one thousand tons a month, not
enough to be a serious factor, wherefore their efforts to cut the
route were perfunctory. Until our air power in the theater became much greater, we wanted them to go on thinking that.
Wherefore one acted dumb and suffered in silence.

In April the fabled General Chennault came to Washington.
It was strange to catch a glimpse of him in the corridors, for
since well before America entered the war he and his Flying
Tigers had seemed a sort of glorious myth, faintly confused
with *Terry and the Pirates.* He brought with him a plan for
aggressive air warfare against not only the Japanese in China
but against the home islands of Japan, based upon a great increase in the tonnage over the Hump. His plan, incidentally,
never materialized, partly because of Japanese advances which
robbed him of his forward bases, and later because of concentration on B–29's as the weapon of air attack. His ideas carried
conviction. It was not until just about the time of his departure that the dreadful slump in April tonnage became known
in Washington. It was attributed to the Chowdah Monsoon
and to temporary, remediable causes.

In Mid-May A.T.C., which that month was heading towards
an even lower tonnage, was told to achieve 5000 tons in July,
7500 in August, and 10,000 in September, the latter level to
be maintained thereafter. I say "told" advisedly. Headquarters

and General Alexander both doubted that it could be done, but they knew how strongly the highest authorities, including the President, felt about supporting the Chinese, and they flew at it. This undertaking was formally known to A.T.C. as "Project 7." Less formally, it was called first "The July-September Objective," and later "The 10,000-ton Objective."

The route was in no way equipped to handle the required traffic. The Wing, to meet the requirement, needed the completion of eight new airdromes and delivery of 9918 tons of equipment. For the first month it would have to have a flow of 7000 tons of gasoline, 7000 tons of cargo, and 200 tons of airplane spare parts and base supplies. The full project called for an increase of 93 C–46's, 25 C–47's, and 24 C–87's. There are points in this narrative at which it is impossible to avoid slinging a mass of figures at the reader. This is one of them. All of the above meant additional personnel, to a total of 2490. Especially important was the question of flight personnel, who had to be competent to fly medium-heavy and heavy transports under extremely difficult conditions. The Ferrying Division furnished forty-eight of its best four-engine pilots. The domestic Air Forces were called upon to provide 220 first pilots with 1000 hours' flying time, and promised that they would provide the "cream of these graduating classes," along with 189 co-pilots, 60 navigators, 193 radio operators, and 28 aerial engineers.

Ignorant persons, or merely hostile ones, have recently attacked the then administration for failing to give full support to Chiang Kai-shek *during the war*. To one who followed our efforts day by day, it is quite apparent that he received more than might reasonably have been expected. The Hump Operation was from this time on the best-nourished of the Command's activities. C–47's promised to the Russians, some of them actually en route to Alaska, were taken back and sent to India. At all times, no matter how urgent the demands elsewhere, the India-China fleet was increased. The most effective method of helping the Chinese, as has been noted before, was to keep the air arm well supplied; at first this meant little more than feeding the budding 14th Air Force, later it extended to the Chinese-American Composite Wing and to the Chinese Air Force proper. Chinese troops were flown out of China, trained and equipped by the Americans in India, and then returned to action. These procedures, of course, allowed relatively little cargo to be turned over directly to Chinese officials, and thus insulated the flow against graft. No doubt this grieved certain of the Chinese — one cannot, of course, accuse Chiang of being in this group. I followed this operation minutely from the inception of the Wing in 1942 until the end of hostilities two and a half years later, and I do not see how possibly one more ton could have been delivered to China.

The July objective was based on the fallacious assumption that everything from the selection of personnel to the construction of runways and hard-standings would proceed exactly on schedule and as planned. A multitude of separate agencies were involved. Construction in India was performed principally by the Empire, and arranged for through the Theater authorities. It will be remembered that A.T.C. was not subject to the Theater. The bulk of the personnel were, as noted, to be furnished by the domestic Air Forces. So it went all along the line.

One factor which gave this project a boost, and probably was important in creating the belief that it could be achieved, was the remarkable mass delivery of thirty C–46's to the Wing in the end of April and beginning of May by a group of Northwest Airlines and T.W.A. pilots led by five A.T.C. pilots. A number of the civilian pilots remained in India for a time, and several of them flew the Hump. The story of this flight is so excellently summarized in *Air Transport at War* (pages 216–233) that it would be merely repetitious to treat it here.[1]

---

[1] Mr. Cleveland's account is drawn from a very full narrative written by Mr. Roosevelt der Tatevasion of Curtiss-Wright. Mr. Cleveland says, correctly, "Submitted to Army authorities for censorship, it was at once classified 'secret.' . . ." I was, reluctantly, responsible for this. The story was submitted to me at the start, I realized that it was gorgeous stuff and well written, but loaded with detailed, secret information. Censoring it would have left nothing but tatters, so I had it classified. Mr. Cleveland's chapter on India-China (Chapter VIII) manages by a curious process of omission or perhaps of shifted emphasis to give the impression that the

This auspicious development was partially neutralized by
the difficulties which the India-China Wing, like all other users,
encountered with the C–46. It acquired the same foul reputation there that it did elsewhere. The historians of the India-
China Division (as it later became), although they were, by
profession, objective and detached, yet wrote of this aircraft in
its early evolution with a bitterness they could not entirely
avoid. On the other hand, perhaps more C–46 fans eventually
developed among India-China pilots than in any other branch
of the Command.

The monsoons were on. Washington did not fully grasp the
effect this would have upon construction. On the first of July
it was running fifty per cent behind schedule. Thus, out of
ninety-eight hardstandings, only forty-nine had been completed, and in the bottomless goo created by the months-long
rain, no plane could be parked except upon a constructed
surface. The planes themselves were slow in coming. All along
the line, the preparations to make the actual tonnage possible
were lagging. Essential supplies piled up mountainously at
Calcutta while the ground supply line to Assam bogged down.

By mid-June another, potent source of trouble became apparent. The organization and procedures of the Army are intended to eliminate the element of human weakness as far as
possible. Many of what seem its strangest and most rigid formulae are devised to this end. No system has ever been devised
which will eliminate that weakness altogether. One of the
forms in which it is most apparent is in the matter of the transfer of personnel: rarely indeed does one encounter a commander who, when called upon to furnish another outfit with
so many men of a certain category, does not pick out the poor-
est he has — regardless of the nature of their mission. It would

Hump operation was very largely, if not chiefly, an airlines one. (" . . . the
men of air transport, working in and at the bidding of the Air Transport
Command . . ." page 234.) C.N.A.C. stayed on the route throughout the
war, but *proportionately* its achievement was small — through no fault of
its own (see pages 87–88). American airlines flew C–87's from August
through November, 1943, and more credit to it. It delivered about 2500
tons to China in that time.

be untrue and unfair to say that the 409 pilots and co-pilots furnished to the India-China Wing by the domestic Air Forces were personally in any way inferior. Their later achievements over the Hump refute any such suggestion completely. But they most certainly were not of the level of skill required. Despite the specifications and the promises, many were single-engine and fighter pilots. The twin-engine experience of others consisted of a few hours in comparatively light trainers. The twin-engine men with 1000 hours, "cream of the graduating classes," simply did not materialize.

Their arrival in India meant, not that more pilots were on hand to fly the Hump, but that some of the best Hump flyers had to be taken off the run in order to set up a regular transition school for the newcomers. The number of pilots available for productive flying was actually decreased.

In June, 1887.9 tons were delivered over the Hump, in July, 2716 — a little more than half of the objective. September's total was 4624, still short of the July objective. It may be mentioned that in July Kunming Field was flooded. Several planes were damaged by landing in the water, and the pilots took to the dangerous expedient of landing and taking off on the dispersal areas. On September 8, the monsoon overhung Kunming with a ceiling of 1000 feet. At nine o'clock in the morning, ten planes were stacked up over the field. Later there were twenty-five. To land they had to make an instrument let-down and as the conventional aids were not available (a radio range was installed at Kunming later that month), they did so under guidance of the control tower, a tricky procedure. One circling plane's engine failed and the crew bailed out.

I mention these items to give some idea of what the A.T.C. men were facing. Record should be made, too, of the belief of the coolies that, by cutting across close in front of the propellers of a taxiing plane, the whirling props would cut off all the devils that usually trailed along behind them. Many of them, unhappily, cut their manoeuvre a little too fine.

The Japanese appear to have gained some idea of what was forward. There was, in fact, little hope of long concealing from them the rate of traffic over the route. In the second half of

1943, eleven aircraft were known to have been shot down. As many aircraft simply disappeared in flight, without having had a chance to communicate, it may be presumed that the full number shot down was considerably larger.

In honor to the airlines, it must be remembered that this was not a simon-pure military operation. C.N.A.C. continued in the game, and from early August to November 28 American Airlines operated nine C–87's, six round trips a day, from Chabua to Kunming. Seldom have civilians been called upon to serve under conditions so closely approaching combat, and they responded gallantly.

General Alexander is a supremely honest man, nor does he pull his punches when punches are called for. His special report to Headquarters for the month of June gives a splendid picture of what was involved in setting up Project 7. A lengthy quotation from it is fully justified.[2]

*   *   *   *

Engineering:
  a. Certain aspects of the maintenance situation in India are pertinent. Maintenance personnel is inadequate at this date throughout the Wing but new personnel is arriving daily. Both officers and enlisted personnel in this category are relatively inexperienced. It is necessary for the Wing Engineering officer and his one Staff Assistant at this date to make frequent trips to Squadrons in order personally to perform maintenance work. Climatic conditions impose extraordinary hardships as regards both personnel and aircraft. Except on rainy days, maintenance work cannot be accomplished because shade temperatures of from 100° to 130° Fahrenheit render all metal exposed to the sun so hot that it cannot be touched by the human hand without causing second degree burns. This means that maintenance work is carried on largely at night. Personnel who work at night suffer from an inability to sleep by day because of the excessive heat. In the Assam area, First and Second Echelon repairs are accomplished only at night whether

[2] I understand that these reports are a happy collaboration between General Alexander and St. Clair McKelway, then a major on his staff. To me, they are military classics.

it is raining or not in the daytime because all aircraft must be alerted for instant dispersal during the day in case of enemy air attack. There are no nose hangars or shelters available for maintenance work. Ships are parked in mud on high ground while maintenance work is in progress. Portable maintenance stand shelters are inadequate in number and frequently useless because motor transportation to tow them from one aircraft to another is not available. There is in this Theatre a critical shortage of wire, electric bulbs, floorlamps and portable power plants essential to night maintenance work. Abrasive dust on dry days plays havoc with aircraft engines all over India. The Hump operation requires engine powers of 65% or more, thus cutting down the engine life-span. The excessive heat also has an unfortunate effect on hydraulic lines, fittings and valves, which break because of the expansion of hydraulic fluid caused by high temperatures. Heat also causes vapor locks in gasoline lines involving delays in getting engines started before take-offs. At this date the Tenth Air Force Service Command is taxed to capacity and is unable to keep abreast of ICWATC[3] Third and Fourth Echelon maintenance and repairs. It, too, is expanding, with additional personnel, equipment and supplies authorized and enroute from the States. New C–87's arriving from the States at this date cannot be immediately converted into gasoline tankers for the Hump haul because the Air Service Command capacity for conversion in this respect is filled. The Air Service Command established its main depot at Agra only to find that Agra has the largest percentage of abrasive dust in all of India. It is moving by degrees to Calcutta where this condition is less menacing.

Health and Morale:

a. In the month of June there were among Wing personnel 36 cases of malaria, 45 cases of dysentery requiring hospitalization, and 30 hospitalized cases of other ailments and diseases. In the month of June there were 9 venereal disease cases. Virtually all personnel suffer from chronic dysenteries of the non-amoebic variety which do not require hospitalization but cause losses of man hours and represent a morale factor. The Wing Surgeon estimates that during August and September, when malaria in this area reaches its peak, 20 per cent of all per-

---

[3] *I.e.* India-China Wing, A.T.C.

sonnel will have it. In general, however, health is good at this date. The supply of fresh vegetables and fresh meat is scarce and is growing scarcer. Vitamin tablets appear to make up for this deficiency to a satisfactory extent. The native population of Assam is faced with a food shortage due to transportation facilities from Calcutta and other southern points and this affects Quartermaster Supply. The local food shortage is not critical at this date but British civilians expect it to become critical before the monsoon is over. Some sources predict food riots in Assam this summer. Plans have been made to transport food supplies from Calcutta to Assam by air for the native population in the immediate vicinity of our airdromes if and when such a situation exists and providing that native unrest interferes with our operations. These plans are held in this Headquarters at present and have not as yet been coordinated with or approved by the Theatre.

b. Morale on the whole is good. There is a widespread feeling among personnel that by the grace of God if by no other means they will be sent home or to another Theatre after one year's service in this area. The fact that such a plan is wholly impractical does not lessen the vividness of the popular dream. Consideration is being given to some means of combatting this harmful fiction by means of propaganda emanating either from the States or from this Theatre or both. An instance of the prevalence of this feeling was that the recent morale talks given to troops in this Theatre by Colonel Rickenbacker were in most cases failures as a stimulant to morale simply because he said that personnel should be prepared to stay here and fight for a long, long time. That statement of all the statements he made was the one remembered and repeated by a majority of personnel of all ranks, and repeated with long faces. In some respects however the widespread grousing among personnel is healthy and is not a morale factor. The proximity of the enemy serves to maintain morale at a sound level. Enemy activity invariably raises it still higher. A Special Services Officer with the rank of Major arrived at this Headquarters ten days ago and is instituting a Special Services program. Other Special Services officers are enroute or expected soon from the States. There has been no Special Services program or personnel prior to this date in this Wing.

*   *   *   *

Supply:

a. The supply situation is critical and may be expected to remain so for some weeks and months to come. It is fully understood that shortages in a combat area are normal. Motor vehicles, including refueling units and transporation required for the movement of air crews from quarters to landing strips, are beginning to arrive in Calcutta. Refueling units are needed to handle not only the increased aircraft allotments but to take care of aircraft already on hand. Transportation for air crews from quarters to landing strips is particularly required in this area, due to British airdrome design which conventionally places quarters from three to five miles from landing strips. Unfortunately the equipment now beginning to arrive in Calcutta arrived simultaneously with the monsoon. Vehicular equipment cannot be moved to Assam by highway because the roads from Calcutta to southern Assam are impassable, with numerous bridges out and extensive sections of highway under deep water. The other two means of transporting these vehicles and other essential heavy equipment from Calcutta to Assam are railway and river boat. Both these facilities are congested at this date. British troops numbering 100,000 are being moved from Calcutta and environs to the Manipur Road area in connection with the Burma campaign. All United States Army Forces in the Assam area are undergoing extensive expansion either as a supporting measure to the ICWATC expansion or in connection with other Theatre projects. All need equipment and supplies and all must depend upon railway and river boat transportation from Calcutta to Assam.

b. Priority for rail transportation from Calcutta to Assam is allocated by the Tenth Air Force by means of liaison with British Headquarters in New Delhi. Roughly, two-thirds of the available rail transportation is allotted to the British and one-third to American Forces. Ten (10) broad gauge wagons (freight cars) per day are allotted at this date to all United States Army Forces in the Assam area for the transportation of essential war materials. One (1) broad gauge wagon per day at this date is allotted to this Wing. Requisition for 81 broad gauge wagons to haul from Calcutta to Assam essential vehicular equipment including refueling units now in Calcutta was entered by this Headquarters on June 20. How many will be obtained is not known at this date. The number requisitioned would haul to Assam in about ten (10) days per train the essential equipment now in Calcutta. At the rate of the present allotment of one (1) broad gauge wagon per day it would take two (2) months to move this equipment to Assam. It comes by rail to Bonggaigon, south of Assam; from there it is ferried across the Brahmaputra River and thence driven up the currently useable Assam highway to the Assam airdromes of the ICWATC. Steps are being taken through channels and out of channels to obtain the necessary priority for moving this equipment here by rail as rapidly as possible.

*   *   *   *

g. River shipment from Calcutta to Assam is slow, congested, and generally unsatisfactory but the rail situation is such that river shipment may be utilized in the near future in favor of rail. A major breakdown of rail facilities between Calcutta and Assam is neither inconceivable nor unprecedented during the monsoon season. Such a breakdown would cause essential equipment to be stranded at some inaccessible point enroute from which it would not be extricated for weeks. At many such points there are no parallel or even neighboring highways. Priority for river boat transport is more difficult to obtain than rail priority because of the acute shortage of river flats and the fact that river transportation is utilized for hauling gasoline and other essential war materials from Calcutta to Assam for shipment over the Hump to China.

*   *   *   *

Faulty and insufficient communications at this date seriously affect the efficient operation of this Wing. A harried Staff Officer recently remarked with grim humor that with teletype, telephone and radio communications what they are, quicker results can be obtained by starting a rumor. A top priority PX message to this Headquarters concerning the expected arrival at Chabua of Madame Chiang Kai-shek got to this Headquarters after she had come and gone. The S–4 of this Staff on a recent Tuesday wired this Headquarters from Calcutta asking for certain instructions, flew up here to Chabua on Wednesday and on Friday his message came through and was laid on his desk. During the recent visit of Colonel Eddie Rickenbacker, teletype messages to Jorhat and Tezpur informing the Commanding Officers of his expected arrival to speak to the troops and award decorations got to those stations sixty-four hours after he had arrived and departed. These incidents are illuminating when it is remembered that the stations of this Wing are strung out over several thousand miles of territory from Karachi to Kunming; that roads between Assam airdromes are virtually impassable now that the rains have come; that transportation is at this date insufficient to meet the needs of pilots going from quarters to landing strips, much less for travel between airdromes; and that Assam airdromes are from 15 to 170 miles apart. Signal Corps and AACS communications systems in this area are undergoing extensive expansion at this date but it will be weeks before this expansion is accomplished. Point-to-point communication has been augmented by the setting up of equipment belonging to the First Transport Group at Chabua, Jorhat, Tezpur, and Calcutta. This small unit is controlled entirely by ICWATC and handles emergency and routine administrative traffic between these points when other means are lacking or are broken down.

An Air Traffic Control System is being set up as a necessary adjunct to increased air traffic in this area. It will be handicapped and for a period rendered inoperable by the present communications facilities. The route over the Hump is narrow and shallow. To the south is the enemy and in recent weeks there is some evidence, though inconclusive, that he is setting up anti-aircraft units in regions over which pliots are sometimes forced to fly because of turbulence or icing conditions on the usual Hump route. North of the usual route are mountain peaks too high to fly over. At too high an altitude over the usual Hump route are icing conditions; at too low an altitude are the tops of mountains. Through this limited air space our planes will be flying simultaneously from India to China and from China to India in order that full use may be made of the limited base facilities now available. Air traffic control is therefore essential. Flight radio operators will be used for the air traffic control system because no other experienced radio personnel are available at this date. This is being accomplished as newly arrived radio personnel complete their training course after their arrival in India. They require a course in radio technique after their arrival in India because their previous training is not sufficient to enable them to perform their duties.

The daily life of the men was miserable. PX supplies and other good things came through irregularly and fitfully, even to Assam. In China a bottle of whiskey fetched as high as seventy-five and even a hundred dollars American money, and American cigarettes were priced in proportion. Food supplies to Assam broke down from time to time, and the men kept up their grinding rate of work on cut-down C–rations. At one time for nearly a month they were issued a three-quarter ration. In China, food was furnished by the Chinese Government. It was adequate, but it was not good, and the Americans sickened of rice-flour bread. Chinese whiskey was used for lighter fuel, it was burned in lamps, and in desperation it was drunk.

And yet, there was a counter-factor. All the men knew what they were doing and why. There was a pride in wearing the C.-B.-I. Theater patch on their shoulders and in belonging to the fabulous Hump operation. They were in the war, and no two ways about it. No matter how sticky the going became, how their weariness mounted, how awful the weather in which the ground crews worked or through which the flight crews were asked to fly, somehow they never let go.

The tonnage steadily increased, but still the objective was not reached. Alexander literally wore himself out; weary and sick, he was relieved on October 15th by Brigadier General Earl S. Hoag. Later he took over the Caribbean Division for a time, and then went on to other key pioneering jobs in the Pacific. Hoag took up with a drive like Alexander's. He was, of course, favored by the ending of the monsoon and the beginning of the best period of Hump weather. Alexander had the dirty part of the job. To his successor he turned over a route on which the necessary construction was well advanced, many items of radio equipment had been installed, and the crews were trained. This, however, does not detract from Hoag's achievement. He inherited no bed of roses. I make the comparison in justice to Alexander. Later, among persons emphatically not in the know, I heard rumors that Alexander had been relieved because he had flopped. This is absolutely untrue. He was relieved because he had burned himself out; his achievement was a great one, and he was justly and rightly decorated for it.

In October, the tonnage rose to 7359. In November, a month of most "favorable" weather, it fell off to 6490. In this month twelve aircraft were missing in flight — indeed Hoag had inherited no soft snap. In December, by relentless driving, the mark was at last reached and exceeded. Every eleven minutes throughout the month a plane took off for China, and at month's end the glorious total of 12,594 tons had been carried over the Hump.

As a matter of interest, I checked accident figures for January, 1944, and August, 1945 (in the first month the amount carried to China increased by another 800 tons). In January, 1944, one aircraft was wrecked for every 218 trips over the Hump; every thousand tons delivered to China cost 2.94 lives, an American life for approximately every 340 tons.

In August, 1945, the operation was nearly a normal one. The Japanese had been driven well back, we had full air supremacy, Mitkyina had been retaken and the route, well equipped with modern aids, ran over the lower, eastern Himalayas. One aircraft was lost then for every 2309 trips, and each 1000 tons cost 0.189 lives.

Though the objective was reached three months late, the accomplishment was so great, and done under such terrific difficulties, that the President moved to give the Wing a Presidential Unit Citation. The Adjutant General's office protested that these citations were given only to combat units — it had previously blocked citation of the engineers who built the Alcan Highway on these grounds. The President felt that the Wing was as good as in combat, and overruled the Office. For the first and only time in our military history, the Unit Citation was issued to an organization which had not actually engaged in battle — that is to say, which although often shot at, was not equipped to shoot back. The real shock to the military authorities came when they inquired how many ribbons should be shipped, and were told, 11,000.

Some of the men did manage to shoot back. One enterprising crew in a C–47, having a Bren gun on board, spotted a Jap fighter in a clearing. They buzzed the plane, strafed it and killed the pilot. Another C–47 pilot, disgusted with the eternal Assam-China shuttle, set up a deal with his flight engineer one time when he was due to stay overnight at Kunming. By means unknown to me they acquired a number of small bombs and some extra fuel. They bribed the guard at the parking area with cigarettes, and took off after sundown. The Japanese had a replica of the DC–3, which perhaps accounts for their unchallenged passage to a point near the coast. When they found a goodly port with plenty of Japanese shipping, they let down, and the engineer had wonderful fun dropping bombs out the door. They returned to Kunming, very tired, but filled with a great sense of release.

From the time of meeting the "Objective" on, the Wing never turned back. General Hoag was transferred to command of the European Wing on March 15, 1944, being succeeded by Brigadier General Thomas O. Hardin, formerly technical adviser to the Bureau of Civil Aeronautics. One day in August the men of the Division, as it was then, believing that he was to depart in the near future, declared "Tom Hardin Day." On that day they accomplished 569 trips, delivering 1300 tons. By the end of August he had pushed the Hump tonnage up to more than 23,000 tons. On September 3 he was relieved, to take charge of A.T.C. operations in the Central Pacific. His successor was General Tunner, the builder of the Ferrying Division. General Tunner's splendid achievement of his new assignment led logically to his later post in charge of the airlift to Berlin.
Division.

The route was still dangerous. Planes went down. Men hit the silk, landed in the jungle, sometimes walked out or were rescued, sometimes died. Planes simply disappeared, or gave out a desperate "May Day" before they went down to unknown ends. The radios listing men missing continued to come in to A.T.C. Headquarters, but the planes kept moving and the supplies poured in, gasoline, ammunition, trucks, jeeps, medicines, mules, spare parts, anything and everything for war, from extra engines to Paulette Goddard on a U.S.O. tour, and out of China moved ever larger amounts of precious tungsten and other raw materials.

General Tunner was as hard a driver as any of his predecessors, but he approached his assignment from a different point of view. His whole career with the Ferrying Division tended to make him especially aware of safety. The period of urgency was over. The deliveries to China should still increase, but they should do so in a soberer manner. He had the advantages of a well-developed route and an organization which had matured. He laid great stress on bringing down the accident rate. By the end of 1944 he had raised the monthly tonnage by a little more than eight thousand, and had decreased the accident rate sharply. In the following six months he increased tonnage beyond any quantity ever carried by air before or since, with a steady increase in safety and efficiency, and at the same time achieved the greatest air troop movements in history.

As the war continued to progress favorably, his Division engaged increasingly in flying within China, especially in transporting very large numbers of Chinese troops from point to point. This function involved strange and terrible hazards of its own. At one time, when the co-pilot went back into the cargo section to see how the troops were getting on, one soldier complained, the co-pilot thought fractiously. He told him that if he did not like it, he could get out and walk. The co-pilot went back to the flight deck. The soldier followed his suggestion literally. On another occasion, the pilot found that the flying characteristics of his plane had suddenly changed in an unaccountable manner. He went back to look. The door was open and the hold was empty. An entire load of troops, miserably airsick and panicked, had decided to walk out.

In early 1945, the stepped-up tempo of fighting along the India-Burma frontier drew the Division into a new type of activity. In February the 17th Indian Division was cut off in the Arakan sector of Burma by the Japanese, and in bad shape. Lord Mountbatten, inter-allied commander in Southeast Asia, asked the Division to provide twenty-five C–46's to aid in their relief. Twenty-five C–46's and C–47's were furnished within thirty-six hours, to operate under control of the Troop Carrier Command. They continued flying in supplies and evacuating wounded and war-weary personnel until the end of March. Part of their service was in support of the division at Arakan, part in support of resistance against the Japanese offensive at Imphal. Later, twenty more C–46's were asked for and provided to support ground troops until May 20. In all, the A.T.C. planes flew more than 1300 sorties in these two affairs. Although frequently under fire, no plane was seriously damaged.

Ninety-six further sorties were flown to bring in over 2500 American troops and some 4000 tons of supplies to relieve General Stilwell's forces in the Myitkyina area. Tied in with the same critical period of offensive and counteroffensive was the movement of more than 17,000 Chinese troops out of China to Sookerating in Assam, whence they joined the American ground forces. Since all of these activities meant that aircraft were taken off the regular runs, the Division authorities referred to them by the term used for any such side activities — "diversions."

In July, 1945, when the old, low route to China had been reopened and Myitkyina was at last securely ours, the spectacular quantity of 71,042 tons of cargo were flown to China, of which over 50,000 were directly handled by the Division's planes. By then the old, terrible, glorious, man-killing days were over. Thereafter the operations dwindled. The India-China Division did yeoman work in moving Chinese and American troops from the interior to the coast, for a while its network reached widely through China, with a line running as far north as Pekin. Men who had dragged it out so long in the wretched hostels of the Kunming area and forced down the monotonously nauseating Chinese grub revelled in the amazing luxuries of Shanghai, the choice hotels, the European-style meals, the fine liquors, the real, high-style Chinese menus. Slowly the fetid Assam area and the stark neighborhood of Kunming emptied, and the Hump operation was over. Once that remote wilderness carried a traffic such as La Guardia Airport has never remotely approached; in all likelihood never again will anyone save some explorer bring the sound of aircraft engines over those mountains. The last to leave, of course, were the men of the Graves Registration service, searching for the last of the dead.

XII

WASPS IN THE AIR

On September 25, 1942, with the blessing of A.A.F. Headquarters the Air Transport Command initiated an interesting, small-scale experiment when it set up the first squadron of women civilian ferry pilots at the base run by the Ferrying Division's 5th Ferrying Group outside Wilmington. The squadron was headed by Nancy H. Love, a very attractive person who describes herself as a woman who wants to do all the flying she can. Mrs. Love's husband, Major (later Colonel) Robert M. Love, was the Command's Deputy Chief of Staff. This connection undoubtedly had some bearing on the selection of Mrs. Love. There were other factors: She had for some time held a civilian position in the Operations office on the base, she was familiar with ferrying procedure and military formulae, and was known to headquarters as a woman who did business without femininity or fuss. As far back as 1940 she had conferred with General Olds, when he was in the Plans Division of Air Staff, on the possibility of using women pilots in non-combat flying. Since her connection with A.T.C. she had argued the desirability of so using them.

The idea was no monopoly of Mrs. Love's. A more famous flyer, Miss Jacqueline Cochran, had propounded the idea even earlier than the date of the conferences with Olds. Shortly after the Ferrying Command got going, Miss Cochran returned from England where she had seen the beginnings of the British use of women pilots and, with the President's backing, had put in a lot of hard work at Ferrying Command Headquarters on a plan for similar service. Nothing came of this effort, as higher

authorities felt that it was not then desirable. At that time the
Air Corps wanted to give the existing reservoir of male pilots
as much experience as possible in order to prepare them for
combat duty. The introduction of women would merely delay
the program.

Evidently others were thinking along related lines, for at the
time of the conferences with Mrs. Love, the Navy had prepared a bill for introduction in Congress to permit the out-
right commissioning of women pilots in its Air Arm.

The discussions between Colonel Olds and the two women
brought out a fundamental difference of opinion which colored the entire story of our actual use of female flyers during
the war. Colonel Olds and Mrs. Love, and later the Air Transport Command, thought only in terms of the aid that women
might give in carrying out existing missions with a minimum
of disturbance to the organizations they served. The squadron
set up at Wilmington, under the name of Women's Auxiliary
Ferrying Squadron, was to be made up of twenty-five selected
women whose experience approximated that of male civilians
then being recruited. If the women made good, a second
squadron would be formed, and so on until the supply of
women of that level of experience was exhausted. At the very
most, there were not more than two hundred who could qual-
ify. They had to have such background as five hundred hours'
flying time, Civil Aeronautics Authority rating on 200-horse-
power engines, and a commercial license.

The Command proposed to handle these women as nearly
as possible as it did male civilians. Essentially their employ-
ment was a matter of individual contracts. For their own protection they would be organized into squadrons under responsible women leaders, just as they had to be housed sep-
arately. They would not form a separate corps, save to the
extent that, because of their sex, certain special regulations and
practices had to apply, but would be a part of the personnel of
the base to which they were assigned — women doing "men's
work" in wartime.

Miss Cochran's concept was much more ambitious and distinctly feministic. She wanted a thorough demonstration of
women's capabilities, and foresaw women taking over very

large areas of non-combat flying. The demonstration, with its ultimate goal of releasing thousands of men for more dangerous work, was primary; the execution of assigned missions seems to have been secondary. Thus in the plan she drew up for Colonel Olds, she set forth what amounts to a large-scale development of in-service training which foreshadowed the system which the Ferrying Division later established. She felt strongly that women should be tightly organized, a definite corps, and placed under strict command of a single woman commander.

In 1942 and 1943 there was a chronic and often acute shortage of pilots. As was mentioned earlier, General Olds wanted to start hiring qualified women pilots as he was doing men in January, 1942. He desisted on instructions from General Arnold, given in response to Miss Cochran's protest. The shortage continued. Mrs. Love pressed for hiring selected women to relieve it, and so the first Women's Auxiliary Ferrying Squadron was established on September 25.

Almost at the moment that this move was being announced to the public through the Secretary of War's office, Miss Cochran returned to Washington from England. She went into immediate conferences with Air Staff, which decided to put her ideas at least part way into effect. I say part way because to my mind there are indications that the high command never did intend to allow the full scope of Miss Cochran's plan. The record is involved and difficult; in this matter one cannot cite chapter and verse. One finds in it, however, a tone, an effect of talk at cross purposes, which leads one to feel that Miss Cochran was to some extent the victim of the constraint which high-ranking officers felt in dealing with a woman. As Director of Women Pilots, the post to which she shortly was appointed, Miss Cochran was unique in being a civilian and a woman in an upper-level staff position. Her position was made more, not less, difficult by the fact that she was attractive and that she put forth her ideas with vigor. Where the brass would have argued forthrightly with a man in the same spot and when necessary bluntly told him "no," they seem to have felt that a woman had to be yessed along — and then blocked.

The arrangement as made in October of 1942 was that a

training school for women pilots would be set up under Miss
Cochran's supervision, and that the Air Transport Command
would accept its graduates, for absorption into the Ferrying
Division. The Command agreed to this with some reluctance,
especially because it thereby relinquished its right to refuse to
employ personnel whom it might judge as unqualified or otherwise objectionable — a most unusual infringement on the prerogatives of command control. The agreement was made principally at the desire of the Commanding General, Army Air
Forces.

Some time would elapse before the first graduate came from
the school which was established at Sweetwater, Texas. Meantime, out on the bases, the women were flying. Establishment
of the first WAFS squadron produced a staggering burst of
publicity for which the A.T.C. officers concerned seem, with
surprising unworldliness, to have been unprepared. Throughout, the women pilots movement had to contend with an excessive and false type of publicity which at once over-glamorized
hard-working, earnest young women and stood ready and waiting for a bit of scandal or a touch of sex.

Like any other pilots, the women started delivering the
basic types, the Ferrying Division's Class I aircraft.[1] They flew
about as well as men, and were a little more careful about
sticking to schedules and flight plans. They took the rough
with the smooth, flying open-cockpit jobs in foul weather,
standing guard over their aircraft when forced to land at fields
where there were no guards, putting up with good lodgings
and bad.

For all the publicity, there was plenty of confusion about
them. Some people, on hearing that they were ferry pilots,
wondered how frail women could steer those big, heavy boats.
They were taken for nurses, Red Cross workers, girl scouts.
On one occasion when a group of them came into a strange
town, tired and messy and dressed in their flying clothes, they
were taken for some new kind of disreputable women and put
through a painful experience with the local police and provost
marshall — for which the latter was roundly reprimanded.

[1] The system of classes of aircraft is described on page 18.

They had conversations like this, usually with elderly ladies:

"What is that uniform?"

"Women's Auxiliary Ferrying Squadron."

"What is that?"

"We deliver aircraft for the Air Transport Command."

"You mean you fly in them?"

"Yes, of course."

"Who with?"

"With nobody. They're single-seater jobs."

Long pause. Then, in real puzzlement, "But who pilots the planes?"

Altogether fifty women were recruited directly by the WAFS. Thereafter, beginning in the spring of 1943, they received their increment from the women's training school. The early group steadily increased its rate of deliveries. Three accidents marred its record in November, 1942; then there were no more until March. Then, tragically, Miss Cornelia Fort — the second woman to join the organization — was killed in a collision during a flight in formation. Judging by her photographs, one could pretty nearly describe Miss Fort as beautiful. She was twenty-three years old, and was an accomplished pilot with 1100 hours' flying time.

When Miss Cochran became Director of Women Pilots in August, 1943, a further step was taken towards implementing her concept of a special corps of women when all women flying for the Army Air Forces, looked upon as an organization, were designated Women Auxiliary Service Pilots, or WASP's. The Ferrying Division was not happy at having the older designation of WAFS, established nearly a year and already famous, taken away from it. Out of sentiment, it kept the designation on signs, such as over the women's barracks, where it already had been set up — which in turn caused some irritation to Miss Cochran.

From this point on there was a steady push and pull between the Ferrying Division, through A.T.C., and Miss Cochran over the clash between its sole desire to get on with its mission of delivering aircraft and training pilots, and hers to conduct a large experiment. Again I feel that some of this conflict could have been avoided if Air Staff had been blunter with its Director of Women Pilots in regard to the limitations of a staff officer's command functions. In order to carry out her experiment most effectively, she desired and perhaps needed to exercise a control over all WASP's which ran head on into the rights of command control of the operating organizations. Air Staff seems to have preferred to let the lower organization — in this case A.T.C. — carry the burden of setting her straight. From Miss Cochran's point of view, this meant that the Command seemed rebelliously intransigent; from the Command's point of view, that Miss Cochran seemed a wild imperialist. Extremely hard feelings developed all round.

The first women received from the training school turned out to be excellent. By the time the WASP's were established, all but the most recent graduates had gone on beyond Class I flying, and some of the original WAFS were reaching much higher. It may be said now that between the WASP's assigned to A.T.C. and those assigned to other Commands, before the end of their service there was no military aircraft that at least a few women had not flown successfully, including B–29's, C–54's, and the famously hot B–26's.[2]

In the spring of 1944 a situation arose which led to a special form of service which stands to the everlasting credit of the women. It also demonstrated the impossibility of a major experiment such as the one outlined in time of war. As 1943 wore on the effect of the Air Transport Command's commitment to absorb all WASP training school graduates was lightened as other organizations, especially Training Command, asked to receive numbers of them. Nonetheless, the Ferrying Division began to find, as the number of WASP's in its employ reached towards the eventual peak of three hundred and three, that it had more than it could profitably use. This situation derived

---

[2] It was a common joke in A.T.C. that Mrs. Love kept her husband on the jump. Both of them are real flyers, but he, as Deputy Chief of Staff, was preoccupied with administrative work whereas she, even after she became the Ferrying Division's Executive for WASP, got in plenty of flying. Mrs. Love would check out on a plane which the colonel had never handled, putting it up to him to move fast to catch up with her.

from the dual nature of the Division's mission — ferrying and training.

As has already been explained, the Ferrying Division's training program was based on an initial period of ferrying Class I aircraft, of which trainers were the most important type, and in the next step of "upgrading," Class II, trainers again played an important part. By early 1944, instead of there being a flood of these types which all but overwhelmed the meager number of pilots on hand, production had levelled off, and the supply of male pilots had become so ample that they and the WASP's were competing for the flights which were the means of advancement to the higher ferrying classes.

It now became reasonable to accept new women and put them through the *cursus honorum* which led to Class V plus instrument qualifications, and hence to eligibility for overseas ferry service and transport flying, only if they, like the men, could come out at the other end and move into those services. Otherwise, giving them this training merely diminished the rate at which the greatly needed, "finished," male pilots were turned out.

There had been no formal rule that women could not thus graduate and go into overseas service until late in 1943, rather everyone except a few of the women assumed that they could fly only domestically. Very early in the game it had also been assumed that they would ferry only trainers and other light aircraft, but that assumption had long been dissipated as the women went on to pursuits and heavy aircraft. In the end of August, 1943, the Air Transport Command decided that two of the most skilled of the original WAFS, Mrs. Love and Mrs. Betty Hughes Gillies, were ready to make a foreign delivery. General Arnold being then in London, the project was cleared verbally with the Chief of Air Staff, to make sure that there were no objections. The two women picked up a B–17 and flew it to Presque Isle and thence to Goose Bay in Labrador, where they arrived on September 4th.

Normally, four-engined aircraft were dispatched from Presque Isle to the United Kingdom via Newfoundland, but Colonel Tunner instructed the two women to go by Goose

Bay and thence to U.K. via Greenland and Iceland so that they should have shorter over-water hops to make. At Goose Bay they encountered bad weather, which held them back until the following day.

Believing that they had taken off, A.T.C. Headquarters radioed Brigadier General Burrows, commander of its European Wing, that the plane was en route and to be on watch for it. As the two women were waiting at the Labrador base, General Burrows was having dinner with General Arnold. The message was brought to him at the table, and he promptly and proudly showed it to his superior. Equally promptly General Arnold radioed that if the aircraft had not yet taken off it was not to do so, and that until further notice women pilots should fly only in domestic service.

The message reached Goose Bay just fifteen minutes before Mrs. Love and Mrs. Gillies were to take off. Reluctantly the commanding officer there — Colonel A. D. Smith — hurried to the line. Sadly they turned away from their plane, and sadly they returned by transport to the Zone of the Interior. When they reached Presque Isle, they encountered ferry pilots, just returning there, who had taken off for the United Kingdom at the same time they took off for Goose Bay. These men did not know they had been routed another way, and asked them where on earth they had been. They had looked all over for them at Prestwick — where had they landed? It really hurt to have to tell them what had happened.

There was regret throughout the Command when the news came through. Everyone had hoped the flight would be made, everyone had been sweating them out, not alone because it would have been a magnificent first, but because of the known competence and great popularity of the two flyers.

General Arnold, of course, was not personally acquainted with Mrs. Love and Mrs. Gillies. He did not share the Command's assurance of their flying ability. More importantly, the introduction of women pilots into foreign service involved a decision of policy, to which he well might want to give careful consideration before a precedent had been established. Partly in this connection, Miss Cochran later made an interesting point. It was her feeling that in the testing of the capabilities of women pilots as a whole, individual cometlike achievements should be avoided; graduation into important, new assignments should be, not by exceptional individuals but by groups. To which the Ferrying Division would probably have answered that it was unfair to hold back able pilots while waiting for a large group to develop, and that such holding back was not the most effective way to win a war.

One cannot help regretting that these two women, devotedly hard workers, in no sense prima donnas, the founders of women's military flying in the United States (Mrs. Gillies was the first to join the WAFS after it was established), should have come so to the very edge of such a notable achievement, and then been turned back.

The limitation of WASP's to domestic flying was thereafter embodied in an Air Force regulation. This meant that if they reached Class V in the Ferrying Division they would become stuck at the top. Either they could not keep on flying in that class, or else they would prevent the Division from completing the training of the male pilots who were so badly needed. All along the line, now, from Class I to Class V, the women offered a harmful competition with the men. Conditions had indeed changed.

There was one important class of aircraft, however, which did not fit into the upgrading program. This was single engine pursuits, or fighters. As a class, they are the most dangerous of all planes to fly. Enormously powerful, fast, hot on take-off and landing, single seaters throwing the whole burden of flying on the pilot, they call for real skill. Nothing about them is intended for caution or conservatism, they are intended to be handled by collectedly reckless men. In all kinds of flying the accident rate with fighters runs consistently higher than with other classes; thus the Continental Air Force, which was formed from the four home-based Air Forces in 1944, found in that year that the accident rate with heavy bombers was 0.29 per thousand hours, with single-engine pursuits generally 1.34 per thousand hours, and for a single type, the P–39, 2.88. There were always plenty of these aircraft on hand to ferry.

Checking pilots out on them only delayed their upgrading to the foreign flying levels. If the women were to continue to be of real use to the Ferrying Division, pursuit ferrying must become their specialty.

The young women were entirely willing. A number of them had already checked out on pursuits. The Division went ahead with the policy, and at the same time, with a good deal of difficulty and after numerous explanations, the Command arranged to receive no more WASP graduates, and to return all those in hand who could not readily be inducted into pursuit ferrying. From then until the WASP was dissolved in December, 1944, an average of a hundred and forty were concentrating diligently and quietly on a difficult, fatiguing specialty, thereby rendering a significant contribution to victory.

From the end of 1942 on, the question of giving women pilots military status was constantly debated. At one time it was planned to incorporate them in the WAC, but Miss Cochran opposed this. At another, some bright reader of fine print in the Air Transport Command discovered that there was nothing in Army Regulations that specified that an officer had to be a man. It was merely taken for granted. He suggested that they simply be commissioned. This original idea got as far as the General Staff, where authorities who not only read the fine print but also read between the lines put an end to it.

Eventually a bill for establishing a special corps of commissioned women pilots was introduced in Congress, where it ran into heavy trouble. At about that time the Air Forces were releasing a large number of civilian flying instructors who had been working for them under contract. These men naturally felt that they should be taken into the Army as pilots, rather than be drafted as general soldiers. The Air Forces were reluctant to take them on; I have read the testimony before Congress, and other documents, and I still cannot figure out why. The question of incorporating the WASP into the Air Corps became joined with that of taking on these men. Congress was cantankerous, and the Army Air Forces were politically stupid. The upshot of the debate was that the A.A.F. were instructed

to give up the expensive practice of training relatively green
women, in favor of recruiting men who needed very little
training. Any hope of commissioning those women who were
already on the job was killed, although the committee recommended that their services be continued.

The last graduates came out of Sweetwater school in July,
and the school was then closed. In October, Miss Cochran
formally recommended to General Arnold that the WASP be
dissolved. This, too, I find difficulty in understanding, although I have read the recommendation and various post facto
supporting arguments. Certainly any hope of Miss Cochran's
carrying through her original broad scheme was ended, nor —
if that were one of her ambitions — could she any longer anticipate a post rivalling Colonel Hobby's, but the women had been
trained at great expense, they were doing useful work, they
were making an admirable record, they wanted to go on. General Arnold accepted Miss Cochran's recommendation, ordering that all flying by women for the Army terminate on December 20.

The Air Transport Command badly needed its pursuit
specialists. It asked in vain for an exception. On the date set,
all WASP's were grounded. At that time there was a crisis in
pursuit ferrying. A number of these young women volunteered
to serve unpaid until the rush was over, but the Command
could not accept their offer; instead, pilots were diverted from
combat outfits to help with the job.

For two years these women had been doing work strictly comparable to that done by Army pilots. Of the ones assigned to
A.T.C. when their service ended, a hundred and nine were
qualified in Class III, twenty-four in Class IV, flying such
bombers as B–25's and B–26's, twin-engine pursuits such as the
P–38, C–47's, and other such ships, and four had reached Class
V. They had ferried seventy-seven different types of aircraft.
As civilians, they could receive no veterans' benefits, no pen-
sions for those who were injured; there was no G.I. insurance
for the relatives of those who were killed — and in the Air
Transport Command alone eleven died in their country's service. Now, on the recommendation of their leader, they were

wiped out of existence as flyers, and they were understandably bitter.

The two years' experience showed that women have a great potential contribution to make in this field. Perhaps in part because they knew that they were on trial, they were more regular than men, adhered more closely to schedules, and observed flight rules more carefully. This group, physically select, generally could and did continue flying during menstruation. Even including those who did not, they lost less flying time for reasons of physical disability than did their male colleagues. One reason for this was that they took better care of themselves and were less inclined to go on benders.

They could handle all types of aircraft, but on heavy transports and bombers it was found that their smaller stature and relatively less strength of arm forced them to fatiguing efforts. On heavy and perhaps on medium aircraft, most of them, so far as the experiment went, should not undertake long-range, nonstop flights, and hence would not be satisfactory in transoceanic operations. In view of their general record and that of the WAC, there seems to be no reason why they should not be used in shorter-range operations in overseas theaters. Now that we are at peace and have plenty of idle aircraft, a real experiment with a women's Air Reserve might well be tried.

As might be expected, they were a group of lively young women, adventurous, and above average in looks. They were surrounded throughout by hostile observers waiting for a chance to develop scandal. Of course there was some misbehavior, but scandal failed to develop. Their level of conduct, while within normal range, was high. They were often impatient of military channels and procedures, and humanly not above exerting a little feminine charm to obtain their ends.

They got a lot of publicity when they were going strong. Later they were subjected to some venomous slanders in Congress. They worked hard and quietly, and did not use their sex as a reason to turn back from danger.

XIII

BLUIE — LAWYER — FANTAN

FOR THE SAKE OF SECURITY, things, places, and undertakings were known by code names which sometimes had a fantastic effect occurring in the context of talk and messages of war. I have often wondered who dreamed them up. The words had to be such that they were not likely to be taken as merely part of an ordinary sentence. One could not use "gun" or "propeller," for instance, but "Poppy," "Larkspur," or "Grumpy" served admirably. Lists containing thousands of such words were drawn up, and they were allotted in blocks to certain areas, organizations, or projects. These blocks had to be well scrambled: the words allotted to an area should not, for instance, begin with the same letter or express related ideas, lest if the enemy learned the meaning of one, he could deduce others from it. There was a poetic suitability to some: Overlord for the invasion of Europe, Anvil for the correlated attack upon southern France, Carpetbagger for the smuggling of men and supplies to the European underground. Others had a wild hilarity about them, such as Bluie for Greenland, Bolero for the movement of short-range aircraft to Britain via the Arctic, and the curiously suitable Grumpy for Alaska. Perhaps the nicest of all, and the only two-word code name I know of, was the delightfully Chinese term for Madame Chiang Kai-shek: Precious Cargo. This was evolved informally and then stuck. It gave an other-world character to the "PX" message from an incoming plane, "have precious cargo aboard."

For safety's sake, even in conversation between two men completely in the know, one always used the code term, so that its use would be habitual. This did odd things to the conversation. I have heard an officer speak of "Madame Precious Cargo." A man might say, "I'm going to the Bluies," meaning that he would make a tour of the Greenland bases. An officer I met recently, on learning that I had been with A.T.C., told me, "I commanded the advance echelon of the Matterhorn," thus effectively bewildering a number of people. He simply meant that he had commanded the detachment of the then 20th Bomber Wing which went to China to make ready for the first movement of B–29's. The war was over and secrecy had ended, but it was the natural way for him, or for me, to speak of the thing.

Many people handled these words, in message centers and at keyboards, without knowing their meaning. To those who knew them, they were something of a burden. A list of code words and a list of their meanings had to be kept separate from each other, in locked safes, and one had to be careful about consulting them, for one's secretary, or even, in some cases, one's right hand man was not supposed to know of the lists' existence. Preferably, one memorized them. This was most easily done by forgetting the original name, and simply thinking of Ascension as Lawyer or New Caledonia as Fantan. With this, it became necessary to perform mental somersaults, remembering in ordinary conversation, as with one's wife, to refer to Grumpy as Alaska or Fantan as New Caledonia, if those places came up in the normal course of non-military conversation.

In the Air Transport Command, the code words generally referred to places, an ever-increasing string of places around the world, east, west, north, and south. To me, the very phrase, "code word," brings up the picture of the manifold dots strung along the constantly reaching tentacles of the octopus which was A.T.C.'s routes. I have referred frequently to routes, their development, their capacities, their lacks. The public still, I believe, thinks of an air route as being something rather simple, in its essence not much more than a line in the air. In fact, an air route is as complex, as definite, and as tangible as a railway.

First of all, there must be bases, spaced at such intervals as will lead to the most economical flying. Up to a certain point, the nearer the bases are to each other, the better, as an aeroplane carries less gas for short hops, and hence has a greater payload. Landing and take-off, however, are time-consuming and gas-consuming, and more time is taken by the process of refuelling, so that if bases are very close together, it becomes more economical to overfly some of them.

A base must have adequate runways, taxiways, and parking space or "hardstands." The latter expression refers to the necessity of building the parking space so that it will stand up under the pressure of 50,000 or so pounds of aircraft. Nor is a runway merely a smooth surface. A 50-ton machine landing at around a hundred miles an hour strikes a terrific blow. If the runway is to continue in permanent, frequent use, it must be of a construction surpassing the finest of highways.

There must be a control tower, to "talk the planes in" and control incoming and outgoing traffic. This means voice-communication radio, so that the control tower operator can speak directly with the pilot. There must also be longer-range, dot-and-dash radio with which dependable communication may be maintained with aircraft at a distance. In order that the base may be found even when covered with a solid blanket of clouds (overcast to us, "undercast" to the flyer), there must be directional beams, both of the "beacon" type which causes a needle on a special compass on the instrument panel to swing towards it, and of the type known as a "radio range" which gives dot-and-dash signals when the pilot is to the right or left of his course, a steady hum when he is "on the beam."

On the base there must be a meteorologist, able to interpret and keep constantly up to the minute the meteorological information which comes in from the supporting network of weather stations which extends to vast distances.[1] This, of course, implies a correspondingly vast communications network. This requirement resulted in the very close affiliation established between the Air Transport Command, the Army Airways Com-

[1] In the airman's jargon, "weather" has two meanings: information as to the weather, and bad weather. He will say, "give me the weather," and "we ran into weather this trip."

munication Service, and the Air Weather Service during the
war, a functional relationship which led to placing the two
Services within the Command after the war ended.

At certain points on a long route, there must be the means
of lodging and feeding crews and passengers, which in terms of
such operations as the A.T.C.'s in wartime means a thousand
or more guests at a time at busy stations, and there must be
everything necessary to serve and perform at least emergency
repairs on the aircraft. Home stations must be able virtually
to rebuild the machines.

Equipping the base to render all these services to aircraft
on the ground and in its immediate vicinity is not the end of
the requirement. Air traffic, like ground traffic, must be controlled. If possible, constant contact should be maintained
with the planes in flight between stations, for readiness in case
of trouble. Collisions occur in the air as well as on the ground,
therefore each departing plane is assigned a level at which it
must fly. It departs under the air traffic control of the base it
is leaving, which feeds the pilot information of changes in
weather ahead, and informs him if for any reason he must
change his course or altitude. At regular intervals, even if the
base has no information to forward, the radio operator in the
aircraft reports to it. This may be at fixed intervals of time,
or on passing certain landmarks which are referred to as
"check-points."

At mid-point, the plane is turned over to the base at which
it will land, or to an intermediate one which it will overfly. As
it approaches its destination, it is warned of traffic over the airport, told to circle at a given point and altitude until the sky
is clear, brought in over the airport, again placed in readiness,
and finally cleared to land on a certain runway. By this time
the pilot has been told what wind, precipitation, and visibility
he will have as he reaches the ground, and the barometric reading by which to set his altimeter for complete accuracy.

With all precautions, crashes occur. If they occur on the
base, there are fire-fighting and first-aid equipment always
ready. If they occur off the base, but the plane has been in contact and given warning, there is rescue equipment, to be flown

or driven to the scene. The last distress signal is "May Day," which is simply a rough English phonetic equivalent of the French *"m'aidez."* The plane may go down without giving notice. When it fails to report at the next time when it should, it begins to be regarded as "overdue" — an ominous word. When it remains overdue longer than can reasonably be accounted for, it is considered lost, and search begins.

By the end of the war, air traffic control across the oceans was as exact as between any two of our domestic stations. It was an amazing thing to watch in execution, with a couple of hundred American and R.A.F. planes over the Atlantic at the same time. It had reached to this degree: A C–54 reported that it was three hundred miles off the Irish coast, at which point it began steady contact with the station at Redbrae near Prestwick in Scotland. Redbrae, Cornwall, and the Azores triangulated the plane by radio beam, and told the pilot he was off his course. The pilot checked with his navigator and said he thought not. Half an hour — a hundred miles — later, they triangulated him again. Then Redbrae asked for his compass reading, which he gave. Redbrae advised him, "your compass is off seven degrees east, your location is now such and such, your new course into Prestwick, by corrected compass, is so and so."

This Transatlantic Air Traffic Control, a joint undertaking of the A.A.F., the R.A.F., and the Canadian Government, was literally miraculous. The men at Redbrae picked up a B–17 with engine trouble off the Irish coast, and set it down on an emergency landing strip in Northern Ireland which had no communications. Radio is a wonderful thing and we know a lot about it, but it is still black magic. A C–54 coming in to Prestwick was unable to make contact either with the Prestwick control tower or with Redbrae, but remained in perfect communication with Goose Bay, Labrador. The weather was thick, the ceiling over Prestwick was only about seven hundred feet, and there was a good deal of traffic in the air. Prestwick got Redbrae on the telephone, Redbrae talked to Goose, and Goose talked the C–54 down onto a runway more than 2000 miles away.

For all of these activities, there must be supply, on a large scale. With, not hundreds, but literally thousands of aircraft in flight at any one time, there must be an unending flow of gasoline, fuel, spare parts, machines, equipment, medicines, clothing — far more than the aircraft themselves could supply. This means surface ships, freighters, tankers, railroad cars, trucks, camels, elephants, packhorses, dog teams, bearers, pipelines.

In the item of aviation gasoline alone, in January, 1943, when its scale of operations was relatively small, the Command used twenty-five million gallons; a year later it used forty-four millions in the same month, which was one tenth of the entire Allied supply. It went into 1945 consuming this fuel at a rate of eight hundred and three million gallons a year. This vast quantity had to be provided in a constant flow to India, Australia, Hawaii, Alaska, Britain, Brazil, Central Africa . . .

All of these things and more go into the building and operating of a route. For all of them there must be men and women, thousands of them, to be fed, lodged, clothed, doctored, disciplined, and when possible entertained and given an emotional breather. They worked in the icy wildernesses of Bluie and Grumpy, the grinding isolation of Lawyer, in the delightful hills of Northern California, on two tiny, desert islands off the Arabian Coast, in the infernos of Aden and of Gaya in India, where in the daytime a man could not touch metal without burning his hand, nor could he sleep, so that the maintenance men worked and snatched their shut-eye in the night.

I landed at Canton Island about four o'clock one morning. Canton is one of those dots in the Pacific about which we used to have such romantic ideas before our men were stuck on them to learn their dull, unending, grinding, remorseless misery. It had some palm trees, a lot of beach, a fine runway, and pretty good barracks. I went to the mess hall for a snack. Half a dozen officers were there, drinking coffee and talking together. Their talk had a weary, irritable quality of knowing each other too well. Their thoughts were worn, over-familiar, conveyed in a sort of code of references and stale jokes.

I introduced myself to them. As I was senior to them all, they accepted this politely and gave me their names, but without interest. Then I told them that on my plane was a very pretty nurse on her way back to the States, and that she would be turning up in a moment. They looked at me in a blank way for a few seconds. Finally one of them said, in a tone of wonder which I cannot possibly describe:

"You mean a real split woman?"

The girl — she was a lieutenant — came in. I introduced her. The men were very courteous and curiously diffident; they all spoke to her, but they spoke briefly, with silences between remarks. She made some mention of the heat, which lay upon us like a blanket wrung out in hot water. One of them had an inspiration. Wouldn't she like a shower? She would, very much indeed. One of them went for a towel and soap, three others led her off. They stood guard over the officers' shower room while she refreshed herself, then walked back with her to the plane. They had done a favor for a pretty girl, and they were plainly pleased.

Of Canton Island the base historical officer wrote: "Canton is a hard place to get used to. At first there was a good deal of psychological trouble and several men committed suicide. Later they learned to adjust themselves better."

Maiduguri is a small station in Nigeria on the southern edge of the Sahara. The soil is dusty sand, the vegetation sparse, consisting mostly of spindly trees rather like mesquite, and sharing with it the characteristic of giving no shade. Before the war the settlement consisted of half a dozen Britons, including the Resident, who represented the Empire. Here we built a fair-sized base — I think about three hundred men were stationed there. A permanent haze of dust rose to a height of about two thousand feet. Directly above one the sky seemed wanly blue, but if one looked at an angle, the blue disappeared into a dingy, blackish smudge. Sand was everywhere, on the floors, in the beds, in the mess hall. An irritated cough, known as "the Maiduguri crut," was endemic. The heat, likewise, was permanent.

The afternoon I got there, the surgeon received his promotion to major. The only other major on the post was the commanding officer, who was away, and there were no gold leaves to be had at the PX. They tried to break into the C.O.'s desk, where it was believed he had an extra pair (they rifled his billet in vain), but it was a steel desk, and they could not force it. I presented the doctor with the leaves off my trench coat, not only to his great satisfaction but to the delight of the entire post.

To Maiduguri came the usual alleviations: movies ranging from excellent to grade Q, an occasional U.S.O. team. Otherwise, about all the diversion available was in such games as handball, which it took vast energy to play in that heat, and a tour of sightseeing which in time grew utterly monotonous.

A couple of miles from Maiduguri lies the native city of Yerwa with a population of 50,000 black Mohammedans. It is the capital of a dignified personage known as the Shehu, who rules over some five million subjects. For urgent reasons of health the city was off limits except for guided tours. Outside the walls was a market at which one saw the desert Arabs with their camels, an occasional pygmy or flat-lipped Ubangi, and forest hunters dressed in leopard skins and carrying sheaves of spears. Over foods and faeces alike the flies swarmed. One looked but did not touch, then drove on to the great gate in the high, adobe city wall. About the gate were the lepers clustered, begging. Within, the streets, deeply sandy, wandered irregularly under the shade of fine trees with irrigation ditches alongside them. On either side, under the trees, the brownish adobe houses were packed, most with little gardens attached. The walls and roof-lines were curved and irregular, the tricks played with the plastering suggested a Hollywood's architect's dream. Although one knew that the city was a breeding ground of amazing and widespread infections, and the beggars were magnificent in their sores and skin diseases, the impression was one of shade, coolness, cleanliness, and peace.

The deep sand of the streets created a strange quiet. A black nobleman would ride past in Arab robes and headdress, his horse adorned with a silver-mounted headstall similar to those the Navajos used to make and having the same type of cruel, elaborate bit. On either side of him armed retainers would trot, holding to his stirrups. The bit would jingle, but there would be no other noise. The feet were soundless.

One drove about in the jeep, crossed the central square, observed the grim exterior of the Shehu's palace, the jail, and the central garrison. Inescapably, at some point the jeep would pass along one of the many streets of prostitutes. The tall, young, black women lounged in their doorways gracefully. Their robes were brilliant, they wore massive jewelry on their arms and ankles, about their necks and in their ears. On their heads they wore folded pieces of richly colored cloth. Their eyes were heavy-lidded, languorous, and they watched the white men pass with incurious, measuring, wise glances. There was a look about them of ancient knowledge, arrogant and weary of itself. One thought of the Song of Solomon's "Thou art black but thou art beautiful, Oh my Beloved," and at the same time remembered that in these sinuous bodies were diseases as ancient as their knowledge, as dark and frightful as Africa itself. One made the sterile tour and returned to the refreshing, cleanly drabness of the base, usually pretty well exhausted by the heat and dust and the intense beating of the sun.

In any sizeable company of men there are always a few fools. Under conditions of monotony and loneliness, a few men become temporarily slightly mad — the condition generally referred to in the Command as "bushy," or, in the Pacific, "island happy." The prostitutes sneaked to the edge of the military area at night, and a few men made use of them, almost always to their deep regret afterwards.

From near Ungava Bay below the Arctic Circle to well above it in Baffin Land were strung the three stations known as the Crystals. At Crystal Two in the first year of its operation the little company of men saw no one except for an occasional Eskimo from the time the boats left in October until the end of the year. There were many days when they could not leave their house at all, even to make weather observations. They practised carefully, under the leadership of a Major Crowell, a Maine man with Arctic experience, the art of getting on peaceably together. The radio operators taught the surgeon their skills; in return, having found an Eskimo baby who had been badly burned, he let the troops take turns in helping him in an elaborate skin-grafting operation which became their chief interest. In January a Northwest Mounted policeman came through with a dog-team on a routine patrol. In March a Hudson's Bay Company trader and his wife came by, trading for furs. In May a plane landed, in June the boats returned. As I remember Crowell's account, they were some twelve men all told. They did not get bushy, God knows why. I have known an officer on a much larger base in Greenland to break into tears on saying good-bye to a casual acquaintance who was heading for the States. It may be that the smallness of the detachment at Crystal II was an advantage. The two officers ran it informally. Everyone studied everyone else's specialty. In addition to the treatment of the baby, there were interesting medical treatments of Eskimo dogs. Also, when the raging winds and desperate snowfalls did not lock them in their house, there was hunting.

These descriptions should be written, not by one who has briefly visited a few points and learned of others through interviews and through their histories, but by those who lived on the bases and knew all the loneliness. In the newspaper published by the Command's Central Africa Division appeared the following joke, complete as I quote it. The bitter inference of its incompleteness speaks volumes.

"Newcomer: 'How long have you been out here?'

"Old-Timer: 'Twenty-seven months.'

"Newcomer: 'Oh, then you'll be going home soon.' "

Natal, Brazil, was a comfortable, almost luxurious post. I enjoyed my quarters, found the officers' mess splendid, and the officers' club delightful. One evening in the club I got to describing the wretched, inglorious drabness and frustration of a Washington officer's life. I made a good thing of it, the officers heard me through, and I got several laughs. When I had finished, one of them said, simply:

"Your wife is with you, isn't she?"

It was sufficient.

Very kindly, Mr. James R. Patterson, who as flight officer flew for the India-China Division, has sent me a description of Chanyi in China for inclusion in this book, and I include it with delight:

Chanyi, China, was Charlie Yoke in the radio facility charts for the China-Burma-India Theater, and the Yoke part seemed significant to many of the men stationed near this festering Chinese village some eighty miles northeast of Kunming. From home, it was a good million light years. When you looked on the map it appeared you were precisely on that point of the globe farthest from any place where you could sip a chocolate soda, inhale nice, clean drugstore odors, and watch the neon lights.

At ground level Chanyi's weather was something like Denver's — cool in the summer and cold in the winter — but with higher winds and more frequent clouds and rains. A spring flood at the field was S.O.P.[2] Like other quaint customs in China its weather was brewed with its own reverse formula. A rising barometer meant bad weather and a falling barometric pressure meant good. Our weather forecasters never could explain this very satisfactorily, but they proved it was true.

There were about five hundred of us after A.T.C. took over what had been an American Volunteer Group field early in the war, and began to station men and aircraft there. The field had one rock runway, a narrow scar on the valley floor between two ridges of 8000-foot mountains. The only pleasant feeling this field ever caused in a pilot was a keen sense of thankfulness at being once more on the ground.

The hostel area in which we lived was cocked on the side of a hill above the field and village. Under a Reverse Lend-Lease agreement, the Chinese Government furnished our food and quarters. By Chinese standards it wasn't bad; by American it was awful. The Chinese love rice and bean sprouts and some kind of degenerate spinach which our boys called seaweed. For the first two weeks it was not unpleasant; after that the Ameri-

[2] Standard Operational Procedure, a term which came to mean any fixed way of doing things.

can palate revolted. There was a bread of a non-yeast type that could be rolled into a rubbery ball and was about as digestible as armor plate. The pork was pretty good but very rarely on the menu, while the beef, brought to maturity but not what you would call fattened on the sparse vegetation of China, had to be ground into hamburger before our jaws could cope with it. Our mess officers never lasted very long. They came down with a mental disorder that must have been something akin to combat fatigue. Under the Lend-Lease arrangement, the cooks had to be Chinese, and being Chinese of the rural western provinces they had an intense and continual curiosity as to the nature of the foreign particles lining their nostrils. It drove the mess officers nuts. We were not very happy about it either, especially since our mess boys — the Chinese waiters — indulged in the same habit.

With plenty of time to mope between flights, it probably was not unnatural for our thoughts to turn most frequently to good, sound American food. Our regular diet was so unusual that we made a great fuss when we received at rare intervals maybe a case or two of "C" rations, or best of all, Spam! No fooling.

Thinking about food was only our Number One daydream. Next in order came (2) Home; (3) when we would be eligible for rotation; (4) mail; (5) the wife or sweetheart; (6) the next jungle ration of liquor; (7) promotion. One home-loving captain even had his wife take an intimate little snapshot of the family icebox with the door open, and mail it to him.

The commanding officer understood our needs but there was not much he could do about them since virtually all of our supplies had to be flown in. Volley ball and basketball games interested some of the younger men, but the older ones couldn't see wasting that much energy when their stomachs were already flat. There was a dayroom for enlisted men and a club for officers, where you could rehash all of the current rumors only slightly less comfortably than in your own quarters.

One of our happiest diversions was going to the movies, two or three times a week, or as often as we could get a film to show. The theater was really a chapel where services were held Sunday morning and Sunday night. Following the Sunday night service a film was shown, so that the only way to be sure of a seat was to attend church. Our chaplain, really a regular guy, was well aware of the reason for the packed congregation and tailored his program accordingly — a short sermon and lots of hymn singing.

Our tastes in movies would have surprised Hollywood. A dressing table with a delicious blonde exposing quite a lot of herself under filmy lace might attract a whistle or two. What set the audience wild was to see pictured a heaping banquet table or one of those Park Avenue buffet suppers. The Chinese down in the village of Chanyi must have thought on occasion the Mengyis were cheering the end of the war.

The gentle opiate of reading was also widely sought. A good murder mystery or a fast-moving Western could float you completely away from the cracked walls of your quarters, the rats feasting near by on your shaving cream, and the charcoal smoke seeping from your gasoline-barrel stove. Nobody cared much for non-fiction or any kind of solid reading. That took reading in low gear; what we wanted was something on which the mind could be thrown into freewheeling while you rolled along.

The better books — from our point of view, that is — were scarce. Even the paper-backed overseas editions were hard to come by because of a barter system that developed. A man with a couple of good novels would not sell them. He held on until he could make a trade for a book he hadn't read.

One enterprising bibliophile at Chanyi was lucky enough to receive a copy of *Forever Amber* from the States. Since there was not at that time any book of comparable value in the whole of China, he organized a one-volume lending library. His rental rate of five dollars for a maximum of three days was eagerly accepted, allowing him a comfortable margin above his overhead, depreciation, and whatnot.

Gambling was only a minor entertainment among the men of the 1342nd Base Unit. There wasn't much point to winning since about all you could do with the money was to send it home, and it was no fun losing either. Heavy drinking was no better since it only made you yearn the more for a girl with clear, white skin, some dreamy dance music, a starched table-cloth, and ice in thin goblets . . .

Don't imagine that Charlie Yoke was a virtuous little outfit, all sweetness and light. It was just that the brand of sin available in Chanyi was strictly *boo hao*. When a crew got a trip — say to Calcutta — you found that they were all mere men.

Some of the more gallant, motivated by a desire to improve Chinese-American relations and other urges of a less laudable nature, conceived the plan of inviting certain of Chanyi's young ladies to the hostel area. Before entertaining the visitors, they would lead them to the shower rooms, ceremoniously hand them soap and towels, and then bow towards the water taps. Probably there are many in Chanyi who ponder upon the quaintness of American customs. This ruse to make Miss Chanyi presentable was not very successful, however. The girls were not enthusiastic bathers, and even the most highly scented soaps could not wash away the strong aroma of garlic, cheap tobacco, and charcoal smoke that clung to them. Also, the colonel was not amused.

Probably the most harmless pastime indulged in in this little outpost of the A.T.C. was the practice of growing a mustache. A few of the younger pilots fresh out of flying school were hard pressed to produce anything of note, but the older men found a fine, manly satisfaction in sprouting hair all over the lower quadrant of their faces. A man could express his individuality in his mustache, choosing his own pattern of adornment and with unlimited time for it to reach its full flower of develop-ment. The really unfortunate ones were those who thought-lessly had grown mustaches in former years and worn them overseas; there was no exhilaration, even in China, in shaving off a mustache.

The most fun anyone ever had in Chanyi (except, of course, the farewell party the night before you started Stateside) was to participate in an informal buffet supper with your room-mates in your own quarters. Nearly every room in the hostel area had some kind of makeshift stove. One of the most pop-ular heating units was a gasoline blowtorch, which could be so employed as to heat two canteen cups at the same time. These impromptu feasts usually followed the receipt of a package of food from home, but not necessarily. Some pretty tricky dishes could be prepared from no more than a few spare parts of "K" rations. Of course, a can of baked beans or a box of crackers from home could really make the meal a celebration.

Jim Windham from Italy, Texas, once received a can of fried sausage and a can of blackeyed peas from his mother. The men who had snorted at Windy's tales of the pre-eminence of Texas came around mighty fast to make their peace when they heard of the Windham windfall. Charley Ripley's relatives lived in exclusive Oyster Bay and Rip was one of the most popular men on the base. His packages from home contained boneless turkey, fine cheeses, and rich chocolate.

To enjoy an evening snack in Chanyi to the fullest, the weather had to be bad and all flights cancelled. A little Yuan wine started things going. Then everyone rallied round with his contribution of food. Some coffee from one, noodle soup from another, a can of sardines from a well-guarded footlocker. Then a careful division of the repast, while you talked about what you would do and the fun you would have when you got back home.

You always said it as if you never had a doubt but that the day would come. This was just an existence that had to be lived through. The other guy might lose an engine on take-off (on a field with an elevation of 6121 feet that was not good), or meet a Zero going into Sian. It wouldn't happen to you. Or so you told yourself.

It happened that Major Richard E. Falconer, the Historical Officer of the Command's Southwest Pacific Wing, backed up his formal reports with magnificently written personal letters. From a series of these I compile something of a view of the Wing Headquarters establishment on Leyte in the Philippines shortly after the landings there, omitting, regretfully, certain passages of truly brilliant but unprintable English:

In Mid-November I journeyed to Leyte to watch the birth-pangs and labor pains of the first A.T.C. detachment to enter

this combat zone. We lived about 400 yards south of the Tacloban air strip, in a camp area with the 308th Service Group. I spent two or three weeks there and got the bloody hell strafed and bombed outa me — the actual statistics show that between October 26 and November 15 there were 148 actual strikes on the strip. Red alerts were lost track of — the figure got astronomical and the boys lost count. By the time I arrived all had quieted down — only twelve to fifteen reds a day and of those only four or five were bombings. That permitted us all to get about two hours' sleep a night, total, between raids. Who the hell said air supremacy? If that was air supremacy I'll take vanilla. I have previously in my life been scared, several times, but these bombings when you lie in your foxhole and grab dirt and you lie and hear that damned double kerump-kerump walking down the strip directly toward you and the earth shakes in around your ears — well, it scares the hell out of me, I can state without fear of contradiction. The Nips haven't killed any of our outfit yet although three or four Purple Hearts have been awarded. Now, December 18 (only seven shopping days till Christmas), there have been four days straight without enemy activity — a good sign, I think.

[Wing Headquarters having been established at Leyte.] We are ass deep to a tall cow in mud, it rains inches daily, paper goes to pulp and typewriters rust overnight. We have no communications we can depend on. We have lost touch with our rearward base units. We have about a hundred inexperienced, jittery, trigger-happy boys trying to make a livable campsite out of this raw jungle swamp. (I nearly got killed last night by a dumb bastard who said Bang! — Halt! instead of Halt! — Bang! — the latter being the preferred sequence, it gives you time to hit the dirt, knowing that these lugs aren't going to wait for you to identify yourself.) Well here we are. The ship carrying our tentage and supplies was loaded end of November and after 15 days at anchor in Hollandia was still there when my group pulled out. I understand that it is on the way now, however, and will be here in a week or so. At the moment I am writing by candlelight on a bitched-up machine which throws me ten times to the line.

As an ethnologist, you'd be fascinated by these people here. The Visayans are a lunatic combination of Chinese, Spanish, and Portuguese, with, I think, a touch of the Poly- and Melanesian stirred in for good measure.[3] They have been brutally treated these past years, but that has failed to break their naturally cheery, happy and very, very gay natures. They are full of song and smile and courtesy. A clean, self-respecting lot, very different from the degraded natives of New Guinea. They are all Christian and go to church every Sunday, and fight their cocks in the afternoon. Sunday is the big day when every man jack is seen converging on Tolosa with a rooster under one arm. They gather in the square and argue and squabble and bet their fool heads off, then set up the fights. Later, toward dusk you see them headed homeward in single file along our road, most of them with a limp, bloody bird hanging head downward. Taking him home to eat after his downfall. I could go on all day. I like these folks fine.

We have such a hell of a time with paper here that it's really funny. The stuff is so loaded with moisture that it sticks, wraps itself lovingly around the roller, disintegrates, wrinkles, tears. The headquarters is abuzz all day long with obscene remarks about the behavior of paper. Envelopes by the thousand have sealed themselves securely. A man works all day, every day, opening envelopes and powdering the flaps to prevent recurrence. Then they have to be sealed with glue because the gum is destroyed. I have half a squad tent for me and my two boys, which is adequate space. We are in dirt, of course, and our engineer bitched up the ditching in the tents — 14 of them ganged up in twin rows of seven with the flaps hooked up to make a continuous cover of canvas — and when it rains we just drown out. Not from above but from below. The ditches are grade-lined in reverse. Our engineer discovered that water does not flow uphill without assistance. A lake forms in my office every time it rains — which is daily with five-day jolts of continuous performance occurring frequently. These are part of the fun but they do slow down and reduce the efficiency of HQ, which after all is a paper outfit.

The food remains good. We lived like princes on fresh beef, steaks, and turkey and capon (!) for a while. We are now back on C-ration stews, etc., but our mess officer is a lulu and has a trick of making even these tiresome foods taste good. He is a professional restaurateur from Seattle and stands at the entrance of the mess hall — coconut log frame roofed with

[3] Major Falconer has not studied Anthropology.

tarps — and beams like a good mine host. Three times a day. Just like back home. He loves to feed people — and aren't we lucky for that!

Did I tell you that some Filipino girls have set up for business down the road? The price is one mattress cover per copy, three covers or 20 pesos for a night. I haven't sampled it, thanks, although I hear that they really give a man the ride of a lifetime. The EM are using up all their covers and sheets. One Joe got six months' stockade for stealing a sheet from a colonel's tent. Some day I am going to do an essay on media of exchange in this part of the world. In Australia it was cigarettes, in Guinea it was liquor, here it's mattress covers and clothes.

And then there's the one about the pilot who came into Owi Island strip to land and set his plane down on the dust cloud which rolls to 200 feet above the coral. He taxied two thousand feet on the dust, at which point it thinned and he fell out. Was he surprised!

None of these sketches is complete, nor taken as a whole do they form even an adequate sample. A few other bases will be briefly described in the further course of this narrative. I should like to tell of many more, the relative luxury of Casablanca, of Atar, a tiny Bedouin town deep in the Sahara, possessing notable peculiarities, where the life was so grinding that three months was deemed the most a man could stand but some men asked for further duty there, of the Bluies in Greenland, Whitehorse and Tanana Crossing on the Alaskan Route, of the sybaritic joys of Amberley Field near Brisbane, that veritable Capua, of the steamy isolation of Amapa in Brazil, of Atkinson Field in British Guiana, where from time to time a shipment of respectable young ladies to attend officers' club dances was obtained through the bank in Georgetown, and of a good dozen more. At its largest, the Air Transport Command comprised some two hundred and fifty base units; at a rough guess these operated on more than three hundred locations the distribution and variety of which may be imagined from those named in this chapter. All of this, too, went to make a route; all of this made up the war for thousands.

BLITZ CLOTH

HARDLY ANY GRADUATE of the Army who writes about it can refrain from putting in his two cents' worth about what has come to be known as "the brass." I see no reason why I should not have my fun, too. Nor is this little essay entirely inappropriate at this point. In the last two chapters I have been working my way around to a sort of profile of the Air Transport Command. If we define brass in the narrowest, most recent sense as meaning generals, the Command had lots of them. It made them and it broke them. I've described some and shall describe more; it's inevitable. Intelligent understanding of generals requires some grasp of the factors, generally little appreciated, which influence their very being.

The term "brass" has evolved considerably. It was originated in the first world war by the British as "brass hat." This had no reference to gold braid, but referred to the red band around the hats of staff officers. These worthies often visited the misery of the front lines briefly, then returned to what the combat soldiers believed were wildly sybaritic luxuries of châteaux far behind the lines. The shortened term has come, in American usage, to be almost synonymous with rank, so that we even run into the expression "little brass," referring to lieutenants and captains, and perhaps field officers.

Taking the term in both connotations, perhaps I could be accused of having been mildly brassy. I was a minor staff officer. I ended my service on the pinnacle of a lieutenant colonelcy — or should I say the hanging valley? No power has given me the gift to see myself as others see me, so I shall simply duck that issue.

I claim no great knowledge of generals, but I have had slight, and usually pleasant, acquaintances with several, and in the course of my duties enjoyed a worm's-eye view of them of which they were unaware. My most difficult experience with a general was when, as a captain, I found myself in awed conclave with H. H. Arnold himself. At that time he wore four stars upon each shoulder. In the middle of the conference it occurred to me, horribly, how useful that shoulderful of silver would be for striking matches, and for the rest of the period I sweated in fear lest I go mad and try it.

Few people seem to realize the curious influences to which the average general officer of the recent war was subjected, influences which made it difficult for him not to become obnoxious. These fall into two principal divisions.

Our top men, such men as Generals Marshall and Arnold, were eminent and accustomed to high office before the war. There was nothing in the positions they achieved in the war to throw them off balance. The sudden, enormous expansion of the Army, however, precipitated a lot of men into general rank from the grades of colonel, lieutenant colonel, major, and even captain. Before the war, the average American had no interest in the Army. Army officers were not considered chic. They were ignored, omitted from our interests. Most of them lived rather drab, sheltered lives, anticipating an extremely slow rate of promotion which, when they had served for some forty years, might bring them at last to a colonelcy. That rank meant enough of a pension to ensure a modestly comfortable old age. They were obscure. It was likely to take them fifteen to twenty years to reach the grade of major, which meant that they married and started their families on small incomes. They economized, and closely followed the various little devices (such as travel allowances) by which they might occasionally ease the tight financial pinch.

The picture changed suddenly. With absolutely no invidiousness or inferences let us take a specific case, that of my own commanding general, a man who was never a run-of-the-mill, humdrum officer. In the spring of 1941 he was a lieutenant colonel — which meant, incidentally, that his promotions had

come somewhat faster than average. Outside of the Army, no one
had heard of him since he got in hot water standing up for Billy
Mitchell. In April, 1942 — about ten months later — he was a
brigadier general commanding the Ferrying Command, an outfit which was very much in the public eye. By the following
fall, some fourteen months after he had been inconspicuously
busy in Florida with silver leaves on his shoulders, he had become a major general. His pay was approximately doubled.
He was so much in the public eye that his Public Relations
Officer had a big job. Later he became lieutenant general,
which meant more glory but no more pay. Under him, on his
staff, were men who in civilian life were national figures in
various lines. Many of them, had they met him at a social
gathering in, say, 1938 or even later, would probably have
passed him up in favor of someone whose occupation or name
was of greater interest.

Is it any wonder that he showed a certain, rather naïve en-
joyment of his new position? That one could occasionally
detect him basking in the limelight? A transition such as this,
accompanied as it is by astonishing accretions of power, is a
terrific experience to which to subject a human being.

The second influence is that of his subordinates. A good
commander wants to be surrounded by subordinates who will
deal with him honestly, frankly, and when necessary firmly. In
a strong headquarters, the top staff men, those with whom the
commander makes his major decisions, usually are so qualified.
Yet I have known surprisingly able generals who allowed themselves to become surrounded, even at this level, by a crew of
gifted sycophants who, while they carried out their duties effectively, devoted themselves to undermining their commander's
character for their personal benefit.

Unhappily, in any headquarters many of the lower staff are
mere yes-men when they come up against the big boss. On the
whole, I think that the civilians in uniform are more inclined
this way than the regulars, but that impression may come from
the relative scarcity of regulars under my observation at that
level. These people do not offer the great man only what
might be called the negative of assent; they take the positive

action of offering him indulgences and special treatments which he himself would not have thought of. They almost force him into unfortunate behavior. I have known a few men of solid position in civilian life who made very nice wars for themselves by carefully studying the weaknesses of their generals and then playing up to them, even developing them. These men had the advantage of life in the great world; in all things except warfare and aviation they were far more sophisticated than their victim. Setting such exceptional characters aside, it remains true that many run-of-the-mill minor officers almost forced their generals into unfortunate behavior. I can illustrate this by two examples.

A high general went to an airport to greet an incoming Very Important Person. While he waited in the commanding officer's office, word came that the V.I.P.'s plane was delayed. It was past lunchtime and the general was hungry, so the executive officer went to the PX and got him a snack. When the general had consumed this, the control tower announced that the V.I.P.'s plane was in the traffic pattern. The general rose, asking, "Is there anything to pay on this?"

The two officers answered, "No." The general said, "Well, thanks," and went on out to do his manners. As a result, the executive, a lieutenant colonel, was out forty-five cents. He was furious, and told all his friends about the way the great man sponged on his inferiors.

The last chapter contains some description of what life was like at Leyte when Southwest Pacific Wing Headquarters first moved there. The commanding general was Alexander, who formerly had commanded the India-China Wing. As the description tells, Leyte was a miserable hole, drowned out in rain. A real Regular, General Alexander detailed people at once to see to housing for the personnel, which meant managing for enough poles, logs, and boards to get the tents out of the mud. Building materials were scarce. One of the officers so detailed made up his mind to make a hit with the commanding general, and accordingly proceeded to build him a real, tropical house with two good rooms and a wide porch and a real floor. The general was too wildly busy to pay much attention to what was going on, but he did twice tell the brown-nose to stop his construction and distribute the materials to the officers and men. The little officer was sure he knew better. In the end he'd please the general, so he finished the house.

General Alexander was presented with a *fait accompli*. He was too strong in his convictions to be trapped, however. He wanted to make the building into the enlisted men's day room, but as it was centrally located in the staff officers' area, and away from where the troops were billeted, he finally decided to use it as an officer's club. He continued to live in a tent like everyone else.

Multiply these two incidents by thousands. Allow for the reasonable doctrine that the commander of a large organization must, for reasons of efficiency, have a modicum of extra comfort. Add the effects of the dizzying rise in rank already described. The wonder is, not that so many generals went slightly haywire in their personal behavior, but that more did not do so. This still does not justify such fantastic contrasts as the one I saw at Casablanca, where the general lived in the fabulous splendor of the Villa Maas, a domicile which even a Hollywood star would consider with admiration, while the enlisted men were billeted and messed in tents — including the enlisted men who ran the Villa. When one encounters such contrasts, however, one should always enquire whether it was the commander himself who chose his palace, or whether it was picked out for him by a smart little major, either with an eye to his own advantage or following that instinct one finds in some little men which drives them to belabor the great with favor.

I do not want to whitewash every high-ranking officer who gave in to the vices of power and privilege. I want only to point out that it takes a strong character and a level head to avoid being carried away by the combination of power and sycophancy. How often have I heard certain of the little men say, "You can't say 'no' to a general." I was a little man myself, yet I have said "no" to generals, including once, in an unimportant matter, to General Arnold — and had my opinion accepted.

The life of the high brass is not entirely so pleasant and secure as people generally believe. The command principle turns a man loose to do his job — and failure is likely to mean his head. If a lesser officer proves unworthy of promotions he has received, he may not be reduced in grade until he has had a trial in which his rights are well protected. In theory, at least, even an enlisted man may not be "busted" without a hearing and the making of a record. A general has no such protection. I believe that the Army would do itself a favor, and clear away some serious misconceptions, if it now publicized the number of general officers who received the axe during the war. The Air Transport Command made generals — a round dozen from the regular Army and five from the airlines — but it also broke them. Three — four if you include the Hump operation before the Command itself took over — good enough men with good enough records, but not of the strength which great undertakings require, received those orders which read in part: "will proceed to Washington, D.C., and on arrival report to G–1, War Department General Staff for further assignment. On arriving in the Zone of the Interior this officer will return to his permanent grade of . . ."

XV

THE BIG TEAM

A REGULAR ARMY has, on the surface at least, definite homogeneity. However much they may have differed originally, common training and experience since early manhood give the officers like exteriors. The long-service enlisted men who are an army's backbone acquire a similar, common patina. War suddenly threw ten million civilians into the Armed Services. They came in their infinite varieties, the good and the bad, the weak and the strong, the wise and the foolish. I have had occasion to describe a few of the outstanding men of the Air Transport Command. Here I want to describe a few others, leaders and followers, famous and unknown, to give some picture of the face of the Command.

In the last chapter I discussed some of the influences playing upon general officers. Against this background of privilege, strain, and responsibility, let me describe two generals, one a West Pointer, one a civilian whose military training consisted in being told to keep his coat buttoned and to return salutes.

General Arnold personally selected C. R. Smith of American Airlines to be number two man under General George. He was commissioned a colonel, and returned to civilian life a major general. C. R. Smith is a big man, a Texan, with the best of Texas qualities. In his official dealings he wasted no time (I use the past tense, as I am describing what I saw during the interlude of war service), he was terse and he wanted others to be terse, yet he had an unhurried quality even in his briefest dealings. He liked to add the two or three extra words, the mild touch of humor, which made his subordinates feel that there was friendliness and personal awareness in his relations with them.

He was utterly informal and profoundly democratic. He could afford to be, for no one could for a moment imagine that his unmilitary ways indicated that he could be trifled with. He enforced the true discipline of a powerful personality. Anyone could approach him: I have known a buck private who thought he had had a raw deal to go to his office and get a hearing — and yet he was never swamped by little matters.

Somewhere in his early career he learned to type professionally. Behind his desk in headquarters he had a typewriter into which fed an endless roll of memorandum sheets, separated by perforations. When he had an idea, he swung his swivel chair, typed four or five pungent lines, and sent the memo on its way. When you walked into someone's office holding one of these blue slips in your hand, you did not need to explain. At the sight of it you were asked, "What's C.R. up to now?"

He is a practical man, a man of action, who also has a real gift at expressing doctrine and theory, and he was a forceful, effective negotiator with Air Staff and other authorities. His fault was impatience with subordinates who were wordy or timid in disagreement. In this, I think, he failed to allow for their fear of differing with a general. If you thought he was wrong, you wanted, first of all, to make absolutely sure that you were right. Then you wrote a memorandum or prepared your brief, verbal statement, as concise and direct as his own — which meant you had to be blunt. To this he listened, and if you convinced him, admitted frankly that he was wrong.

He was personally more widely known in the Command than anyone else. I have never heard his name mentioned other than with admiration and respect, often with affection.

My West Pointer is that same Brigadier General Edward H. Alexander who has been mentioned so often. He is another big man, dark, with deep-set, dark eyes and a face which would seem craggy were it not for his expression of warmth and charm. He is a quiet-spoken man, quietly friendly with his subordinates, earnest about his business, intense.

He is a thorough flyer, a man who likes a hot plane. A private B–26 is his style, and those who ride with him when he is in a hurry sometimes wind up with their hair on end. As the incident of the special building at Leyte shows, he stood by the basic military doctrine that an officer's first duty is to his subordinates — something which all too many officers, regular and volunteer, thoroughly forgot during the war. Alexander had no patience with officers who coddled themselves while their men were in discomfort. There was a base commander on one of the Southwest Pacific's innumerable, depressing islands, who worked out a deal for himself by which the through plane from Australia regularly dropped off steaks for him. The rest of the outfit was on C-rations, Spam, powdered eggs, and other such famous delicacies. Nightly in solemn state this commander sat alone at a table in the mess, in the sight of his officers, to the open knowledge of his enlisted men, and consumed one fresh Australian steak. When Alexander heard of this he issued an order, general in tone, pointedly specific in intent, to the effect that all officers, regardless of rank, would partake only of the common food of their messes.

During the war Alexander seemed driven by an inner fire. My personal belief is that, as a relatively young man, he could not quite forgive himself for not serving in combat. Having worn himself out in the India-China struggle, after a month's leave he took command of the Caribbean Division, with head-quarters agreeably situated in West Palm Beach. He married a beautiful woman. His health mended. He was not content to sit out the second half of a savage war in the luxury of Florida. He was offered, and accepted, command of the Southwest Pacific Wing, another hard, crude pioneering job of the type he was so well equipped to handle. Accepting command of a subordinate Wing, a subdivision of the Pacific Division, was technically a step down; the malicious could interpret it as a form of demotion, but that was of no importance to him. It meant forward area service; it was a job of great importance, and it was up his alley, so he took it eagerly.

His chief weakness came out of this same drive. He himself handled too many matters which ordinarily are attended to

by the staff. As the appropriate staff officer was likely to have
started on the matter also, this created confusions.

Put these two men side by side in uniform. If you spoke
with them briefly you would be likely to decide that the professional soldier was more likely the civilian in uniform. He
was less gruff and less brisk. He had a gentleness of manner
and a look of the dreamer which we do not associate with
military men.

The peculiar, even sometimes fantastic, duties of a historical
officer threw me into closer contact with the Command's deputy chiefs of staff than with any other of the top group of officers. I became genuinely fond of both of these men. Their
unlikeness beautifully portrays the make-up of a citizen army.

Colonel Robert M. Love was young for his rank and position.
In civilian life he ran a small, non-scheduled airline outside
Boston. When he went overseas on a mission, his usual procedure was to ferry a B–17, and characteristically, as he went
along the route he presented himself as a ferry pilot, making
no fuss over his true status, thereby learning things about how
these pilots were lodged and handled at different bases which
he could never have discovered if he had aired his brass. He
had a remarkable number of facts ready in his head. He made
quick, bold, sound decisions. His talk, even on serious matters,
was informal, lively, and full of humor; this humor and his
related sense of the ridiculousness of occurrences was an excellent outlet for what in other men would have been exasperation. I have never known another man whose immediate
subordinates were so deeply his friends.

His opposite number and successor, Colonel James H.
Douglas, Jr., was quite different. He had been a distinguished
Chicago lawyer. Infinitely patient, he listened carefully,
thought long, and moved, as lawyers will, only when he had
conscientiously made sure. There was no flash about him. He
got his results by thorough thinking and by working late into
the nights, keeping at it to the verge of breakdown. He did not
have Love's circle of intense friends, but the more you worked
with him, the more you liked and respected him. His closely
observed judgments of the men with whom he worked were

penetrating and fascinating to hear. You knew that when the pinch came, and you had to tell your story and ask for support, Douglas would listen to you and stand by you.

Such men as these and many others, all different, were the staff and the commanders. Some, as I well know, were stupid, some lazy, some incompetent. There were men to whom the war was merely an incident which they would allow as little as possible to interfere with their private pleasures. That the majority had devotion and abilities comparable to those I have described is proven by the outcome.

All the ability in the world at the various staff and command levels would, obviously, be useless without the men who fly the planes. I wish I could name and describe them all, those pleasant men, mostly young, sometimes callow, all endowed with a certain quality arising from their chosen way of life which marks them off, with all their human variations among themselves, as clearly as cowpunchers or seamen are marked off. I remember them on innumerable bases and on thousands of miles of flights, inclined to be casual about their uniforms, given to very limp caps worn rakishly, friendly by habit. Their reading ran to Superman and detective stories, although this was by no means universal. If a groundling officer visited the flight deck when the flight was quiet, he was usually offered one of the pilots' seats, and often enough he was handed a head set and Sparks was told to get the B.B.C. or Tokyo Rose, or whatever the available radio entertainment was. They were very kind about letting a near-sighted, wingless, interested groundling play pilot for a little while, taking the stick in straight and level flight on a clear day while they coached him. The younger ones, bachelors, drawing overseas and flight pay, gambled for fantastic sums in all the currencies of the world. Many of them had short snorters which reached the length of the bar in any officers' club, each bill representing another strange land in which they had set down a ship. They gave, many of them, an effect of carelessness, but if you watched their faces in landing and take-off, or when there was some trouble, any such impression was instantly dispelled.

They ran somewhat older than the combat pilots. There was,

for instance, "Pappy" Turner, forty years of age, tall, half bald, with a humorous face and slow, easy way of talking. Before the war he was a Northwest Airlines pilot. Turner happened to be in Greenland with a B–17 bound for the United Kingdom when another ferry crew crashed on the notorious Greenland Ice Cap. For a whole, long, dreadful winter, operating out of a primitive, ill-equipped base, whenever it was possible for a plane to keep the air he flew over those men, dropping supplies in a curious sort of makeshift bombing manoeuvre. He and his crew did their own maintenance. By their remorseless persistence they kept six men alive from November to April, when rescue finally reached them. One might well have considered both the crew and the plane war-weary after those months, but they were kept on in Greenland. Far to the north the Germans had established a secret weather station. Turner was provided with a bombardier, and having never had any combat training, took part in the farthest north bombing missions ever accomplished by American flyers. After which he went on, delivered his B–17 to the United Kingdom, and then returned to a wife who had just about given him up.

One of the men down below on the Ice Cap, Lieutenant Spencer, looked more like the public's idea of a pilot, tall, blond, young, with a casual roughness of manner, and the characteristic trick of hanging his cap on the edges of his head. His appearance disguised a sensitive perception of beauty, thoughtfulness of others, and a habit of deep reading. In those icebound months he proved himself a true and steadfast friend. Like all of those who came out of that adventure whole, he returned immediately and willingly to ferrying, in which he continued to the end of the war.

The cream of the transport pilots was made up of men of great experience and skill. Major James H. Sammons was typical of these. Before the war he was superintendent of a steamship terminal, president of an aircraft sales company, operated a flying school, and flew aircraft under charter — a busy man. He was in his middle thirties, of medium height, quiet in appearance and manner. There was nothing showy about him, he was simply an extremely good pilot. He began flying for the Ferrying Command on the old trans-Atlantic shuttle and went on from there until there were few parts of the earth to which he had not guided a transport. He was one of the picked men who piloted for the Yalta Conference, and through an error in briefing was nearly brought down by German ack-ack over Crete. His short snorter bore the signatures of half the great of the war. Meeting him casually on the base or in the cockpit of his plane — where he was a pleasant host — you would never read in his quiet, friendly manner the long list of great enterprises in which he had taken part — the trans-Atlantic shuttle of 1941, the opening of the route across the Sahara to Oran, the service into Okinawa, and so many others.

By no means all of the fine pilots came out of civilian life. Some of the very best were Regular Army. One such was Richard C. Kight, who piloted Willkie on his trip around the world. The trip was notable in itself because from Moscow to Chungking and from Chungking again to Fairbanks the route lay over almost totally unknown territory, as dangerous to cross as any wilderness or ocean. Kight is another Texan, but not at all typical. He is slender, not tall. He is built, and looks, like a western horseman. He is perceptive enough to have derived, partly from his contact with Willkie, partly from his own wartime observations, a clear grasp of the importance of just treatment for all nations and races if we are to have lasting peace.

In China, he had an interesting experience. There was no field at Chungking capable of receiving his C–87, so the plane and crew remained at another town while Willkie was taken to the capital by DC–3. The local Chinese general, a charming, elderly man, invited the crew to dinner, along with a couple of missionaries to serve as interpreters. Before dinner, the general and his wife received them. The young men were a long time away from home. Regardless of race, costume, and language, in the general's wife they recognized a mother, and they seem to have managed to become quite cozy with her. When the meal was ready, the lady rose to withdraw. The men begged that she be allowed to stay, and to this the general agreed. It was, the missionaries told them later, something that had never happened before. The Americans must have managed to break precedent with charm and innocence, for after dinner the general entertained them by showing them his most beautiful paintings. Before they left, he asked them to autograph one of the finest of these. Kight said the custom seemed strange, but you could see it was a great honor, like being asked to autograph someone's Rembrandt.

Although not yet thirty, Kight was too able to remain in pure flying. He became Alexander's right-hand man in the India-China Wing, and went on from there to other key posts and a colonel's eagles.

Among so many thousands of flyers, not all could be famous. Some ferried aircraft. Some flew transports across oceans and continents. Some flew the Hump. Many operated milk runs in strange places: from Port Moresby to Sidney, from Khartoum to Cairo, across Scotland, or across Central Africa. They ran risks, became horribly bored and homesick. Some of them were killed.

They had strange experiences, such as those of the India-China flyers with the coolies. There were fields where they had to circle overhead until cows or elephants were herded off the runways. There were Arctic runways on which the mist lay to a depth of six feet until the first plane landed; where that plane had passed, the mist remained parted, standing on either side like a wall. There were the amazing things that the Northern Lights do to radio. There was the battle-shocked enlisted man who sat on top of an inboard fuel tank, smoking a cigarette, until the agonized co-pilot talked him out of the compartment.

When I think of pilots on the long runs, one scene, often repeated, comes back to me as a sort of summation. You go up to the flight deck in the middle of the night for a smoke. Whichever pilot is then on duty motions you to the empty co-pilot's seat. He sits on the left-hand side, his face faintly shown by the reflection of the fluorescent lights on the instrument panel, or, more warmly, by the glow of his cigarette. The dials in the panel and overhead, their figures, marks, and needles delicately lined with the violet light against the black

of the panel look like a magical arrangement of skeletons of
butterflies, framing the wide windshield. Through it, you see
stretching below you an endless, gray-white ocean of clouds, or
an endless, far blackness which is the ocean itself. Ahead and
above are the stars, from an altitude of nine thousand feet or
so as clear as ever you saw them in Arizona or New Mexico.
The plane is full of the rising and falling drone of the engines,
a sound like organ music, like a deep-pitched hymn sung by a
tremendous chorus. You sit and smoke in a companionable
silence, you exchange a word or two. You look at the contours
of this young man's face as the glow picks them out, and then
ahead into the vastness into which he is staring, and you begin
to understand the distant quality you have noticed in flyers'
eyes. After a time it will often happen, if the pilot believes
you know enough to understand, that he will lean towards you
and say in a voice of deep warmth, "Listen to those beautiful
engines!"

The world's imagination tends to concentrate on pilots, and
writers do the same, forgetting that aircraft are flown by a team
which, on the big transports, includes navigators, radio operators, flight engineers, and flight traffic clerks. Especially I
think that navigators have received much less than justice. The
navigator has no one to spell him off. Aboard a plane travelling at two hundred miles an hour or better, he must be constantly at work in order to keep track of the flight. He catches
catnaps, but that is all. Hour after hour he makes his exact
observations and performs his complex calculations, pinpoint-
ing the plane's position. I have seen them at the end of long
missions, unshaven and haggard, still covering the paper with
their incomprehensible figures, calculating wind and drift, to
bring the plane to land at one exact spot, and I have seen them
deeply humiliated when their estimated time of arrival proved
to be ten minutes in error.

The planes are flown by crews, and for each plane and crew
there must be on the ground many men and women performing a thousand tasks which range from maintenance of the
plane itself to billeting transients. Much of this work is dull,
safe, unglamorous. All of it is necessary. Among these, too,

there were all sorts and conditions of people. I think of Colonel Stephen L. Gumport, a very pleasant young doctor with a passion for flying who, as Captain Gumport, went to the Gold Coast and brought the hospitalization rate down from a locally accepted forty per cent to somewhat less than two per cent. A definitely young Lieutenant Steinway found himself in command of a handful of men on a god-forsaken island, mostly sand, off the Arabian coast. They ran a stand-by airfield, where planes generally put in because of trouble or bad weather. Occasionally the local sultan let them come to the mainland to hunt gazelles. They fished. It was a place where the troops should have gone nearly crazy, a place from which they should have tried by every means to escape. Steinway handled himself and his men so well that, when some of them were listed for rotation to greener pastures, they begged to remain.

The enlisted men were just as varied as the officers. There was, for instance, an ingenious master sergeant in North Africa who sold an airfield which his unit was abandoning, to a local Frenchman for 30,000 francs. This sergeant was the only man in his unit who spoke French. On the eve of the unit's departure, the Frenchman, delighted by his bargain, gave a party for the commanding officer. As the sergeant interpreted, no unfortunate information was communicated. The C.O. was touched by the Frenchman's affection for the Americans. They pulled out the next morning, and immediately after they left, the purchaser, going to view his property, was apprehended by the advance guard of the French unit which was taking over.

At the A.T.C. base in Manila I was guided about by a Sergeant Beard, who worked at Base Headquarters. Beard turned out to be a nephew of both the historian and the scout leader. For an hour or so I enjoyed with him one of the few really civilized conversations of my war experience. In Maiduguri in the middle of Africa I encountered a Staff Sergeant Roybal who had come from his father's ranch in the hills of New Mexico to become a competent and respected line chief in this far place. He had then been in Africa over two years, and although he still spoke with a slight Spanish accent, his native tongue came slowly to him. Under the permanent overcast of dust we talked together, both of us remembering the clear skies over the snow-capped Sangre de Cristo Mountains. There was a Pfc. Hansell whom one of his officers described as a screwball of purest ray serene, a slight, blond young man who eternally forgot to wear his necktie, or his cap, or some other required article. Once, accompanying an officer on a mission to Persia, he offered to go on when the officer was forced to turn back. In his own way — which I cannot imagine — he established valuable liaison with one branch of Persian Gulf Command Headquarters, and en route had a very interesting conversation with an English Brigadier, to whom he gave some cigarettes.

It would be a gross injustice to leave the women out of this description. It happens that, outside of the WAC's who were assigned to Headquarters and those who worked under me in an activity which was specialized and rather set apart from the main line of operations, I had little contact with them. I have already written of the WASP's, and later shall have occasion to pay tribute to the flight nurses. Of WAC's, I can only relate my general observation that as a whole they were fine soldiers. Like their more glamorous sisters who ferried aircraft, they were characterized by the quality of being volunteers — those who served overseas doubly so — and of determination to prove that women belonged in a war.

Of all the inconspicuous, hard-working, loyal men I met, one sticks particularly in my memory. He typified many. His name, according to my short snorter, was Lieutenant Jimmie Weaver, he was a Pennsylvanian, and from his general appearance, small, rather dark, wiry, I should put him down as being of Welsh extraction. Our acquaintance consisted chiefly of a couple of flights across Scotland in the plane he piloted. When we returned to the big base at Prestwick, we talked together at leisure, being drawn to each other by a common interest in Latin America. Before the war he had barnstormed in South America, and become engaged to a Uruguayan girl, with whom he corresponded regularly, longing for the day when he could return and marry her. We spoke a little Spanish together, and discussed the virtues of Spanish women, which are many.

Weaver had joined the Ferrying Command early in the

game. As a ferry pilot, he had crossed the oceans and earned the three theater ribbons when the greater part of the Army was still in training at home. He had been seasoned in that first year of war, when the routes were primitive and hazardous. Like his fellows, he had had his long tours of ferrying duty within the United States, in the course of his in-service training, and like them had griped and cursed at an assignment which kept him safely flying minor aircraft while the combat men were pouring overseas. At those times he sang a parody of Casey Jones about his heroic service "Ferrying a B–T into Dixie Land." Then, as he progressed, he took the big bombers over the Atlantic and the Pacific to all the distant places. Now he was assigned to the routine, humdrum piloting of a C–47 around Britain, a day-in, day-out service without glory or glamour, but only the irritation of the constant foul weather and low visibility of the British Isles in November. He still wore his three ribbons, which had become rather frayed by the end of 1944. There was no going home after thirty missions for him, there were no automatic Air Medals and Distinguished Flying Crosses, no battle stars. He probably never would have more over his pocket than he had earned in 1942, although up his sleeve was slowly creeping a golden ladder of overseas stripes. He would stay on, flying where he was told to fly, until that thing called Washington, which was as unknown, mysterious, powerful, and incomprehensible to him as it is to the average Indian on his reservation, decreed that he might come home.

We had a couple of drinks of watery, war-time Scotch whisky at the bar, then as we went to chow, I stopped to speak to a friend, so he went in alone. I ran into him again as I came out, pacing the hallway, shaking with helpless anger and humiliation. At chow he had sat next to a "happy warrior," a P–38 pilot who had completed his missions and was now on his way home via A.T.C. with his ribbons and oak-leaf clusters and battle-stars brilliant and new upon his chest. There had been technical talk of flying, and Weaver, who had been a pilot while the pea-shooter boy was in school and seen service overseas while he was making up his mind to volunteer, took exception to a procedure he described. The fighter pilot rounded upon him, wanting to know by what right he put his two-bit's worth in when all he did was chauffeur a lousy transport up and down Britain. The young whelp got away with it for the same reason that so many of his fellows got away with much the same thing, which was also the reason why it hurt the men of A.T.C. so badly. No matter how well they knew the needfulness of their job, no matter that you do not pick your assignment in the Army but you do what you are told, no matter what their inner reservations about some of these gay young blades, no healthy man could help respecting the ones who had been in mortal combat. No man worth his salt in the Air Transport Command who did not have deep within him a regret that his duties would not lead him into combat.

Therefore they took it, and they got it on the chin, the nasty catchwords, "Allergic To Combat" and "Army of Terrified Civilians." These were said, not with a smile, but with full intent to wound. It happened to me again in 1947, when I encountered a man who had been an officer (and served with outstanding heroism, I assume) with a Troop Carrier outfit. The men up front know very well how necessary to them are the men behind them. They know that they are under fire and that others are serving in safety, not through choice, but through the decisions of an authority from which there is no appeal. Yet among the ones up front there is, at least in the American Army, a proportion which cannot abide the thought that anyone failed to endure what they endured, and who exploit the honor which all men willingly pay them to enjoy themselves with sneers and insults.

This was by no means universal. The thousands of wounded who found themselves within the United States forty-eight hours after the stretcher-bearers picked them up, the tens of thousands of ground troops whose battle service ended with that single swift ride home, were often touchingly grateful to the organization which so carried them. Curiously, it was our fellows of the Air Corps who were the worst.

You could not argue with them. Somehow you could not suggest that three years of desolation in one outpost after another could in any way be compared to their months of death and horror. You could not in any way compare thousands of hours of flying all over the world to even the briefest of combat missions, nor indicate that air raids on your base were comparable to battle, nor bring yourself to inquire just how much enemy interception this particular returning warrior had, in fact, encountered. All you could do was take it, and the men of the Air Transport Command did take it. They did more, they poured it onto themselves. Their real pride in their great achievement warred with an inner shame that they, personally, had not been shot at.

It was characteristic of these men that morale was highest on those bases which were either under enemy attack or overwhelmed with work under difficult conditions. Given a poor runway, inadequate equipment, a foul climate, too few men, and aircraft coming through at a rate that had all hands working far into the nights, desk officers unloading cargo, mechanics dreaming up repairs that are supposed to be made only at the great depots, and morale went up like a balloon. The planes going through told them that they were important in the war. They could see that what they were doing supported the men up front. Their unrelenting efforts placated them for not being up front themselves. While it lasted, they were content.

Of all the bases I visited, the morale was highest at two: At the base in northwestern Scotland where a handful of men, in darkest secrecy, ran a shuttle line across enemy-occupied Norway to Sweden, and at Okinawa where another handful did the work of a hundred or more under nightly air attack.

Such was the Army of Terrified Civilians. The ones I have described do not add up even to a sample. They knew they were not heroes. They had a job to do and they did it. Late in the game, flights over the Hump were recognized as partaking of the nature of a combat mission and those flyers began collecting medals.[1] On the whole the A.T.C. men expected nothing but the long work, and the satisfaction of having a part in making something new and great.

[1] This was principally the result of persistent efforts on the part of Brigadier General Earl S. Hoag.

The units requisitioned them by M.O.S. — Military Occupational Specialty — which is indicated by a number. Send us a 501, a 274, both in the grade of corporal, four privates 042's, a 9003 not higher than captain, and a second lieutenant 2421. Thus they were requisitioned and thus, in the main, Headquarters Personnel secured them from wherever they might be had. Sometimes the request was more specific: send us one Portuguese-speaking propeller specialist. In the wholesale moving of men you have to be impersonal, to get and send out "warm bodies" and trust to the law of averages to provide the necessary innate abilities. The good personnel officer — and A.T.C. Headquarters had many — was personal and human when he could be, but that was not often.

They were shipped out by air and by boat, the 501's, 274's, 379's, 2010's and the rest. They worked hard, learned new skills on the job, got promoted, even got decorated. They went on benders, went A.W.O.L., got into fights, and landed in the clink. They went off their heads. They wrote home desperately. They studied the local botany. They got married. They stole. They prayed. They were men and, later, women, human, varied, unequal. They rose to emergency after emergency, worked around the clock, and made the whole vast machine function.

XVI

THE BLACKBIRDS

EARLY IN 1944 the Air Transport Command became engaged in an enterprise small in scale, but nonetheless notable, the running of a transport service across occupied Norway to Sweden. This project was dreamed up by Colonel Bernt Balchen, the aviator and arctic explorer, and a Colonel Milton M. Turner, both of whom were in the Plans Division of Air Staff at the time.

Sweden, theoretically neutral, encircled by the enemy, accepting with a straight face Allied chidings for her sale of ball-bearings to Germany, had allowed a large number of Norwegian air cadets in civilian clothes to complete their pre-flight training on her soil. She also harbored an increasing number of American flyers who had crashed or made forced landings within her borders, to whose escape under certain circumstances she was willing to close her eyes. In order to strengthen the country against Germany, it was highly desirable, if possible, to deliver to Sweden certain supplies to obtain which, otherwise, she was forced to render favors to the Nazis.

The free Norwegians themselves were making some flights to Sweden with C–60's — fast Lockheed Lodestar transports capable of carrying fourteen passengers. The British Overseas Air Corporation also ran a line to Stockholm, apparently in an irregular manner. Some of their flights were made with Mosquitoes, the famous, very fast and beautiful little fighter-bombers. These aircraft could scurry across the dangerous areas even in the short period of the northern summer night, but they could bring out only one passenger and handle only a small amount of cargo.

The normal, peacetime route from the United Kingdom to Stockholm would be entirely over the water, but the Skagerrak and Cattegat were alive with radar, anti-aircraft, and fighter patrols. In practice the only practicable route was by sneaking in across Occupied Norway, and that was no cinch. There is to my mind something wonderful about this idea of running even a small transport line across an area which the enemy occupied in force and guarded watchfully.

The project was proposed in 1943. The British opposed it. They were reluctant to see American air transportation, which had already established itself so solidly in so many parts of the world which Britain had regarded as her own preserve, become established here, too. This should not cause one to become too angry with the British. I can state with considerable assurance that A.T.C. established no route or service during the war that was not required for purely military reasons; nonetheless these services were effective salesmen for post-war American aviation. The British could not afford to have as fine transport aircraft as did we, they could not maintain their bases as lavishly. Fighting as Britain was, on a financial shoestring, she fed her troops on a diet compared to which our C-rations were sheer luxury. She could not offer to passengers as fine food nor as comfortable lodgings as did we. The British were quite right in looking upon every extension of A.T.C.'s activities as a potential advantage to the United States after the war, and not unreasonable in sometimes suspecting the purity of our motives. We reacted in the same way. When the British opened an amazing service from the United Kingdom across the Atlantic to Florida and Mexico and thence via Clipperton Island and the South Seas to Australia, everyone with whom I talked was convinced that its *raison d'être* was post-war competition. In the matter of the shuttle to Sweden, the British suspected that our service would be superior to theirs and foresaw, correctly, that in the end it would develop into a direct United States-Sweden line via Iceland. Hence they opposed the project.

As Secretary Stimson has remarked, disagreements such as these were "brothers' quarrels." In the end, this operation became possible only through extensive British co-operation.

Sweden approved the proposal in January, 1944. To protect her neutrality, the shuttle would have to have the appearance of a simple, civilian, commercial one. A line to be known as the "American Air Transport Service" would be licensed to fly to Stockholm. Its crews must wear civilian clothes, the aircraft must be unarmed, and carry only the usual civil airline markings — in this case, as they were American planes, "NC" numbers such as we see on the wings of every airliner.

Control of this operation, which was given the code-name "Sonnie," was lodged in the Air Transport Command and Colonel Balchen put in charge. Five B–24's were turned over by the 8th Air Force, which also provided the flight and maintenance crews, the rest of the personnel being drawn from A.T.C. The B–24's were stripped of guns, painted black, and their bomb bays remodelled to carry passengers in moderate comfort.

Sonnie was based at Leuchars (pronounced lōōkers) on the cold Scottish coast not far from Dundee and from Saint Andrews of the famous golf course. It is a pretty little town or large village, with a church the west end of which, singularly beautiful Romanesque with a strong French influence, was built in 1244. Outside it is a large R.A.F. base, on which the A.T.C. detachment was given quarters and a hangar. The village is pretty, but that part of Scotland, beautiful from the air and from the ground, is also a land of mists, rains, penetrating chill, and leaden skies. Under the circumstances, plenty of cloud cover into which to dodge was to be desired.

Operations began in April, 1944. British Overseas Air Corporation facilities at the Stockholm airport were put at the Americans' disposal, and maintenance personnel, in civilian clothes, were stationed there. This detachment became a formally established unit, an "operating location" of the main base at Leuchars, on October 18. As may be imagined, as soon as the first B–24 landed at Stockholm, where it parked alongside Lufthansa aircraft, the Germans who swarmed about the airport formed a pretty clear idea of what was going on, and alerted their coastal patrols. Continuation of the service was made possible by the Norwegian underground, which maintained a steady stream of intelligence to London. Combat intelligence — changes in the basing of enemy patrol planes, radar, and anti-aircraft artillery, patrols over new areas, anything that would affect the choice of a corridor — was relayed to Leuchars through the R.A.F. Each flight was individually planned, and briefed as for a combat mission.

The route ran north and east from Leuchars until it approached the zone of heavy German patrol off the Norwegian coast, then turned eastwards across the widest part of Norway, between Oslo and Trondheim. The distance was eight hundred and seventy miles, requiring about five hours' flying time. Some two hours of this were spent in the zone of enemy air superiority. If a plane were forced down over Norway, the crew faced the prospect of being captured in civilian clothes, and presumably treated as spies. In the event of such a landing, they would put their hope in the vigorous Norwegian underground.

In summer the planes took off late in the afternoon, in order to come over the enemy-patrolled area in the short darkness, and reached their destination about five-thirty in the morning, once more in full daylight. In July of the first year operations were greatly hampered by a period of very clear weather coinciding with midsummer; the following December and January, furious winter storms all but stopped operations. Eastbound the flights carried personnel for the Stockholm end of the line, supplies for those personnel, occasional special passengers, and a considerable tonnage for Sweden. Included in this were B–17 spare parts with which the Swedes could repair the less damaged B–17's interned there. These were sold to Sweden to strengthen her air power. Westbound they carried first the air cadets, later the interned American airmen, and at intervals a quantity of the ball-bearings which the Germans so greatly desired. In summer, with morning landings, the passengers were reloaded on waiting C–47's and whisked away without ever having left the hangar beside which the planes landed. In the winter, with the long nights, the transport came in around midnight and the passengers were allowed some sleep.

The planes took off from Stockholm, knowing that their departure would quickly be reported to the enemy in Norway. In the uncertain protection of darkness, following a corridor which they believed was not covered by radar, they crossed the mountainous backbone of Norway and then, flying high, the narrow coastal area. If there was cloud cover beneath them, they breathed easier. The plane roared across the enemy area, a jet-black figure hurtling through the high dark. The men in the cockpit strained their eyes to one side and the other, above and below and ahead, and wondered what might be on their tail. They at least could look out, the passengers packed in the bomb bay were entirely enclosed and could see nothing. They just hoped. At last they encountered the welcome challenge of the British Coastal Patrol, and knew that from that point on they would have fighter cover.

The winter schedule led to a colorful procedure. All hands at Leuchars except the guards and other essential men on duty turned in shortly after eight. They were waked about eleven, had a mug of coffee, and proceeded through the chilly darkness to the hangar. The hangar was a huge cavern, a kind of skeletal Madison Square Garden, dimly lighted and mysterious. The offices, adequate enough shacks of crude boards, huddled insignificantly along the bottoms of its curved sides. They stood around waiting. The incoming transports observed radio silence until they were near to home; each time they sweated them out. Then they were coming in, a pair of grim, black objects briefly, tersely declaring themselves. The minimum of runway lights was turned on for the shortest possible time, and then the planes taxied up alongside the hangar, guided by a single flashlight. The NC numbers on their wings seemed somehow ridiculous.

The bomb bays opened and the men got out. They were herded rapidly into one of the offices. The ones I saw were returned internees; they made a curious impression. For months they had lived the pointless life of internment, idle, well treated, eating well. Now in thrown-together civilian clothes they looked soft. The quality of the soldier had disap-

peared. They told great tales of that land of beautiful blondes, of the pro-Nazis and anti-Nazis, and of the Krauts whose presence they had to endure. One young man told me how, the evening before, a woman had wept on his shoulder over her husband who had just gone off as a volunteer to fight for Germany.

However easy their life in Sweden had been, however grim the missions they had flown, however narrow the margin by which they had landed alive in neutral country, there was not one of them who was not eagerly happy to be back in the hands of the Army Air Forces.

There were forms, and measures which were more than forms, to be observed. For reasons unclear to me, they remained as civilians until they reached their next base, where they would be refitted. The British immigration and customs officials, deadpan, went through the motions of the usual inspection of visitors. They made the matter as simple and rapid as possible, provided the men played ball. Those who had pornographic pictures must surrender them. They must declare their watches and their ski sweaters. More important, they must divest themselves of Swedish money, matches, and other articles which would betray the fact that they were fresh from Sweden.

They were in a mood to comply, and naïvely pressed curious Swedish candies and Swedish coins upon the officers around them, not realizing that it was just as much a violation for these men to have them as for themselves. No harm was done, as there was not a man there who was not intent on guarding the secret.

On top of the Sonnie mission the detachment at Leuchars was handed another, a branch of the activity known as "Carpetbagger," which was the delivery of air-borne supply and personnel to the underground in various parts of Europe. A.T.C.'s share, supplying Norway, was given the code name "Ball." It was undertaken at the request of Special Force Headquarters of the O.S.S. in London. This was a welcome mission to Colonel Balchen, and one for which he was well suited, both in his intimate knowledge of his native country and in his natural daring. Six war-weary B–24's and additional crews were provided for the Ball project. These aircraft were armed and carried Army Air Force markings, and their crews flew them in uniform.

Activities at Leuchars were now surrounded with a yet deeper blackout of secrecy. Following a common custom, the personnel within the organization developed their own informal code words in order to protect the formal ones. Because of the impression one received from the Liberators in their black paint, their mission, and especially the supply to the underground, came to be known as Blackbird. It was a good name, although I thought of ravens, or better, condors, when the great planes came in in the dark.

Blackbird flights were carried on from July to September, 1944, and a few additional flights were made later. There was no possible scheduling of these missions. The weather had to be right, the disposition of German air and ground patrols, and the situation of the Norwegian patriot groups had to be suitable. Ground mists and low fogs caused many missions to be aborted. When all went well, the blackbirder flew in the darkness, with the navigator working overtime, until, well inside Norway, some such landmark as a lake or a mountain was recognized. To spot such landmarks in the dark, the planes flew low once they were past the coastal defenses. From the landmark, the blackbirder flew on a given course until the signal was seen — usually three men with lanterns standing in an L formation. The tiny dots of light were hard to spot, nor was it an easy matter to drop the packages so that they would land close to the right part of the L. It was even more difficult when there was a man to be parachuted down. Everything had to be quick and exact. The roar of the plane making passes at a low altitude would soon draw attention, the enemy or his spies were never far. A quick drop on the right spot meant a quick escape for the plane, and a good chance for the patriots to collect the supplies and get away.

Many times the underground reported that they had heard and even seen the plane, but been unable to attract its attention. Sometimes the wrong landmark was picked up, easy enough at night. Once, searching desperately for their target, the men in the plane mistook a farmer walking along a path with a lantern for the signal, and dropped their cargo. Fortunately he was a patriot. He got the stuff hidden, and then communicated with the underground.

On one of the first missions, Balchen went along as a passenger and counsellor. When the drop had been made, he told the pilot to turn to a bearing leading north. After a time he told him to alter his course slightly. The pilot told the navigator, "Follow me if you can. I don't know where I am." They flew for perhaps half an hour longer, until they saw a snowy mountain rising before them.

Balchen said, "That's the highest mountain in Norway. I wanted you to see it. We can go home now."

Sixty-four missions were flown in all, of which thirty-seven were successful. A hundred and twenty tons of supplies were dropped. Two aircraft were lost. The first crashed in a forced landing near the Norwegian coast, killing all on board.

The second crash, although it involved much less loss of life, was more spectacular. A drop was planned in the far northern part of Norway. This was a part of the plan for crippling the *Tirpitz*. Observing how close the destination was to Russia, the men at Leuchars asked that the Russians be warned, in case they found it expedient to go on to Murmansk or Archangel instead of making the long flight back to Leuchars, but they were advised that word could not be got through before they made their flight.

On this particular mission the pilot was Lieutenant Colonel Keith N. Allen, the base operations officer, a man whom I heard spoken of with great affection and respect. Over Norway the Number One engine developed trouble. When they were over the target area it caught fire. Allen feathered his propeller, and, without alternative now, headed for Murmansk after completing his drop. They approached Murmansk with their lights on, and making all the signals they knew how. The radio operator frantically tried to establish some sort of communication with the ground. They passed near the battleship *Archangel,* and she, as well as the shore batteries, opened fire on the B–24. A shot set the Number Two engine ablaze. Allen ordered the crew to bail out, but before he could follow them the plane exploded in mid-air.

Excited Russian WAC's fired on the men in the water, and it was some time before anybody could be persuaded that they should be allowed to explain themselves. When the Russians learned the truth, they were extremely apologetic. The wounded were hospitalized, all were well treated, and Colonel Allen was given an elaborate military funeral.

The belated amends did not greatly lessen the bitterness of the men at Leuchars. The whole incident indicates excessive trigger-happiness on the part of the Russians. Of course, it must be remembered that acting like a friendly plane, coming in with lights on and landing gear lowered, in order to lay a few bombs on the right spot, was a known trick of the enemy's, and presumably of our side as well. Nonetheless a burning engine can hardly be faked, the searchlights must have caught the A.A.F. insignia on the plane, and a B–24 is one of the most easily distinguished of planes. A C–54 can easily be mistaken for a Focke-Wulf 200; in fact one C–54 flown by a T.W.A. crew was shot down, under conditions of bad visibility, by Spitfires for that reason, but there was nothing on the German list much resembling a Liberator. The action of the women soldiers in shooting at the men in the water betrays a general overexcitability and lack of true discipline. The Russian policy of shoot first and look later cost us the life of a fine officer. It contrasts vividly with the restraint of the British on several occasions when C–54's made similar unannounced landings.

The materials supplied to the underground were assorted and curious. One drop included a large number of copies of *Life,* which the underground managed to place among the German and quisling publications on the tables of the principal hotels. This procedure seems to have caused great pain to the Nazis, and equal delight to the patriots. Planes were requested to buzz the home of certain quislings and go through pretenses of signalling them, with the result that the collaborators became suspect and in some cases were arrested.

While the detachment remained at Leuchars it was always undermanned. The hours were long and irregular, and tension was inherent in the enterprise. Everyone, from the commanding officer to the cooks, worked with willingness. They were deeply proud of what they were doing and uplifted by a sense of its importance and its very danger. The type of double duty visited upon them is illustrated by the work done by Mr. MacDonald, a Counter-Intelligence Corps Agent who, for lack of available officers in the European Division, acted as Intelligence and Provost Marshal Officer. It was his duty to receive the daily combat intelligence from the R.A.F. and our own sources, keep the secret maps in the briefing room up to date accordingly, interrogate returning crews, and brief the outgoing ones. Since he was also responsible for security, he instructed and took charge of the passengers arriving from Sweden. As Provost Marshal he was in charge of the guards, a group of overworked military police who maintained a cordon around the area, patrolled everywhere, shepherded the passengers, and did extra jobs outside of their regular duties. Mr. MacDonald was upheld in his overload of work by the fact that he was something of a prima donna, but it was not only that characteristic which made him the happier the hotter things got. The success with which he handled his assignment is shown by the secrecy which remained so long inviolate, and above all, by the many planes which completed their flights without encountering the enemy.

In November, 1944, Sonnie and Ball moved from Leuchars to Metfield in East Anglia. Better flying conditions obtained at the new location, and as the base was American-controlled the unit was more comfortable. Shortly after this time the Germans must have succeeded in tracking down the line of the operation, for while Leuchars received sporadic attention from adventurous German raiders, Metfield was twice subject to more formal air attack, and was a target for buzz bombs. The route from Metfield was longer — twelve hundred miles by the shortest way — but the service was regularly maintained.

There now occurred an activity which was called "When and Where." Although far from large, it is of special interest as illustrating the crucial part that well-organized air transport can play. It is not stretching the facts too far to say that the ability to deliver a small, select amount of cargo — in this case passengers — changed a minor part of the course of history.

In late 1944 the Western Allies seem to have begun to grasp the idea that Russia would be slow to evacuate any country she liberated. The Germans were beginning to pull out of Norway; the Russians were moving across Finland to the Norwegian border. It was felt important to have Norwegians ready to liberate themselves. At this point Sweden seems to have abandoned all but the last vestiges of neutrality, as she allowed A.T.C., through Balchen's unit, to base C–47's with A.A.F. insignia at Lulea at the northern end of the Gulf of Bosnia, standing by to take Norse police troops, the Norse flag, and a hospital to the vicinity of Kirkenes at the extreme northeastern end of Norway, confronting Petsamo in Finland. The well-armed and equipped Norwegians were referred to as "police," presumably as a faint gesture towards continued Swedish neutrality.

Lulea is some sixty miles below the Arctic circle. Kirkenes, at the tail end of the Lap country, is slightly less than 250 miles above it. This meant that in midwinter the planes had to contend with intense cold and very long hours of darkness. On December 28 they picked up a fourteen-ton field hospital, fourteen nurses, and twenty-eight medical officers and enlisted men at Väseres near Stockholm, and flew them to Lulea. The go-ahead signal for the main operation came on January 12. Some fourteen hundred "police troops" plus the hospital and its staff were flown to Kirkenes. As a result, severe suffering among patriots released from concentration camps in the area was alleviated, and the tip of Norway facing Finland was liberated and occupied by the Norse before the Russians could move in. When and Where continued making flights as needed for the assistance of the Norwegians until the first of July, by which time it had completed 572 missions.

The German grasp on Norway and the air above it weakened rapidly. In the long nights of early 1945 the Swedes made flights to the United Kingdom in converted B–17's. In April the Air Transport Command put C–54's on the route, slower than the B–24's and having a lower ceiling, but much more efficient as transports. By summer the planes were coming to Sweden direct from Iceland via Oslo, a branch line ran to Finland, schedules were published. The planes now were bright silver and bore the Air Forces star. Sonnie and Ball and the heroic nights were over, the blackbirds had ceased flying.

XVII

THE BRIGHT BLUE YONDER—CRASH !

IN THE PACIFIC, the infantry standing in line for chow used to sing "Off we go into the bright blue yonder," and then slam their mess kits together with a terrific crash. It was fair enough commentary on the high accident rate inevitable in combat flying with the hot combat planes.

There is a fundamental difference between the philosophy of combat flying and that of transport and ferry flying. The principal types of combat flying are generally thought of as bombing, and fighting or pursuit, but to these should be added the functions of the Troop Carrier units, not only in delivering air-borne troops but in bringing supplies to the front lines. In all such flying the primary interest lies in getting the plane to, or over, the target, whether it be literally a target to be bombed, an enemy plane to be shot down, or a front-line strip on which to land with fresh ammunition. The mission is a one-way one; only when it has been accomplished does *primary* interest turn to safe return.

Combat pilots, including Troop Carrier, are conditioned accordingly. They are truly brave men. Risk, great risk, is their habit. Such men are likely to be of a dashing temperament, impatient of rules, forgetful of safety.

Constant insurance of safety was inherent in the mission of the Air Transport Command. If a bomber was delivered to India, that delivery must be made smoothly, on time, and without damage to the bomber. The pilot must fly his aircraft at the speed, manifold pressure, revolutions per minute, rate of fuel consumption, which would least wear the engines, so that

191

after thirteen thousand miles of travel he could turn over a machine as nearly as possible ready to go immediately into combat.

The transport must not only reach its destination safely, it must keep shuttling back and forth without major interruptions, or fail in its mission. Both Troop Carrier and A.T.C. planes carried passengers, but in different senses. Troop Carrier units brought troops directly into combat, in the teeth of anti-aircraft fire and enemy interception. The operation could not be made safe, it was undertaken with an expectation of losses. The Air Transport Command moved thousands of passengers between the Zone of the Interior and the active theaters, and between the theaters, movements which required that the men arrive safely. It was the mode of travel of skilled enlisted specialists, staff officers, generals, cabinet ministers, presidents, and the sick and wounded. Safety had to be its watchword. Its pilots had to be conditioned accordingly, its routes correspondingly equipped.

I do not by any means mean that A.T.C. pilots were a group of stodgily cautious flying chauffeurs, any more than that the combat flyers were wild men. We have not yet reached the stage when the timid can be good pilots. Strategic necessity called for such operations as Sonnie and the Hump, and many others, some of which are noted in this account, more omitted. There were always the special occasions when the book was thrown away and the only objective was to deliver the stuff. Nonetheless, the general difference in philosophy obtained in all but a few, exceptional operations.

No matter what the rules and precautions, crashes will occur. The causes are manifold. Mechanical failures will happen, no matter how careful the inspections, how remorselessly careful the manufacturer, the mechanics, the flight crew. The modern flying machine contains thousands of vital parts, many of them at once intricate, delicate, and required to function under violent stresses and fantastic changes of temperature. When I contemplate the guts of a big aircraft, I find myself leaning to the conclusion that nothing so complicated can possibly work; it's all an illusion, like the flights of Peter Pan. The remarkable thing is, not that some failures occur, but that they occur so seldom.

The greatest cause of all is simply the frailty of human nature. The momentary carelessness of a tired mechanic, the decision that a part can remain in service a little longer, may send an aircraft to destruction. Pilot error, a term which covers everything from a minor flaw in technique to a wild disregard for elementary rules, is bound to recur. When something goes wrong in the air, you cannot just draw up to the curb and park. There are many other occupations just as dangerous as flying; in fact, normal, organized transport flying may today be classed among the safer ones. What still makes us stop and think is the dreadful finality of an accident.

Although every accident was carefully investigated, the causes of some remain utter mysteries. The causes of others were strange and unpredictable.

In 1943, P-38's were ferried across the Atlantic in small flights convoyed by heavy bombers as mother ships. One such flight, after it was fairly well on the way to Iceland, turned back because of very bad weather ahead. As they approached the coast of Greenland the P-38's were running low on gas. The leader radioed the nearest base. He was answered, not by the base, but by Germans, either in a submarine or at the then undetected, secret weather station in northern Greenland. The Germans had cracked the code. They told the leader that the field towards which he was headed was closed in, and that another, more distant one, which was in fact closed in, was open. The flight became lost, and the fighters ran out of fuel. One of them picked a smooth spot on the Ice Cap which covers the whole interior of Greenland, and made a normal landing. After he had run about two hundred feet on the snow his wheels broke through the crust and his plane flipped over on its back. Mercifully, he got out unhurt. The rest of the flight landed with their wheels retracted — "belly landing" — in safety. The men were rescued shortly, but six fine aircraft were lost, as even if repaired, it was impossible for them to take off from the Ice Cap.

On January 14, 1943, C-54 number 42-32939 took off from

Miami for Natal en route to the Middle East. It had come down the previous day from Washington, and carried a crew of nine and twenty-six passengers, staff officer specialists on important missions. This was a T.W.A. contract plane; the chief pilot, Captain Benjamin H. Dally, had been with the airline since 1938 and had 7947 hours and 49 minutes flying time, 53 hours and fifty minutes of which had been in C–54's. The flight from Miami to Waller Field in Trinidad was routine except that the number four engine overheated. At Waller Field the flight engineer gave the engine a working over. Captain Dally became suspicious when he found the rear compartment door open after the plane had been standing empty for some time. Investigating, he found a screwdriver near the IFF set.[1] He gave the ship a thorough inspection and found nothing wrong. Shortly before midnight he took off for Belem, Brazil. In the early morning, native fishermen in the swamps and lagoons along the coast of Dutch Guiana saw the plane pass overhead. About half an hour later it came back, flying low, and then with a terrible noise flew into the trees and mud. The C–54 broke to pieces on contact with the ground. Engines and parts of wings were thrown far ahead of the main body. No one survived.

This was the second worst accident in the history of aviation; even today it stands among the bad ones. It was minutely investigated, but no good explanation of it has been offered.

Shortly before midnight on January 17, two days after the C–54 went in, C–87 number 41–1708 took off from Accra to Natal. The pilot was Captain Orval Elwes. He carried a load of U.S. Army and R.A.F. passengers. As he had a strong tail wind he planned to make the trip non-stop, overflying Ascension. This aircraft just plain disappeared. On February 5, Brazilian soldiers at Ponte Negra sighted a life raft. It was picked up. On it was the desiccated body of Major Arthur Mills, and papers and effects of the rest of the passengers and the crew. There was no log or document to shed light on the

[1] IFF: Identification, Friend or Foe. This was at that time a highly secret gadget which gave off code signals on a special frequency automatically and picked up corresponding signals of other planes.

mystery. There were bones and tails of fish on the raft, and a colonel's eagles bent to form fishhooks.

It was apparent that the plane must have been ditched, and that the men on board evacuated it successfully, but in a great hurry, as they did not have all of their survival equipment on the raft. The ensuing investigation, stimulated by the shock of two major, fatal accidents within two days, was minute. Captain Elwes was one of the best pilots in the Africa-Middle East Wing, he was not overtired, had not been drinking the night before departure. The records of the rest of the crew stood up equally well under examination. The usual inspections of the aircraft had been properly made, the engines had not had excessive service, there had been no unusual incident. No messages had been received from the plane after it took off. The probable explanation of this was that, with a heavy load of gas, fumes often entered the cockpits of C–87's, so that use of the radio, with its exposed spark, was dangerous until a portion of the fuel had been consumed. The best theory, and it is only a theory, is that the transport was shot down by a German submarine, crippled, but still able to ditch.

An interesting cause of accidents is a condition known to Arctic pilots as "flying in milk," when the sky and the ground are both white and there is no horizon. It is impossible then to judge one's height off the ground or one's position by eye. Under these conditions one pilot made a careful landing, only to find himself still seventy-five feet up in the air when he expected to touch the snow. Another, flying towards rising ground, heard a strange hissing sound and, to his amazement, saw his airspeed indicator drop to thirty-five miles an hour before he realized that he had made a perfect belly landing. One pilot in Greenland believed that he was still over the lower coastal strip when in fact he was too far to the east and flying a few feet above the high Ice Cap. He banked for a turn, his wing-tip touched the ground, and a crash occurred which, in the end, cost the lives of five men and crippled another. It was the survivors of this strange accident whom "Pappy" Turner kept alive as told in Chapter XV.

Sheer custom leads to carelessness. A contract C–54 with a

T.W.A. crew disappeared tragically shortly after it took off from Iceland, homeward with a full load of wounded. This was the only time that wounded were so lost. Investigation as to the cause of the accident got nowhere until another plane, passing through the same base, had its engines cut out shortly after take-off and, by God's grace, cut in again. The plane returned. Inspection showed water, a very small amount, in the fuel tank. It then developed that the ground crew had become just a little sloppy in putting gasoline into the tanks, which they did with equipment which was somewhat obsolete and required special care. The ground crews on this base, incidentally, were not a part of A.T.C. Long habit, intense cold, and boredom had led the men to drift into practices which caused one disaster and narrowly missed causing a second.

At an island base in a totally different part of the world, another contract carrier's plane took off on a regular, scheduled flight, carrying passengers. A few hundred miles out it radioed distress signals and its position before it ditched. About half the personnel on board were finally rescued. The investigation brought out an instance of how a smoothly functioning, veteran team can outsmart itself; how two very small departures from routine procedures which must often seem burdensome can cause death. The aircraft landed on the island with enough fuel left in its tanks for several hundred miles' more flight. Routinely, as he had done hundreds of times before, the pilot filled out his form, calling among other things for a couple of thousand more gallons of gas. He went further. The contract ground crew were so experienced, the team worked so smoothly, that the pilots had fallen into the habit not only of filling in the request for fuel, but of checking off the line which said it had been provided. They knew that automatically the gas truck would come along and fill her up. This time, for some reason, the truck did not come. A ground official, checking the plane, looked at the form and saw from it that she had been fuelled. The crew came back on board. It was raining hard. The flight engineer looked at the gauges. They were low, but it was his experience that they were inaccurate, and he concluded that they were not registering. Because it was raining so hard, he did not go out on the wings and measure the fuel by hand, as it was his duty to do. He had done that hundreds of times, and the tanks had always been full. So the transport taxied to the loading point, took on its passengers, and departed.

It is not easy for men to learn to trust the elaborate instruments which extend our vision so far beyond our senses. This is the same psychological factor which must be overcome to make pilots really easy about flying on instruments. It seems especially true of radar. Until he has seen it work, an observer has an inclination to feel that when the scope reports something unusual, the machine is at fault. It's just a queer flash out of place, it has all the character of a disorder in the machine. It is hard to believe that those misplaced dots can be as portentous as the book says. The incident at Pearl Harbor was by no means unique.

Aircraft departing from the A.T.C. bases around San Francisco were tracked by radar, after the manner of the Transatlantic Air Traffic Control already described. Month after month went by without any sign of a plane off course. The men who watched the scopes had never seen them really proven. They had never seen anything unexpected of them.

Then one night a B–25 took off for Hawaii. The navigator, in correcting for the declination of his compass, added the correction instead of subtracting it, thereby doubling the error. The radar men saw the signals on the scope which indicated a plane heading far to the north of its course, but they did not believe it. No report was made. The navigator evidently was not on his job, for he did not discover his mistake until the plane was well on its way to Attu and fuel was low. The crew discovered their predicament too late. There was nothing for them to do but radio for help and fly desperately in the darkness, hoping against hope that a Navy vessel would come in sight. None came. That last hour in the cockpit must have been a dreadful thing, with the final, inescapable necessity of ditching, and then the rubber rafts and death in the subarctic ocean.

Anyone who has seen aircraft prepared for overseas flight and the care with which the various crew members are briefed in their special duties knows how little margin for error is allowed. On top of this the radar tracking system was well able to detect and immediately correct any deviation after take-off. A doubling of human weakness frustrated the entire system.

All men have moments of folly; some are permanently fools. The ugliest fool of all is the one who endangers not only himself but others. Not even the strictest military discipline can always restrain such men. An aircraft is a great temptation. A young man who has become master of his machine is naturally inclined to show off, and there is no method of showing off more impressively than stunting at low altitudes and "buzzing" — that is flying over a person or thing so low as almost to touch it. Buzzing is strictly forbidden by military and civil law. It leads to court-martials, severe fines, dishonorable discharges. Still some fools will do it.

The cases are manifold. There was a pilot who had orders to ferry a B–25 over a route which would take him past his home. He wired his parents and his fiancée to stand out in the pasture and watch for him at a certain hour. They did, along with his younger brother and sister. The pilot buzzed them to give them a thrill, misjudged his altitude, and destroyed his plane, himself, his crew, his father and his fiancée.

There are other rules that, sometimes from long habit, men forget. Once I helped pick up the pieces — and I mean pieces — after a B–24 and a C–46 had flown into each other. The bomber was on a long-range cruise technique training flight, which meant that it had two relatively new pilots and a long-experienced pilot-instructor on board. The C–46 was flown by a civilian contract crew, also of long experience. There were scattered clouds, but they ran into each other in the clear, at a height of only about two thousand feet. At the last moment they seem to have seen each other, and made a desperate effort to turn away, too late.

Staring at a fragment of a web belt with a brightly shined, officer's brass buckle still attached to it, I tried to imagine what had happened. Both aircraft were violating a fundamenal rule.

They had not stuck to their flight plans, which would have kept them much higher in the air, and at altitudes a thousand feet apart from each other. The B–24 men were nearly home after a long flight, instruction was over, they were taking it easy. Both planes were flying on the automatic pilot. How often have I seen it, the pilot with his feet up, reading a book, glancing from time to time at his instruments and adjusting "George," the co-pilot perhaps catching a little shut-eye. But the men I saw kept to their flight plans, and never went long without looking through the windshield. It took just a little extra carelessness, fatigue, overfamiliarity with an often repeated run, the thought in the minds aboard both planes, perhaps, that it might be fun to drop low enough to see the pretty women on the beach, to bring these two great machines hurtling together, with miles of empty air around them. At the last moment someone looked up and gave a cry. The pilots wrenched at their sticks and jammed their feet down on the rudder controls. With an intense, fantastic slowness and at awful speed the two aircraft swung, the men's hearts prayed frantically, and the wings struck together.

One of the oddest losses of an aircraft, perhaps, in all history occurred to an Air Transport Command C–87 in January, 1943. The war was a great laboratory. Planes were tested as they had never been tested before, and curious weaknesses showed up in time. About this time Liberators all over the world were plagued by an epidemic of tail flutter arising from a structural fault which was quickly remedied. This flutter could develop so badly that the plane became unflyable. It manifested itself erratically.

The C–87 in question took off from Miami for Natal with a load of cargo, one passenger, and the usual crew. It reached its assigned altitude of 9000 feet and flew for a short time without incident. Then tail flutter began, and shortly became so bad that the passenger was unable to stand in the cabin. They turned back. As they approached Miami, the C–87 kept losing altitude. They dumped the cargo. It still lost altitude, shaking violently and "mushing" in the air. The pilot judged that he could not make a landing, so he notified the field and turned the plane out to sea. As soon as they were over the water, he pointed the plane northeast, set the automatic pilot, and the crew and passenger bailed out. One was drowned, the others shortly were picked up.

The C–87 continued flying. Through the automatic precession of the gyroscope which controlled it, plus probably the effects of the flutter, it flew in a circle not less than 1250 miles, westward and then southward over the United States, waving its tail, to crash when it ran out of gas on a mountainside not far from Monterey in Mexico.

The Command steadily improved the safety of its operations, although in the nature of things, they could not achieve a peacetime level. The available figures are uncertain and somewhat confusing. As good an indication as any of the improvement is in the simple pair, of 0.1 fatal accidents per thousand hours of transport flying in 1943, 0.04 in 1945.

Any accident to an aircraft was the subject of intensive investigation. These careful inspections had an interesting outcome. From time to time structural weaknesses or faults of manufacture were encountered. Reports of these were passed along to the factories, with the result that a fault discovered in some remote part of the world would bring about the detection of a careless inspector or an incompetent workman at home.

Since accidents were bound to occur, the Command early turned its attention not only to every possible device of prevention, but also to search and rescue. That story deserves a whole book to itself, the devotion of the rescuers, their gallant deeds, and the techniques which they developed make absorbing reading, even in the stilted telling of official reports. In Alaska they learned to parachute sled dogs. For doctors, parachuting became routine all over the world. The bases on islands and coasts maintained fast "crash boats" with crews always on the alert, able to take to sea with the same speed with which fire engines set out to a fire. The rescuers were equipped to search the jungles of Brazil, and in the Sahara struck bargains with the Arabs.

I have several times mentioned the men who were stranded

on the Greenland Ice Cap and kept alive by Captain Turner. Their story has been told in detail elsewhere, and need not be repeated here, except to mention the extraordinary device by which the men were finally reached. The Command secured the services of Colonel Bernt Balchen for this rescue, which occurred long before the Sonnie Project was thought of. It was Balchen's idea to try landing a Navy Catalina on the snow as if it were landing on water. With Lieutenant Bernard W. Dunlop, U.S.N., as pilot, the Catalina twice landed and took off in this manner.[2]

Of all developments of search and rescue, the most spectacular was in the India-China Division. Losses of aircraft on the Hump were heavy. As there was seldom a chance of making an emergency landing, the men bailed out. Mostly they landed in heavily forested, tropical mountains inhabited by head-hunting Naga tribesmen, and sporadically patrolled by the Japanese. Many men were badly injured in landing, others contracted tropical illnesses.

Because rescue depended upon relations with the tribesmen, and upon knowledge of the disposition of enemy troops, and also partly because no one was making it his primary business, Major (later Lieutenant Colonel) Robert Wright, the Division's Assistant Chief of Staff, Intelligence, took over the problem. The Naga tribes were on the whole friendly to the British, even more so to the Americans, and soon developed a distaste for the Japanese. The British already had an information network through the hills. Far in the interior were some missionaries who stuck at their posts throughout the war. Wright established relations with them and developed the network yet more elaborately. He devised a special silk patch, to be worn sewn on the flyers' jackets. These patches carried the message that the wearer was an American and a friend, and that a handsome reward would be paid for his safe return, in Chinese, Burmese, South Shan, West Shan, and Sgaw Karen. The prom-

[2] The whole story of this crash, the men's survival, and their rescue, is dramatic, to put it mildly. It is told in "The Long Wait," which forms the second portion of *War Below Zero*, Houghton Mifflin Co., 1944, by Balchen, Ford, and La Farge.

ise of the reward was a real one. Delays, the filing of vouchers, would not do. Wright kept a safe full of gold coins in his office, ready for payment night or day. His office was a mere hut, the safe not large. He had it chained down, but its presence was a constant source of worry to him.

Search for downed flyers was conducted by air. For this an informal unit was organized, using whatever aircraft could be obtained. Later this evolved into a more formal search and Rescue Squadron, equipped with B–25's for searching and with liaison aircraft, and later helicopters, for actual rescue. Until he was killed when his B–25 was shot down on December 10, 1943, this unit was led by Captain John L. Porter, a remarkable and daring man. It was he who, earlier in the game, flew the search C–47 from which a Jap Zero was destroyed on the ground with a Bren gun.

Conducting these searches in unarmed transports was doubly hazardous, as it was necessary to fly almost at tree-top level, up and down along the contours of the steep hills, and enemy fire might be encountered at any time. The sweeps might well reach deep into Japanese-held territory. B–25's, tough, fast, and well armed, were especially suited to such missions.

When, between the natives, the missionaries, and the search planes, a party was found, whether simply stranded in the jungle or in the act of what was called by the miraculously inadequate term of "walking out," the problems of rescue ensued. If the men on the ground signalled that they were in good shape, and it was determined that they were in the hands of friendly tribesmen, it might be sufficient simply to drop supplies to them. In other cases, mixed teams of Americans, Ghurkas, and natives went in through the jungle trails. Often it was necessary to have a rescue team, including a surgeon, parachute down to them. The first to do this was Lieutenant Colonel Don Flickinger of the medical corps, who with two aides dropped into Japanese-occupied territory to assist a party of twenty who had bailed out of a C–46 on August 2, 1943. With the greatest difficulty this large party was led to a safe area. Among its members was a radio commentator. When radio communication was finally established with the party,

the first message that came through to the anxious listeners outside was from the commentator, asking that the Wing communicate immediately with his agent in the United States to
arrange for magazine sale of his story on the best possible
terms.

When helpers parachuted down, they ran much the same
risk as had the men below, of being killed or crippled trying
to land among the dense, tall trees on the precipitous hillsides.
I use the term "hills" following local usage. The main area
of these operations was in the Naga Hills, named for the head-
hunting Nagas. These little eminences, dwarfed by the Himalayas, rise to heights of ten thousand feet, more or less. Later in
the game, when helicopters were on hand, matters were
simpler. When there was no clearing to which an injured man
could be brought, it was practicable to clear a small area on a
hill top, on which a helicopter could land.

One rescue can well enough stand for many. As I have said,
this subject could fill a book, and that book would contain not
one but several absorbing chapters on the India-China area.
The one I have selected is the rescue of Lieutenant G. M. Collins, a P–51 pilot of the 10th Air Force. On July 29, 1944, a
C.N.A.C. pilot flying the Hump route saw a man parachute
near the head of the Gedu River, well up into the wild country. He reported the incident as a matter of routine and Search
and Rescue carried it on file. The man could, of course, have
been a Jap. There was no report of an A.T.C. bail-out or lost
plane for that area.

On August 25 the 10th Air Force finally reported to the
India-China Division that Collins was missing, probably lost
in that neighborhood. A ground party started in, with rescue
planes dropping supplies to it, but was forced to turn back.
The country seemed impenetrable. Nagas were sent up the
Gedu. Well up the river they found Collins, a living skeleton.
They brought back a note he had written on a map taken
from one of the caches which by then Search and Rescue and
co-operating organizations had distributed through the jungle:

Somewhere in hell. I am the pilot who crashed and am
coming in with Nagas. I need medical supplies, quinine,

mostly sulfa for millions of boils that are rotting my limbs off.
. . . Cigarettes would be nice, and please, please, soap and a
sharp little pocket knife. . . . I am ashamed asking for so
much.

The Nagas reported that Collins was unable to walk without
help, and had malaria badly. It was obviously urgent to get to
him, but the jungle was impassable, the monsoons, in August,
were full on, and the rivers were flooded. In this as in many
such undertakings, A.T.C. teamed with Military Intelligence
Service X, the intelligence group devoted to bringing flyers out
of Japanese-held territory.[3]

Carrying walkie-talkies for communication, an M-I-S-X
officer parachuted to one village, two A.T.C. officers to another.
The latter pair hit the right one. They found Collins. A pow-
ered pontoon boat made its way up to the junction of the Gedu
and Tarung Rivers, a considerable distance below where Collins was, but as far upriver as it could be pushed. A rubber
raft was dropped to the group. Painfully and in considerable
danger, Collins was floated down the swollen Gedu on this,
until the party reached the boat on September 13. As they
came down the river, a rescue plane followed overhead. From
there they were brought out without further incident. The
account, unhappily, does not tell how the M-I-S-X officer got
out.

When Search and Rescue closed its books at the end of 1945,
some time after operations over the high Hump had ended, it
reported that 509 aircraft crashes were "closed," 81 still "open."
Of this total of 509, 328 involved A.T.C.'s own planes. At that
time, 1314 men were known to be dead, 1171 had walked out,
345 were still carried as "missing." By then there could be
little doubt as to the fate of the missing men, although search
activities continued for some further time in the faint hope
that somewhere one of them might be alive in God knew what
hidden native settlement. The majority of those who were

[3] During the war, M-I-S-X published a very interesting little periodical
giving the distribution of enemy forces, location of trustworthy natives,
underground organizations, routes, hiding places, points of contact, etc.
for practically the whole of the "Co-Prosperity Sphere."

found dead died in the crash of their planes or in making their parachute landings. Some died later, of injuries or disease, a few were caught and executed by the Japs, a very few fell victim to hostile natives.

Concentration on these activities in Southeast Asia should not be taken as a slight to similar rescues in other parts of the world. As the problem was nowhere tougher than here, and this was the area in which the greatest number of aircraft went down, it is natural to single it out for description. There was a similar experience everywhere. We developed our air transport system in a hurry; our first interest was, of necessity, to get the ferried aircraft and the transports going to the fronts at almost any cost. When the first losses occurred, local units improvised methods of rescue. Not only the Air Transport Command, but the Army and Navy as a whole gave increasing attention to saving lives. Survival became a subject of intensive study, local efforts and experiences were brought together, new equipment devised, kits for dropping in the Arctic and the tropics, wonderfully compact and complete, other kits to be attached to the men's parachutes as permanent equipment.

No soldier was so humble that, if he were lost in whatever desolate place, there was any hesitation about exhausting all possibilities for finding him. The crash of that B–17 on the Greenland Ice Cap involved, in the end, the Air Forces, the Ground Forces, the Navy, the Coast Guard, and the Canadian R.A.F. It was my duty to monitor incoming and outgoing messages concerning the rescue, and I can testify to the intensity of interest. In such cases, the jealousy and lack of cooperation so often noticed between the Army and the Navy seemed to disappear.

When human lives were involved, when there were lives to be saved, every step that was taken was followed closely at the very top. The messages came and went in a volume that would have sufficed for a minor campaign. From Assam, in the nature of things, the reports came to take on a routine quality, usually sent in weekly. They gave the names of any men newly missing or who had walked out, as well as totals of those with whom contact had been made, of those who had walked out to date, and of those still unlocated. There would be a report that the wreckage of a C–46 number 12–3456 had seen, "total loss, crew not sighted, search continues." From time to time in the curious message code the report would say:

SEARCH PARTY REACHED CHARLIE FOUR SIX NUMBER FIVE SIX DASH SEVEN EIGHT NINE ZERO BODIES IDENTIFIED ALL DEAD PILOT FIRST LIEUTENANT JOHN ROGER ATCHISON ASN OBOE ONE TWO THREE FOUR FIVE NEXT OF KIN MRS WALTER MIKE ATCHISON MOTHER TWO ZERO ELM STREET WICKFORD ILLINOIS CMA COPILOT SECOND LIEUTENANT FRANCIS JIG MACREADY . . .

XVIII

UP THE ISLANDS

DURING 1942 AND 1943, the Air Transport Command's activities in the Pacific were limited to its single main line from San Francisco to Hawaii and thence via the southern islands to Amberley Field near Brisbane in Australia, plus a curious, looping "milk run" to a string of remote islands with names such as Tontouta and Funafuti, which used to spell romance to our imaginations in earlier, more innocent days. The milk run was set up chiefly at the request of the Navy, to carry mail and certain supplies to its lonely men stationed on these islands. In the very first, barnstorming days, the crews of the old Ferrying Command were right up front, as has been told, but the later service lagged far behind the battle lines. Nowhere was the gibe, "Allergic to Combat," hurled more bitterly.

This lack of aggressiveness had several causes. Until the end of 1942, even at Hickam Field on Oahu, the great Hawaiian base, A.T.C. was a lodger of uncertain status and without authority. Beyond there the bases were controlled by the 7th Air Force until one reached Amberley Field, and even there it was some time before the Command achieved a satisfactory settlement of its status. Within the Southwest Pacific Theater, the Directorate of Air Transport controlled transport activities. This was a joint Australian-American organization. It sought at first to exercise a sort of reverse control of A.T.C. through controlling its activities, cargoes, priorities and passenger lists at Amberley, and even tried to divert its aircraft or change their schedules. Defeated in these attempts, it remained clearly hostile to any expansion of A.T.C.'s services.

Overriding local factors was the grand strategy of the war, which at that time concentrated on the attack against Germany. The Command of necessity concentrated its resources on strengthening its services to the eastward, both to Britain and North Africa, and for its heavy commitment to China. For the Pacific in the early period it could spare only the comparatively limited number of major transports flown under contract by Consairways and United Airlines.

All these were inhibiting factors. Nonetheless, in going over the record, one cannot but feel that there existed, also, an element of mental inertia on the part of the Command. An organization offering a new kind of service, generally little understood if not actually mistrusted, must be aggressive. It must use salesmanship. This A.T.C. headquarters well knew, but until the end of 1943 it made little attempt to push itself in the Pacific. For a long time Captain (later Lieutenant Colonel) Richard Davis, the Pacific Theater Officer, was a lone voice in headquarters, urging that the Command at least realize the full potentialities of its existing capacity in that area.

For all this, there were moments when flashes of the Command's real verve were displayed. One of the neatest jobs that it ever performed is a case in point. At ten o'clock of a night in January, 1943, a colonel of ordinance telephoned Captain J. J. Farmer, who was the Pacific Route specialist of Priorities and Traffic, at his home. (I cannot give exact dates because this transaction was carried through without paper work of any kind. By pure accident I got the story from Captain Farmer nearly a year later.) At his urgent request Farmer repaired to his office, where the colonel sent over by messenger the original of a radio just received from General Douglas MacArthur stating that the troops in the Solomons were about to run out of grenades, the Australian stockpile was exhausted, and their whole position in those islands was in jeopardy if more could could not be flown out immediately. The colonel stated that there was a good supply, amounting to 11,000 pounds, at the Ordnance Depot at Ogden, Utah. At Farmer's request he alerted the depot to have the necessary personnel stand by through the night.

Farmer then telephoned the Air Transport Association, through which at that time all arrangements were made with the domestic airlines. The A.T.A. got in touch with the three cargo DC–3's then nearest to Ogden, and instructed them to unload whatever cargoes they had aboard at the nearest airport and proceed to the depot. They arrived in the small hours of the morning, loaded the grenades, and took off. The third of these had reached Hamilton Field, the departure point in California for the Pacific Route, by eleven o'clock the following morning. There, on Farmer's instructions, two Consairways C–87's were standing by. Both were loaded and had departed by two in the afternoon. They reached Amberley just three days after MacArthur had sent his radio. The situation was so urgent that there was no time for reloading the grenades onto local aircraft. The weary crews had a bite to eat, the planes were fuelled and served, and off they went, civilians or no civilians, for the crude runways of the Solomon Islands. The grenades arrived in time, and the transports returned unscathed. This deal, which compares favorably to the flying of anti-tank gun fuses to Cairo, has gone almost entirely unnoticed. It is a favorite of mine because of its informality, the military-civilian teamwork involved, and the entire willingness of the civilian crews, tired as they were, to take their big planes into an active combat area.

The Air Transport Command was charged with operating and controlling its own routes and bases, but it was not until the spring of 1943 that it achieved this situation in the Pacific. Little by little in that year it did increase its services. In February, at the Theater's request, it opened a shuttle service from Espiritu Santo in the New Hebrides to Auckland, New Zealand. In July it opened another from Port Moresby to Sydney, the chief purpose of which was for the rotation of combat flight personnel to comfort and relaxation in Australia.

G.H.Q. (MacArthur's headquarters were always known by those simple initials) commanded operations which, by the end of 1943, extended over enormous distances. It became increasingly aware of the need of strengthening and ordering its air transport capacity. In November, 1943, it established a theater priorities board, modelled in part upon one set up nine months earlier by the China-Burma-India Theater. This act was a setback to the semi-independent Directorate of Air Transport, which up until then had controlled priorities in the theater. In January, 1944, at the suggestion of Captain Davis, already mentioned, who was visiting Australia, G.H.Q. requested that an experienced priorities officer be provided by A.T.C. to work with the board. Captain Farmer, the man who handled the delivery of grenades, was sent out. It was with G.H.Q. after this event that the Command worked out in full the final details of the priorities and traffic system described in Chapter VII. In April, 1944, this system was formalized by War Department Circular 13.

Meantime, air transportation within the Theater, as distinct from the Command's inter-theater service, was getting into trouble. The Theater had fused its strategic and tactical air transport. Operating over increasingly large distances from Australia into the islands, with ship-borne supplies coming in at the southern part of the continent, it needed steady, continuous, scheduled air transport for strategic use. At the same time, front-line, tactical air transport was essential. The result, given human nature, was inevitable: over and again, in order to meet a combat situation, the rear area was stripped of aircraft and everything that could fly went to the front. Only the two shuttles run by the independent A.T.C. continued their usual functions. The speed with which this could be done, and the tactical effectiveness of the units, were a source of pride to the Theater — but, in each case there resulted a piling up of cargoes to be flown northward, and resultant shortages at the front, which in turn became a dangerous tactical factor.

To remedy this situation, General Kenney, MacArthur's air commander, proposed in January, 1944, that the Air Transport Command ready two Air Transport Squadrons equipped with four-engine planes and turn them over to him. This, he claimed, would provide ample intra-theater service, and he stressed the flexibility which his transport organization had already demonstrated. Placement of the squadrons under his command would include their flexible use. The Command flatly opposed his plan. Its observation of operations in the Southwest Pacific and its many experiences elsewhere had convinced it that this famous flexibility was very bad doctrine, inevitably resulting in serious damage to the strategic service. Aircraft production was good, but four-engine transports were not so plentifully available that they could be thrown away or wastefully used. The Command made a counter-offer to run an intra-theater service under its own control, but in much the same relation to G.H.Q. that the command's operations generally had to the War Department.

While discussions went on, A.T.C. manifested a more aggressive attitude towards the use of its existing service. On February 10 the end of the trans-Pacific route moved up from Amberley, far in the rear, to Townsville on the northern part of the Australian coast, and to Guadalcanal. In March the terminus shifted again, to Port Moresby.

Colonel Love, A.T.C.'s Deputy Chief of Staff, went to the Southwest Pacific early in March to take up where Captain Davis had left off. He made detailed observations of situations in the area, and negotiated for the Command directly with G.H.Q. I have had occasion to point out before the autonomy of major commands; except in unusual circumstances, relations between them are worked out by discussion and eventual agreement, not by flat orders from higher authority. Of course, the knowledge that Joint Chiefs of Staff, and above them the President, are watching and can always intervene undoubtedly leads to greater reasonableness, but actual intervention is rare. This is far from the absolutism most of us associate with military procedure. Its great virtue is that it takes the maximum advantage of the knowledge of those who are most experienced in the needs, capabilities, and methods involved. The negotiations between A.T.C. and G.H.Q. read almost like those between independent powers.

The outcome of these negotiations does credit to the intellectual grasp of the top men of the Theater. A clear distinction was drawn between inter-theater and intra-theater service. Inter-theater service, most of which originated in the United

States, remained as ever under the high control of the War
Department General Staff. The principal change occurring in
regard to this had already been foreshadowed by the moves
which had brought the terminus of the route to Port Moresby.
The termini would continue to move forward as close as possible behind MacArthur's advance.

The intra-theater service would be MacArthur's own strategic airline. The Air Transport Command would staff the
bases largely with its own personnel, and fly its own aircraft
under its command. For this it established the Southwest
Pacific Wing of its Pacific Division. G.H.Q. would tell the
Wing where it wanted the capacity used, and, as it was both
the originator and recipient of the cargoes carried, would assign
the priorities.

At first glance, the arrangement seems cumbersome. The
Southwest Pacific Wing, intended to work closely with the
Theater, was subordinate to the Pacific Division, and it in turn
to A.T.C. headquarters. In intra-theater matters, however,
G.H.Q. worked directly with the Wing. In inter-theater matters the Wing served as an interpreter and liaison between the
two larger organizations. There had to be, inevitably, a close
meshing between air transport within the area and the long-
distance main line which fed it. This the Wing could provide
far better than any organization not part of A.T.C. By having
the aircraft under an entirely separate command the Theater
was, one might say, protected against itself. The very strong
temptation from which a local air commander cannot help but
suffer, to divert his strategic aircraft to meet a tactical situation,
was eliminated. In an extreme emergency diversions could
occur, as they did in India. But such diversions would be requested, not by the air commander with his primary involvement in the execution of his particular mission, but by the top
command, after fully weighing the resultant effects of cutting
off the regular flow of supplies and possible loss of the planes
themselves. In the end, General MacArthur did call for the
largest and most wonderful diversion of all time, which will be
described in another chapter.

The establishment of an adequate force of A.T.C. planes

within the Theater, of course, also released the theater's own transports for purely tactical use, thus increasing the permanently assigned tactical capacity.

The arrangements which I am describing resulted in a very important further development and extension of the doctrine and practice of strategic air transportation. It is for this reason that I give them so much attention. I believe it can be said that more than any other major commander, General Mac-Arthur grasped the full possibilities of the new logistical arm, and exploited them. In the teeth of jealousies and skepticisms the Air Transport Command had extended its routes within various theaters. It ran a number of schedules which were geographically intra-theater and to a great degree served intra-theater purposes, such as the line from North Africa to Italy or, later, from the vicinity of London to various parts of Europe. These services grew up as fingerlike extensions of the main routes; they evolved without explicit philosophy. The Southwest Pacific Theater included what A.T.C. had to offer in its grand plan, and developed an explicit, carefully worked-out relationship which may be taken as a model.

There were flaws in the arrangement. The Command accepted a much greater dependence than usual upon the Theater for "housekeeping." To the Theater's supply and service arms the A.T.C. men were outsiders, late-comers, not part of the outfit. There was no high-ranking general at G.H.Q. to fight for their interests and protest discrimination. As a result they were the last served in food, tentage, plumbing, electricity, in anything and everything but actual operational equipment. The men were well aware of this, it was painfully obvious. They grumbled and cursed, and went on proving that the Theater had been right to call in A.T.C.

This part of the arrangement was an expression of the extreme independence of General MacArthur's theater, which exceeded that of any other. It extended to the handling of airborne transients, elsewhere the exclusive function of the Air Transport Command. Being in the passenger business as one of its main undertakings and being, after all, only a subordinate branch of the Army Air Forces, the Command paid great attention to its treatment of transients, feeding them, lodging them where they remained overnight, taking them to and from billets, handling their baggage. This was a matter of pride, and also of policy, since the Command was lowly enough to be vulnerable to adverse criticism. The Theater had no such interest in a passenger's welfare. It was as close as could be subject to no one. An irate colonel meant nothing to it; if enlisted men were disgusted and wretched, that fact could never penetrate to its Olympus. The Theater was very big. It had a whole great war to fight. What A.T.C. called transient services were a sideline so small as to be almost invisible.

The result was just what might be expected. The drop in the level of those services when one entered the confines of the Theater was startling. It was not just a matter of minor discomfort, but of needlessly bad operation, enlisted men unfed, waiting and lost in an empty terminal, baggage mislaid, a Red Cross girl with a broken arm at two o'clock in the morning desperately trying to drag her footlocker across the platform. It resulted in the gross inefficiency of "no shows" — passengers failing to turn up to board their aircraft, simply because they had not been told that they were due to depart.

The first service under the new dispensation, from Brisbane to Nadzab in New Guinea began on an irregular basis in the spring of 1944 and was established with regular schedules on June 23. In July, General Alexander arrived, taking formal command on August 1. In order to maintain the closest possible touch with G.H.Q., Wing headquarters moved along with it, to Finschafen on July 25, and to Hollandia on August 12. The route extended accordingly.

This shifting of headquarters and bases gave a new shape to the Command's activities. The pattern up to then had essentially been formed in 1942, when the fronts had become stable and attention all over the world was upon massing our forces and supplies against the day when we should once again be ready to move, this time forward. This meant that the Air Transport Command tended to develop routes and bases expected to remain in use on an increasing scale over long periods of time. It concentrated on stability. In order to maintain the integrity without which its operations would fail, it tended to place the headquarters of its wings, and later of its divisions, at points most advantageous for its own activities and communications, and away from theater headquarters.

The Command's customers came to think of it as a supply line which was supposed to reach only to their borders, or to some well-established, major depot well in the rear. There were exceptions, of course, as when A.T.C. planes ran into Anzio during the fighting there, but in the main this was the attitude, strengthened by remnants of antagonism towards an organization which sought to operate within their realms without accepting their command control. Certainly the customers, and probably the Command itself, had not yet realized how best to use its real capabilities.

In our first great offensive, the invasion of North Africa, the Command seems to have been called in at the last moment, as an afterthought. It was assigned an unimportant rôle. In the Mediterranean area, the advantages to be gained from prompt extension of the air transport system on the heels of a new offensive, which meant including it in the advance planning, do not seem to have been perceived. Instead, A.T.C. was invited to extend its routes in a sporadic way, to relieve shortages of transportation after they developed. Such requests, coming without advance notice, could be fulfilled only after delay, as the aircraft in hand had already been committed elsewhere.

Now, in the Southwest Pacific, G.H.Q. integrated the strategic air transport system in its offensive planning. The transport arm would go island hopping along with the Theater. This branch of air transport would be tested in mobility instead of stability. So far as I know, there has been little comment on this change, without which strategic air transport could never have reached its full growth. As the front lines moved forward and the routes twisted, changed, reached out to follow them, one could see new perceptions forming in Command headquarters. The phrase "close support" began to be heard everywhere. The experiment worked, the military airline showed that it could maintain its procedures, its scheduling, its lift, its handling of priorities, on a flexible basis moving closely behind a mobile army.

The routes bent and moved northward, then, as islands to the eastward were taken, straightened, shortened, and moved north again. The military and the contract pilots brought their planes from the States to Port Moresby, Hollandia, Biak. The intra-theater planes shuttled north and south over ever longer distances, bringing the supplies from the Australian stockpiles on schedule. Finally the end of the line was Leyte in the Philippines.

The advance moved through the eastern end of the Netherlands East Indies, islands which comprise a part of the nexus of islands which anthropologists call Melanesia. The Melanesians are not, on the whole, attractive to the eye. Their basic racial stock is Negroid, mixed in varying degrees with Malayan, Australoid, and the racial compound of the Polynesians. They are very dark, sometimes black, frizzy-haired, and have a lamentable tendency to protruding stomachs. The islands they inhabit are rich in many ways. Viewed with complete detachment from any other consideration, they are beautiful. To most of us from the temperate climates, they are plain hell to live in. Their lovely jungles are hot, wet, and full of insects bearing deadly diseases. Other diseases, needing no co-operation, abound. The runway at Finschafen is an artist's dream, with the wall of the sheer jungle, green, tangled, misty, rising all along one side of it. From a flyer's point of view, the arrangement, however artistic, is undesirable, and within that lovely mystery breed a hundred kinds of death and illness. On many islands the jungles came close to the bases, on others there were surrounding coconut plantations. In addition to the insects and diseases, the unchangeably oppressive climate, and the lack of what might be called the amenities of war in an occupied, civilized land or in an area close to the source of supplies, the trees were full of Japs. It was all a man's life was worth to wander close to the groves or the forest.

Nothing that the men on these bases, or the Air Forces in general, suffered can, of course, compare with what the fighting ground troops went through. There is an indescribable difference between taking to a foxhole occasionally, or even nightly, during a raid, and living in one, between the worst of organized messes and cold C-rations which sometimes failed to arrive. When anything is said about what anyone other than these combat troops went through, it must be with the reservation that, compared to them, everyone else lived in luxury.

Nonetheless, it was now the turn of A.T.C.'s men in the Pacific to maintain a smooth, reliable, scheduled airline under conditions as bad as any that those in the Arctic, or Africa, or China had to face. They met malaria and dengue fever and scrub typhus and jungle rot. Their skins turned bright yellow from atrabrine. They were shot at by snipers, and learned what it felt like to have Japs infiltrating the tent area night after night. They built their own camps — though they were not equipped to do so and the Theater was supposed to do this for them — went through the usual elaborate manoeuvres to obtain such luxuries as flooring, pipes for shower baths, or mess tables, got sick, swore and sweated in the heat, drank fantastic alcoholic concoctions, ran short of sleep, were shot at, along with everybody else. And like everybody else, they kept Headquarters running effectively, maintained their airlines, and did the job they were supposed to do.

If the southern islands offered unusual conditions for a smooth transport operation, Leyte was plain impossible. A thumbnail sketch of life there has been given in Chapter XII. At Leyte, they felt, it always rained and the rain always steamed. The welcome they received from the natives touched them; they were inspired by the fact that at last we were driving back into the territory Japan had raped from us ourselves, and the realization that this push was bigger than anything they had supported before. They could also tell plainly that the Japanese were really fighting back. The runway was strafed and bombed, not a few times, but over and over again, there were parachute attacks and, at the outset, regular ground attacks which came menacingly close to the base.

The Americans landed on Leyte on October 15, 1944. On the 9th of November the first A.T.C. plane took out a load of

wounded. Early in December its base personnel were established at Tacloban air strip, and on the sixteenth of that
month the first elements of Wing headquarters arrived. The
Command's commitment was to evacuate one thousand sick
and wounded a month to Biak, which would be done principally by the Wing's intra-theater aircraft, plus evacuation on
a "special mission basis" along the main line to Saipan north
of Guam. This meant also the delivery to Leyte of about
one hundred tons a month in addition to what the main line
aircraft brought in.[1] Only military pilots were used in this operation. All the intra-theater crews were military. By this time
military crews were handling a constantly larger part of all flying over the Pacific, and this particular run was not one on
which one would call on civilians to operate if it could be
avoided.

A transport pilot is used to the approach and landing procedures which are standard within the United States. He ex-
pects to begin talking to the control tower and getting his instructions well in advance, he has been elaborately conditioned
to move as instructed to his place in an orderly traffic pattern,
and to bring his plane down with the runway pretty much to
himself. Such conditions could not obtain on Leyte. The air-
strip was in combat use, with fighters and bombers landing and
taking off. Combat pilots tend to be more casual about these
procedures. Many times, even if they wished to, they cannot
observe them. A fighter almost out of gas, a plane badly shot
up and in trouble, another with a seriously wounded man on
board, perhaps the pilot himself bringing it in with his last
gasp of consciousness, or the plane being landed by a navigator
or a gunner who washed out of flying school — these cannot be
formal or leisurely about getting to the ground.

Into this confusion the transport pilots brought their big
wagons, heavy laden, slow to manoeuvre. They were glad to do

[1] The standard calculation is eight men, with equipment, to a ton.
The wounded would carry little equipment, but this saving in weight
would be taken up by the medical personnel and supplies on board. One
thousand men, then, equals 125 tons, but part of this must be deducted
for the greater load of fuel carried on the flight to the combat area.

it. This was close support. They had vaguely imagined something like this when they put on their uniforms, they had all but given up hope of it as they worked their way up from class to class in the Ferrying Division. They kept their eyes peeled for peashooters in a hurry whizzing over them, prayed that their aircraft would not be strafed on the ground, called forth their skill, and came and went as if they had been flying between California and Hawaii.

There was only one thing which caused the men's morale to drop off. That was the discovery, on certain occasions, that the transports were delivering, not ammunition nor medicines nor any of the urgent things required by troops in violent battle, but refrigerators and some other luxuries consigned to the high brass. They had no way of knowing, nor have I, whether these things were loaded only when the stockpiles of necessities for the front were high, or whether they replaced goods that should have gone first. The idea that their efforts should be put to such use when everyone knew how the troops in general, officers and enlisted men, were living and how violent the battle was, caused disgust and gloom all along the line clear back to Hawaii, but most intensely, of course, on the Leyte base itself and among the flight crews.

Fighting on Leyte, other than the eternal problem of cleaning out Japanese "hold-outs," ended with the end of 1944. By that time, 1945 sick and wounded men had been flown to rear area hospitals. By the time that this island ceased to be an evacuation area in April, 2259 had been thus mercifully removed.

The demonstration of the principle of strategic close support had an effect upon the use made of the Command in many active theaters. Brigadier General William Ord Ryan, commanding the Pacific Division, followed it up actively. He pointed out to the joint Army-Navy authorities in the Pacific that, outside of General MacArthur's area, his Division was called in, sometimes in a hurry, to meet needs which should have been foreseen. This was especially true in connection with the evacuation of both Army and Navy wounded. Both the Air Transport Command and the Naval Air Transport

Service should be integrated into the planning, so that they could be ready to offer the maximum benefits of their capacities. On occasion, subject to the approval of the General Staff, A.T.C. might even be able to transfer additional aircraft from other theaters.

By this time, in late 1944, the A.T.C. main line ran directly across the Pacific through liberated Guam. From the main line, tentacles reached out in many directions over that vast ocean. The Command no longer ran a trickle of transports along a single line to Brisbane; it had become a powerful transport arm capable of many different kinds of operation. To make the fullest use of its capacities and to control what amounted to an empire, in addition to the Southwest Pacific Wing, the Division was subdivided into the Central Pacific Wing with headquarters in Guam and the West Coast Wing with headquarters in San Francisco.

Wherever the Navy was in command or strongly represented, the A.T.C. services were paralleled by those of the ever-growing Naval Air Transport Services, the greatest strength of which was concentrated in the Pacific. This concentration arose in large part, but not entirely, in a natural manner since the Navy itself was most active there. A contributing factor was a war within a war which went on throughout the latter part of the period of hostilities and through 1946, and may, for all I know, be going on still. Except for the Army establishments in the Philippines and Hawaii, the Navy had always been supreme in the Pacific. In Hawaii it had the upper hand, to the extent that patrol sweeps by Army aircraft were strictly limited as to the distance they could go over the water, and that even flights between islands could be made only with Navy permission. The Navy wanted the Pacific war to itself. When it set up the attack upon Guadalcanal, it excluded the Army from its plans with the notorious result that, unable to relieve the exhausted, desperately fighting Marines there, when it finally did call upon the Army for help the Army had to go through the whole business of setting up, equipping, and transporting the relief force. This bit of service chauvinism greatly prolonged the agony of the heroic Marines and cost hundreds of lives.

Now the Army, and especially the Army Air Forces, were reaching out over the Navy's ocean. The 20th Air Force with its B–29's — ferried to their bases under A.T.C. — was operating out of Guam and its neighboring islands. MacArthur's Far Eastern Air Force, a merger of the Fifth and Thirteenth, dominated the western Pacific. Above all the Air Transport Command's nexus of routes threatened to establish the Army as an independently interconnected concern throughout the area.

The Navy met this threat with a three-fold counterattack. First, it dug in in a big way. Its control of surface transports enabled it to provide its personnel with living quarters and to feed them on rations which contrasted violently with what the Army people got. Wherever possible, it established itself as the arm which actually commanded the islands, and wherever this became the case, the Army units on those islands had to fight not for comforts but for necessities. I have spoken before of the violent contrast between the living quarters of enlisted men and of one commanding general at Casablanca. That contrast did not shock me as deeply as the contrast between the comforts available to Naval personnel generally on Guam and the poor food and wretched housing of the B–29 crews at their base on that same island. The nature of these men's missions, the terrible strain upon them, their combat losses, the fact that they, and they alone, were beating down the homeland of Japan meant nothing whatever to their comrades in arms a few miles away.

Their second counterattack was in public relations. Not only did they have a galaxy of public relations talent on the job in the field, but the comforts they could offer, the incomparably superior supply of liquors in their officers' clubs (to which I can testify), and their control of most communications facilities at the key point of Guam tended to lure news correspondents into their arms. The result was that Navy news dominated the wires.[2]

[2] The A.T.C. stationed a Major George Carroll, a quiet, slightly graying, unassuming, and thoroughly delightful newspaper man, on Guam. Single-handed, Carroll should have been whipped. His personal charm,

The third counterattack, and an important one, was through the Naval Air Transport Service. In every possible way N.A.T.S. was pushed to duplicate and where it could to exceed A.T.C.'s activities. If, post-war, the Navy was to retain its dominion over the Pacific, it must prove that the Army's air transport system was unnecessary. This kind of competition, to which the Army, through A.T.C., responded in kind, resulted in needless waste. On the whole, however, the two transport arms themselves got on remarkably well, worked out a good *modus vivendi,* and supplemented each other as often as they merely duplicated.[3]

Both of these organizations were now brought into the advance planning of new moves, notably of the invasion of Okinawa. To make ready for its assigned share in this venture, the Command activated and manned a base unit, held on Guam in condition to move in when required, and set aside the necessary C–54's. N.A.T.S. made similar preparations. Neither side would allow its air transport arm to be omitted from so important a job. This was long-range work; 1420 miles of open water lay between Guam and Okinawa. At the time, we took the task for granted, but if one thinks back to 1941, just three years earlier, one cannot but gasp at the progress which made it possible to plan on continuous, airborne supply to a beach head, and continuous air evacuation of the wounded from it, over fourteen hundred miles of ocean.

The commanding officer of the base unit, Lieutenant

---

his wide acquaintance among newspaper men, and his concealed wiliness enabled him to turn the Navy's advantages to his own use. Correspondents lodged with the Navy invited him in, and over the Navy's liquor he gave them the A.T.C. story.

[3] For the record I should state that these observations on Army-Navy rivalry are not based upon any unfortunate experiences of my own. Tales of Navy discourtesy to Army personnel are manifold, hairraising, and may or may not be true. For myself, in occasional contacts with the Navy, generally with N.A.T.S., I received nothing but friendliness, help in need, and genuine courtesy. My experiences, both in Washington and in the Pacific, and more recently in obtaining certain information for this book, have been uniformly pleasant.

Colonel James W. Luker, landed on Okinawa with the first wave. So presumably, did his N.A.T.S. opposite number.[4] On D–Day plus six, April 8, 1945, Lieutenant General Simon Bolivar Buckner sent out the call for the transports. Through its control of communications at Guam, the Navy was able to get its plane off forty-five minutes ahead of the Army, so that the honor of bringing the first transport to Yontan Field went to Commander Jack Thornburg in an R5D (C–54) with a load of flame-throwers and personnel for the base. A.T.C.'s plane, a C–54 piloted by Captain R. C. Spotts, landed at Yontan at ten forty-five. It carried the initial detachment of base personnel and their equipment, and a fork lift which was thereafter used by both A.T.C. and N.A.T.S. in loading. The flight nurse on board was Lieutenant Nabors. Sixteen litter patients were loaded, along with parts of the first Baka bomb to be captured. The plane took off again at one P.M. and reached Guam at ten-twenty.

The troops on Okinawa could hardly believe their eyes when they saw the big transports come in, and watched them take on their loads of wounded, who within a few hours would be settled in the well-equipped base hospitals of the Marianas. War in the Pacific had never been like this.

Yontan airfield, which the transports used, was on the coast near the middle of the island. From its wide expanse of crushed coral rock, the pretty, rolling, green hills reached to the horizon. After the southern islands, even after Guam, the climate and landscape of Okinawa were heaven, except for the

[4] *Operation Lifeline*, by James Lee, Ziff Davis Company, the semi-official N.A.T.S. popular history and Senior Class Album, says almost nothing about the establishment of the N.A.T.S. unit on Okinawa. In its account of this operation it makes the remarkable error of stating that operations began on *June 5* (page 35). A beautiful example of a half-truth aimed to create a false impression is to be found on page 37, where the author writes: "And of those 24,000 [wounded to be evacuated], the amazing total of more than 17,000 — more than two thirds — were evacuated by air. If there were a register to compute totals of lives saved, a tremendous credit would have to be rung up for NATS." A.T.C. is never mentioned in the chapter; the intention of the omission is obvious. This is the kind of thing which keeps the services apart; when the Russians perform similar tricks, the whole country howls.

excessive rainfall. This was a temperate land, fertile, mild, bearing trees and shrubs which were familiar to Americans. The people of the country, the meek little "Okies," had little in common with the Japanese. Their faces were mild, they were tiny, they had no desire to resist anyone. It would have been a lovely island but for the presence of the Japanese Army, and the home islands of Nippon, ominous, hateful, over the horizon but ever present in one's mind, 350 miles away.

When we captured it, Yontan was a pretty good field, as major Japanese fields went. One of the striking impressions one received in the Pacific was the general inferiority of Japanese engineering and their mechanical equipment. In terms of road-building, runways, grading, and similar activities, they seemed to be fighting the First World War; even close to home they depended greatly upon horses and wagons. Here in the United States we look casually upon the machines we see along our highways and in construction. Never did I realize what they meant until I saw them on the Pacific islands, the enormous D–8 tractors, prime movers, bulldozers, scrapers, scoops, the great cumbersome, competent machines, operated with a sort of bored, triumphant calm by men in goggles, remaking the landscape. The mind boggles at the mere thought of carrying them across the whole Pacific Ocean and landing them on a dockless beach, under fire. But here they were, a source of power which the enemy could not even approximate. Here they worked, and by their work changed the whole balance of the war.

Yontan, as I have said, was a pretty good field. By the time the Seabees got through one of their usual, miraculous jobs of remaking it, it was an excellent one, capable of heavy, four-engine traffic, with wide, smooth runways, ample hard-stands, broad taxi-strips. Equally important, since many other fields had been secured in the initial period of the invasion, the melange of incompatible types of flying which cursed Tacloban was eliminated here. The traffic on the field was manageable without confusion. In addition to A.T.C. and N.A.T.S., the field was used by T.A.G., a Marine transport organization using C–46's, and a squadron of Navy "Buccaneers." These last were a radical modification of Liberators, with the fuselage

lengthened and a single tail, and very heavy defensive armament installed. They were easier to fly than the older, twin-
tailed Liberators, but retained their ruggedness and had an
even longer range. In these the Navy crews went out on long
sweeps over the Yellow Sea and Korea, from which they returned often shot up and with dead or wounded on board,
always exhausted.

With the great numbers of men on the island and the fighting as desperate and long drawn out as it was, supply remained
a serious problem for all our facilities. To cut down the load,
Colonel Luker decided that he could run the base with thirty
men, so thirty, a single plane-load, moved to Okinawa, and in
conjunction with the N.A.T.S. contingent ran an activity for
which ordinarily four times the complement would have been
considered scanty.

The goal was to achieve a "turn-around time" of forty-five
minutes; that is, the planes should land, unload, be fuelled,
loaded, and take off within that time, in order that they should
be exposed to air attack for the briefest possible period. The
chief outgoing cargo was wounded, who had to be put aboard
with care. More often than not, this remarkable goal was
achieved.[5]

Obviously the base was not equipped to make repairs, yet
on such occasions as when transports landed after being slightly
shot up, or when injured B–29's put in on their way back from
Japan, the handful of mechanics performed miracles of ingenuity.

They had a tent area on a pretty hillside among evergreens.
The tents could be used only in the daytime. At night the
officers and enlisted men slept in two Japanese aircraft revet-
ments, artificial caves with concrete roofs, across the open halves
of which they erected sandbag barriers. Crowded, damp, uncomfortable, they gave good protection against enemy bombs
and the falling fragments of our own anti-aircraft fire. They
were also reasonably defensible against ground attack. Even

---

[5] *Operation Lifeline,* cited above, page 35, states that Commander
Thornburg achieved this time on his first flight. He departed with a full
load of wounded, and as the fork lift was not then available, I question
the statement.

so, as one officer who visited the base remarked, when the bombs started dropping and the fragments raining down, you wished that you could pull your helmet down over your navel.

With one or more "alerts" every night, no one got a whole night's sleep.[6]

When the detachment finally got a movie, it took three nights to show the whole picture. Life was definitely not a picnic. But there were other considerations. Faced with a critical shortage of ammunition, on May 20 General Buckner radioed for all available 81-millimetre mortar shells, a prime weapon against the dug-in enemy. The nearest supply was at Hawaii. In twenty-eight hours the Command and N.A.T.S. delivered 36,000 rounds, approximately two hundred tons. Luker's thirty men, and the crews on the planes, could never forget the desperate nature of the fighting the rumble of which they heard, night and day, to south of them. They saw the wounded being loaded, plane-load after plane-load, day after day. From these planes they unloaded tons of supplies, essentials of war, and saw them moved rapidly to the fighting front. They knew what they were there for.

In the first week, A.T.C. evacuated 407 wounded. The base was subjected to eleven air attacks. In the course of April, it carried out 1249 wounded men. Before the fighting ended, A.T.C. and N.A.T.S. between them flew some 17,000 wounded (including a Red Cross girl) to the relative comfort and the safety of the rearward bases. The men worked for all they were worth. Over the headquarters tent they put a sign with Japanese characters on it (it turned out to be a sign for a tailor's shop) to which they added, "Welcome to Yontan, every night a Fourth of July." The mess sergeant was inspired to do such things with C-rations and dehydrated potatoes as I never tasted elsewhere. They were as happy as it is possible for men under such conditions to be. As I have said before, here and at Leuchars with its midnight operations was the highest morale I saw on any base.

---

[6] One's capacity for sleep becomes remarkable. After an alert which came to nothing, I slept right through a sneak raid by a Japanese "bogie" which made a direct hit on a Marine C–46. I was wakened, after the shooting was over, by the brilliant light of the burning plane.

We won control of the air over Okinawa, in the daytime, early in the game. At night the Japs came in from Kyushu, some readily seeking death, many cautious and evasive, with a reasonable respect for their own skins. One night two of their planes landed on the strip, to pour out a group locally known as The Yamashita Marching and Chowder Club, which blew up a number of aircraft and generally raised merry hell until it was wiped out. The fighting went on, the transports shuttled between Okinawa and Guam, while the very, very high brass debated whether the next offensive should be directed against the home islands of the empire, or across from Manila into China, and in the Jemez Mountains of New Mexico in an isolated colony they were building the first atomic bomb.

I do not see how anyone who saw a little of it can write about what went on in these islands without some word about the actual fighting. As one travelled from island to island in the Pacific, increasingly the nearer one got to present combat, most of all in the horror of Okinawa, one felt the terrible nature of the war against Japan. Americans have shown amply that they are great warriors, but they are not warlike. They like neither killing nor being killed. One got it from the men of the Air Forces, but even more from the ground troops, on Okinawa from the Marines and the 27th Division, for it was their hell particularly. The closer they got to Japan itself, the more clearly and terribly they saw what the shape of the ultimate invasion would be. The Japanese turned the southern end of Okinawa into a great prairie dog town. They had always been great ones for digging in, and here, defending long-conquered territory, on the threshold of their homeland, they dug themselves in as they had never done before.

One might shell and bomb and shell, and still in the end men of vulnerable, tearable flesh had to creep to the mouth of each hole and throw in grenades, or the searing, liquid fire of napalm, or on occasion, a bulldozer could be brought up and simply stop the hole solid. It was not only the being wounded, maimed, killed, it was also the nature of the killing. Those men whose duty it was to go into the burrows after resistance had ceased within them came out sickened and praying they would never have to enter another. In every sense it was a hateful form of war; no matter how or with what horribly good reasons our men might hate the Japs, they hated also the kind of killing they had to do, and this on top of their own bloody losses, and the constant sense of "pretty soon, me."

In the name of humanity, they asked, why don't we use gas? We could not kill more than we are killing now, perhaps we should kill less, and we could end this thing.

From the air, the south end of Okinawa looks like the blunt head of an adder. Across the neck, near Naha and further back, our artillery was ranged across the island, from the 150-millimetre cannon in the rear to the light mortars in the front lines. Over the adder-head the attack bombers flew and swooped and swooped again in low-level, precise bombing. Up and down the coast the battle fleet cruised in line, the flames spouting like sun-smitten marigolds from its turrets. All the tip of Okinawa seemed to shimmer, a haze arose from it, the ground smoked with a continuous, thin uprising of dust over all its surface. After a pounding like this from dawn to late afternoon, you thought, no man can have fight left in him. But always, when the attacks were launched, the Japanese were still alert, ready, fighting in the mouths of their countless burrows. It went on day after day, month after month, and there was no end to it until the last gopher-hole had been taken.

It was a nightmare in which the heaviest concentration of fire, the sixteen-inch guns, the bombs, had no effect. This was the foretaste, the sample, from which the imagination could not help from framing pictures of what it was going to be like on Kyushu and Honshu, where not only the main army lay waiting, but every living soul was a Jap.

In the nature of this war we killed civilians. We could not help it. Before ever an atomic bomb was dropped we killed great numbers of Japanese civilians. The two bombs wrecked two cities. They killed indiscriminately. But if they stopped the war, then by their final, dramatic horror they ended the long-drawn, equally great horror which the people at home seem never to have grasped. The two bombs killed their thousands, but they saved far more thousands, Japanese as well as American.

XIX

NEAREST TO HIS HOME

A WOMAN living in Washington patronized an Italian shoe-maker, a pleasant old fellow and a good workman. They be-came friendly. When he learned that her husband was over-seas, he told her that he had a son in the Pacific, and that he had not heard from him in a long time.

A month or so later she went to the shoemaker again with repairs to be made. She saw that he was close to tears as he worked. He told her that there was still no word from his son, and that he and his wife were in despair. The woman re-minded him that if his son were dead, missing, or wounded, he would unfailingly hear from the War Department, and that in this war, as never before, no news was good news. He heard her, but her words had little effect. A week later she returned for her shoes. The old man's voice broke when he spoke to her. He had no heart to go on, he said.

While they were still talking, his wife broke into the shop, waving a telegram. "Poppa, Poppa, he is coming home. He has been wounded and he is coming home in an airplane. It will be here tomorrow."

The shoemaker sat perfectly still for a moment. Then he took one mighty swing with his hammer on the heel he was repairing, and that was the end of work for the day.

This incident represents one aspect of Medical Air Evacu-ation at work. Air Evac, as it was called, was a by-product of the Air Transport Command. It combined humaneness and military practicality in an exceptional degree. It was a task at which no one could help but work with enthusiasm.

Use of hospital planes was by no means unknown before A.T.C. took it up, but no fixed techniques had been developed. Until then there had been rather a variety of cases of sporadic improvisation to meet special situations. Planning for the establishment of medical air evacuation as a standard part of the Command's functions began on October 5, 1942. Many considerations urged the planners on. There was, first of all, the common humanity, one might almost say the delight, of getting these men home. There was the unquestionable therapeutic value to them of being returned to the States, and the equally great effect upon the morale of the men at the front in knowing that this would be done. Keeping the base hospitals overseas relatively free of those casualties who could not be quickly cured nor were unfit to be moved, relieved the strain upon them. It also meant an enormous saving of manpower and in the shipment of supplies. A patient, the medical authorities calculated, occupies all or part of the time of six people, and his maintenance overseas represents ten tons of supplies.

The problem was by no means a simple one of deciding to undertake medical air evacuation and then putting litters in the planes. Many factors were involved. No one knew just how various kinds of sick and wounded would be affected by flight at various altitudes. No one knew just how to equip the planes so that, flying in one direction, they could be efficient hospital ships, in the other, efficient cargo and passenger carriers. No one was willing to undertake transporting the victims of war by a method which might prove unsafe. The medical authorities, especially the highest elements of the Medical Corps, who were unfamiliar with aviation, were not easily persuaded to try the experiment.

The first air evac flight began at Karachi, India, on January 17, 1943. I have the impression that it was bootlegged by the Command. Seven patients were loaded on a C–47, which carried them to Accra on the Gold Coast. From there they departed on January 21 in a Liberator, and arrived at Morrison Field in Florida, where they were hospitalized, on the twenty-third. They were accompanied by Second Lieutenant Elsie

Ott, a nurse who had never flown before in her life. When she reached Morrison Field, her first wish was to be assigned to the Air Transport Command.

The activity grew slowly at first, while techniques and equipment were developed. Experience showed that this was a safe and highly desirable way of moving the sick and wounded. In collaboration with the Medical Corps, an Air Evacuation Wing was formed, subdivided into flights which were attached to the various divisions of the Command. The wing contained a number of doctors and specially selected and trained, volunteer, nurses and medical attendants. The nurses were the now famous flight nurses, remarkable young women about whom, inevitably and justifiably, there gathered a certain amount of glamour. The attendants, enlisted men, have been slighted, not by intention, but because the young ladies could not help being the center of attention.

Usually, a nurse and an attendant were placed aboard an aircraft as a team, unless the load consisted of walking cases not likely to require special attention, in which case an attendant alone might go along. Flight nurses were used as often as possible, because of the morale value of their appearance in forward areas, and because the patients had more confidence in them than they did in the enlisted men, despite the latters' competence. According to the length of the route and the presence of intermediate stops, the team might make the entire flight, lie over at the home base for a rest, and then go out again as passengers, or they might lie over at an intermediate point, such as the Azores or Kwajalein, then replace the next team coming in from the forward areas.

The nurses' presence on some of these bases was a great thing. As an officer remarked on the bare desert of Kwajalein, "They keep you from forgetting what a woman looks like." Their work was by no means pure glamour. One saw them at such points as Biak and Okinawa, in their monkey suits, looking rather bedraggled and having long since got over the excitement of being the only women around. In flight, they were confronted by long hours of steady, responsible work. By the time air evacuation was fully worked out, complex treatments

were continued in the air, under the difficult circumstances of
the tiers of planes with the narrow aisle between, often enough
with the plane rocking like a boat as it battled rough air. There
is neither glamour nor romance, but something finer than
either, in attending to a helpless man who is thoroughly airsick.

Much of the technique was developed locally by the divisions of the Command. Requests for air evacuation originated
locally, from the theaters, and in any case the theaters controlled the priorities, so arrangements were made directly between them and the division concerned. Ordinarily, patients
were given a number two priority. Equipment of the aircraft
themselves was carried out from Command headquarters, distribution of the air evacuation personnel was between that
headquarters and the Medical Corps. Most of the rest was
worked out on the spot.

Thus, many methods of loading were used. In some areas,
the authorities favored the fork lift, already described as a sort
of mobile freight elevator. On this a platform was placed. The
stretcher bearers stepped onto the lift from the ground, were
raised, with their burden, to the level of the plane's door, and
walked in. The objection to this method was that, unless the
man running the lift was expert and very careful, it might
stop or start with a jerk.

In the Pacific, much use was made of a series of platforms,
with a team of bearers on each. The litter was handed from
level to level, and in practice was moved with great gentleness.
One observer has written: "One had only to be on hand in the
dawn hours during the loading of the planes to realize that
these men had their hearts in their work as well as their
muscles." But here there was the awful danger of dropping. It
did not happen, but it might. The European Division favored
a long ramp, which also had its advantages and weaknesses. At
places such as Okinawa, they used what they had.

A great deal of thought was given to the question of the most
efficient in-flight medical chest. Existing chests were too heavy,
and inconvenient for use aboard a plane. Different items of
equipment were needed according to the nature of the cases

being carried. Experiment in this line was continuous and ingenious. One never knew what problem, large or small, would arise next. Fairly standard procedure is for the pilot and copilot of a plane to board it after it has been loaded, and then proceed with their "cockpit check" of the various instruments, which takes some minutes. At Saipan the surgeon observed that the plane became very hot on the ground under the brilliant sun, and felt that these extra minutes during which the wounded lay sweltering were harmful. He protested, and the usual procedure was changed.

Short-range movement of wounded from points close to the front began early. As the Air Transport Command's long-range evacuations became regularly established and increased in quantity, and as the Naval Air Transport Service joined in in 1944, there was a corresponding increase in the same operation further forward, principally with C–47's, flown by Troop Carrier Units, the Navy, the Marine Corps, and A.T.C. There finally developed an air network by which it was possible for a soldier wounded in France or on a Pacific island to be carried to the hospital nearest to his home in the United States in little more than double the actual flying time involved, provided there were no medical complications.

The actual working of A.T.C.'s operation in the European Theater provides a good example of it everywhere. Wounded men were picked up at the front, and, after receiving first aid, moved to temporary hospitals behind the lines. In the early, Normandy, days they were then loaded on Troop Carrier aircraft with little delay; later, there was more opportunity for further attention on the spot and more careful selection of who should be flown back. These men were carried to base hospitals in the United Kingdom, where they were put to bed and sorted into three main groups: those who could soon be returned to service, those who should not be moved, and those who should be sent home. The last group was established in conjunction with one of the Command's flight surgeons, and in this matter the Command had the final say.

The A.T.C. medical officer at Prestwick was notified of the number of patients ready for evacuation. The priorities and traffic officer, checking capacity against the list of higher priority passengers and cargo on hand, advised how many could be moved in the near future. This involved somewhat more complex calculations than usual, as it was preferable to make up whole plane-loads of patients, although mixed loads of patients and well passengers or cargo were made up at times. According to this determination, patients were brought, by ambulance, hospital train, or air, to the holding hospital on the line at Prestwick Air Base.

The types of patient which were not acceptable were: Those in too poor condition to survive, unless moving them would be the means of taking them quickly to a place at which some special treatment might save their lives; those who were dying, near dying, or whose prognosis was fatal; contagious cases; persons in shock; sufferers from coronary occlusion or angina pectoris if an attack had occurred within thirty days; persons with severe anemia; persons who had received transfusions of whole blood within forty-eight hours. It was found that cases with head injuries suffered no ill effects in flight; those with abdominal and chest injuries or respiratory infections could be carried only if the aircraft flew entirely below three thousand feet, which in practice meant that they could not safely be loaded for long trans-oceanic flights. Many psychotics and psychiatric cases improved rapidly from the moment the plane took off for home. One medical observer reported "This change was often spectacular."

At Prestwick, the flight surgeon and the nurses carefully rechecked the patients. The number to go out on the next flight was chosen. They tried to arrange the list so that they should not have too many patients in one load who required extensive treatment or care in flight. According to the nature of the wound or ailment, the patients were then assigned their litter stations on the plane. The litters were in four tiers on each side. Men requiring least attention were placed in the top and bottom tiers. Highly nervous patients, it was found, did best forward. Patients were placed on the left or right side of the cabin, so as to make whatever part of them might need dressing or care easy to reach. Further, in distributing the load, the weights of patients (including such items as plaster casts) had to be considered, and arranged so as to ensure proper balance of the aircraft. In this matter the priorities and traffic officer worked closely with the surgeon.

Operations advised when the transport would be ready. Red Cross girls distributed gifts to the men. The flight nurse made their acquaintance. She, the attendant, and the surgeon went over each case carefully, so that she was well aware of their various requirements. They checked the medical equipment to go on board, and when the C–54B had taxied to the ramp, entered it and inspected the litter attachments and arrangements inside. (The C–54B could carry twenty-eight litter patients; the earlier C–54A, twenty-four.)

The long, sloping ramp was wheeled to the door of the plane. The patients, immensely cheerful, were loaded into ambulances and unloaded again at the ramp. I watched this operation on a Scotch-misty October evening, in company with Lieutenant Colonel Raymond J. Lipin, the Flight Surgeon at Prestwick, who later received the Legion of Merit for his work in air evacuation. Colonel Lipin observed that, on account of the drizzle, it was necessary to cover the men's faces with their blankets. He did not approve of that at all. He remarked that later in the year ice might form upon the ramp. He would have a canopy built for it, which would take a lot of finagling.

The litter bearers were old hands at the game. They worked smoothly, with the manner of men performing habitual actions, but they were in no sense casual. The care they took to avoid jarring was typical of the entire treatment of the patients. The nurse and surgeon met each litter at the door, saw it to its proper place, and one or the other supervised the setting of the litter in its holders.

At this point, cheerful was no longer the word for the men. They seemed permeated by a happiness so deep that it had to be quiet. This was the last lap. They were on board. It was only a few hours now to the States.

By the end of 1944 most transports flew non-stop from Prestwick to Labrador or Newfoundland. The air evac planes stopped at Iceland so that the patients could have a hot meal, then continued to the further bases and finally, some thirteen hours after they left Prestwick, to La Guardia Field. From there, after rest and treatment, the Ferrying Division's smaller transports delivered each man to the base hospital nearest to his home. (Near the end of the war the policy of sending patients near home had to be extensively modified in order to place many of them in hospitals equipped to give special treatments.)

For the nurse and attendant, those thirteen hours were a long grind. They might catnap occasionally, but most of the time they were on the alert. There were treatments needed, patients to be readjusted in their litters, all the needs of the sick to take care of. In the rumble of the engines, a weak call might not be heard. Flight was entirely new to most of the passengers, and it affects men variously. They patrolled the long, narrow corridor through the night, with a nap here and there, a visit to the flight deck to smoke a cigarette, and back again.

Medical air evacuation had begun to roll by the end of 1943. In the course of that year, some 3000 patients were carried. The following January 2000 were carried, and September of 1944 saw a record for the year with 11,189. The biggest month of all was in May, 1945, when 18,537 sick and wounded men were evacuated by air, a little more than half being carried by the Pacific Division. N.A.T.S. took up air evacuation early in 1944. Their "Operational Summary" does not distinguish between patients and other passengers that year, but in 1945 their rate jumped from 1225 in January to 9392 in May, which was their record month also. This method of carrying the wounded did not really get going until two full years after we entered the war, yet one fifth of all patients returned to the United States were carried by A.T.C. and N.A.T.S. In regard to these passengers, incidentally, no distinction was made between Army and Navy. Both agencies flew whatever patients came to hand. In fact, the Command's first major undertaking along this line in the Pacific was setting up five C–54's to carry back wounded from the landing at Tarawa, which was a Marine and Navy show.

The exact timing and all but perfect safety record established by the four-engine aircraft on the great routes could not, in the nature of things, be maintained by the C–47's and C–46's which flew when and as they could between the main-line junctions and the advanced bases and landing strips. If a flight nurse craved action, she could certainly get it by having herself assigned to one of these runs. While A.T.C. took part in them, the story primarily belong to the Troop Carriers, and to the Marines' T.A.G. and S.C.A.T. organizations in the Pacific. I hope that someone will write it.

The type of thing in which A.T.C. got involved was air evacuation from the Admiralty Islands to Guadalcanal, to which it assigned sixteen C–47's in September, 1944. This activity required the Navy's assistance, and the co-operation obtained was perfect. The route ran for one thousand one hundred miles over water, skirting the Japanese-occupied islands of Rabaul and Bougainville. The weather was described as "predominantly stinko." Incomplete records show that these planes brought out 2701 patients, and probably considerably more.

On another, similar run, between Momote and Carney, in the Solomons area, an accident occurred which resulted in heroic action by the flight nurse, Second Lieutenant Mary L. Hawkins. The plane involved was a C–47 carrying twenty-four litter patients, piloted by First Lieutenant George W. Jones. They ran into bad weather and thunderstorms, and part of the time the radio blanked out. Jones seems to have become lost. The plane began to run out of gas. Jones made a remarkable crash landing on Bellona Island, in a clearing only a hundred and fifty feet long.

In the landing, a propellor was torn loose. It flew into the fuselage and overthrew a litter. A patient's trachea was cut. With the help of the medical technician on board, Lieutenant Hawkins made a suction tube from an aseptic syringe, a small rectal tube, and Mae West inflator tubes, and with this kept the throat clear of blood until a destroyer arrived next day to take them off. Other injuries were a recurrence of malaria, a small cut, and one case of hysteria.

This matter of medical air evacuation gives one of the most dramatic and clear-cut realizations of the tremendous change which aviation had created in the nature of war, and by inference, in peace. From the days of Florence Nightingale to World War I the struggle to care for the sick and wounded was overwhelmingly a struggle to get the hospitals and medical supplies to the forward areas. Transporting patients for any considerable distance by litter, wagon, or later by automobile, meant insupportable and harmful, even lethal, jolting. Hospital trains on the rails compete with other traffic. Hospital surface ships are expensive and slow; since they take anywhere from several days to several weeks en route, they must be equipped elaborately, real floating hospitals, and therefore cannot effectively be used for any other form of transportation.

The aircraft move rapidly. They put Okinawa, 1400 miles from the Marianas, within approximately one third of a day from the great base hospitals on the rearward islands. A boat making twenty miles per hour, which is good going, would take three days for the sea voyage alone. Where the plane was loaded directly from ambulances on the runway, to the boats the wounded had to be lightered out. Round trip time by boat was considerably more than nine times as long. Further, because of the relatively simple equipment needed on the fast-flying aircraft, they could be converted in a few minutes to cargo or normal passenger service, and in equally few minutes reconverted for handling patients. The more transports take off for the front in order to evacuate the wounded, the more supplies they bring with them. The two functions do not compete, they complement each other.

What occurred in the war just ended was a transition. With transports capable of carrying, not tweny-four, or thirty, but four hundred passengers coming up, transports with a range which will take them comfortably from Okinawa non-stop to California, we can foresee a revolution in the entire military medical system. This is, of course, providing that mankind in its folly is unable to avoid becoming involved in another war, and as far as the United States is concerned, providing that, granted that disaster, we are fortunate enough again to have our fighting forces based beyond our borders. Given an adequate air transport system, the forward area hospitals will care for those cases which can soon return to duty, the small number of desperate ones which cannot be moved, and otherwise will act essentially as holding hospitals and centers for preliminary treatment for patients who will shortly be returned to the infinitely more comfortable and well-equipped establishments within the home country. It is likely that, not one fifth, nor one half, but all wounded who can be so moved will be moved by air, in transports which on the outward flight carried priceless loads of troops or matériel.

This, which is mercy in terms of hundreds of thousands of people, is a real revolution. In this aspect it is a beneficent one. The strange, new god of the air which man has created has two faces, one beautiful, one frightful. What the great transports can do in taking home the sick, the injured, the victims, that they can also do in carrying to battle the fresh fighting men, the invaders, our own or the enemy's. Always, flying higher, just as powerful and with just as vast a reach and ever more fearsomely equipped, there are the bombers, carrying a different kind of cargo in which there are no elements of mercy.

XX

YOUNG MAN WITH A BEARD

You saw them at the flyaway points for ferried aircraft, at Morrison Field in Florida, Mather Field near San Francisco, Presque Isle in Maine. They tended to be of medium stature or a little over, rather lean, in good physical condition, not at all stupid or heavy looking, and above all, young. The beards they were so fond of raising could not disguise that quality. They were usually not very good beards, perhaps they got better later; they were likely to be rather thin, fine, curly, and to make a circle around the mouth and the lower part of the chin, leaving the lower lip and front of the jaw clear, as in portraits of mediaeval kings.

Before them lay their first real departure from the nest, the long flight over an empty ocean where there were no emergency landing fields, and if all went well, the time when they would pass the point of no return, irrevocably committed to their venture. Beyond that flight, out of England, or Australia, or Saipan, or India, or China behind the Himalayas, lay combat. They were afraid, in part, as any reasonable man must be afraid of known dangers which he has made up his mind to face. They were also afraid with the more difficult fear of the unknown. They had trained and strained towards this final departure month after month, it was their goal, not to be here and readying to go would have been a personal disaster for each one of them, and yet now that they were here, they seemed to feel a bewilderment. A very great change was about to take place. It was the feeling of the canoe caught in the pull of the rapids, the point at which one begins playing for keeps.

These things showed in their faces as they lounged about with an emphasized insouciance. They did not intend that any such things should show. They were combat pilots and crewmen, the pick of the land, teams finely blended and trained and strung up for battle. They were the *raison d'être* of the Air Corps, and whatever might happen to any of them individually, they knew with great certainty that nothing can stop the Army Air Corps.

They would not willingly show a trace of nervousness, they lounged about, consciously apart from the A.T.C. personnel who served, guided, and prepared them, intimate among themselves, the crews tending to hold together. They preferred to wear their monkey suits with various articles stuck onto the awkward-looking pockets in front of their shins. Their weapons might have been checked, or the magazines simply removed from their pistols, but they liked to wear their underarm holsters and their long knives. Their caps were the most flexible obtainable, and commonly they jumped upon them, twisted them, wet them, did everything possible to make them completely limp and give them "that old ten thousand-hour look." They wore these caps adhering miraculously to one side or the extreme back of the head. With numerous exceptions, they tended to affect as much sloppiness as they could get away with. It was part of the casualness, the attitude of the trained and ready airman killing time, sweating out the time until he should be told, "Number Easy eight six zero six, you will take off at zero three hundred hours tomorrow morning."

These were what the Air Transport Command called "tactical crews," the men who were going over in the same aircraft in which they would fight. Observed casually, they looked like a single type; in fact they differed enormously. They came from every part of the United States and every kind of background. Some of them had very recently married, some left behind girls who would wait or who, they knew achingly, would not wait. Some of them painted excellent, sensitive water colors; more of them preferred to shoot craps. The Air Transport Command knew them for a few days while it handled and guided and shepherded them over the first hurdle;

then it turned them over to the waiting combat Air Forces. Many, but not all of them, unhappily, it would meet again when their turn came to be flown home, some as wounded, most as "happy warriors." From a certain proportion of these last, full of confidence now, proven men, it would receive the gibes and taunts of their contempt.

Seeing these crews and their aircraft safe across the water was no simple matter. I have already described the early fiasco of X Mission and the shepherding of the Kit Project A–20's. Later, things went more smoothly. The training of 1942 had been strongly revised, the crews reaching the departure bases thereafter were far better prepared for the flights ahead of them.

The problems began with the mere arrival of combat crews at the bases. At first, for reasons of secrecy, their orders were cut so as to read simply that they would go to Presque Isle Army Air Base, for instance, on permanent change of station. Their overseas orders would be handed to them there. The crews, leaving their last training base in Ohio, Arizona, Texas, or California, on the strength of their orders would arrange for their wives to make yet one more of the many moves these women had learned to make. The young wives would reach Presque Isle either to find that their husbands had already gone overseas, or were "alerted" and held incommunicado. Heartbreaking situations resulted. This trouble was quickly corrected.

At one of the last staging bases before reaching the departure point, all hands were paid, so that they reached the departure base heavy with cash. There were many more bachelors than husbands among them. This was the edge, the place for the last fling. Most acutely at Morrison Field, just outside fabled Palm Beach, they planned on one final jamboree, one night of nights to savor afterwards in the wildernesses. At first they were allowed a certain amount of liberty, but too many of them were too young to be able to resist the temptation to let the girl they met at the bar know, darkly, that they wouldn't be back soon, and from that, as the drinks took hold, that they were members of the best damned B–17 squadron in the world, namely the Leapin' Lena Squadron. Before the night was over, perhaps in the intimacy of darkness and bare arms, there was little they knew that the girl did not know also. They had to be confined to the base.

Those last telephone calls had to be stopped, their letters had to be doubly censored. Not every one of them, by any means, got drunk, chased girls, or leaked his secrets, but the majority had to suffer for the ten or twenty per cent who possessed all the disciplines except self-discipline.

When they landed at the field, all set for that last fling, and found that they were confined to the base, they were, to use an accepted euphemism, tee'd off. The officers among them hit the officers' club with a bang. After a few experiences with pilots taking off in the early hours of the morning after having turned in drunk at midnight, that had to be stopped. No drinks other than a limited amount of beer for tactical crew members. Again the majority suffered because of the minority which could not control itself.

Confined to the base and cut off from the bar, they were more tee'd off than ever. Their irritation, aggravated by suspense, expressed itself in various ways, such as tossing an M.P. into a swimming pool. After one ambitious pilot took his pistol and held up the officer of the day, with the intention of getting from him the identification cards ("AGO cards") which would enable him to take his whole crew to town, it was decided to play safe by disarming crew members upon arrival.

They encountered, also, a type of behavior on the part of the "permanent party," that is the officers and men stationed on the base, which constantly recurs and concerning which it is difficult to draw lines between what is reasonable and what is reprehensible. The permanent party on any base, domestic or foreign, must make a life for itself. If social contacts are possible, it will develop them. With considerable effort and expense, it will create amenities. If a principal mission of the base is taking care of a continuous flow of transients, the transients are likely to drown out the permanent men. They will crowd the clubs, and give to social occasions the rough charac-

ter which comes from the behavior of altogether too many
Americans when they find themselves in a place which is none
of their own and from which tomorrow they will be gone,
never to return.

It arises naturally that the men who must stay put protect
themselves. They reserve certain amenities for themselves.
Within reason, this is fair enough and should cause no resentment. There is reason and unreason. Some of the men passing
through resented all restraints, or could not tolerate seeing
others more comfortably established than they were. On some
bases, mostly overseas, the welfare of the transients was virtually ignored, while the people of the base did very nicely for
themselves. At a few points I myself saw shocking contrasts
along this line.

Both the restraints which the tactical crews brought upon
themselves (as did to some extent the Command's own ferrying crews), and the occasional improper discriminations, bred
hard feelings, although the individual variation was great.

Handling the transients and protecting them against themselves was only a beginning. They and their aircraft were
checked in every possible way. The compasses were tested. The
navigators' instruments were tested and, when necessary, adjusted. Both the pilots' and navigators training and experience
were ascertained, to be sure that as a group they were ready for
their long flight. It was found that many crew members had
not properly completed the arrangement of their personal
affairs — allotments, powers of attorney, wills, and insurance —
so these were gone over. It was even found necessary to take a
look at their orders and make sure that they were properly
drawn. Some of the bases deep in the Zone of the Interior
seemed to have trouble with the wording of overseas orders.

Above all, they had to be put through the elaborate group
of processes which were comprised under the term "briefing."
This word was taken over by us from the English. It originally
referred to the service a solicitor performs for a barrister, when
he assembles and arranges for him the legal data in a case which
the barrister is to take into court. Its general meaning in
aeronautical usage is now well known. In preparing tactical

crews for overseas flight, it meant attempting to familiarize them in advance with the route they were to fly, the radio facilities and signals, the physical conditions and weather they would encounter, landmarks, alternate fields, the character of the field on which they would land, and to impress upon them the flying techniques to be used on this particular flight. There was a delicate balance to be struck. They had to be fully warned of such matters as the inter-tropical front in the Caribbean and how to cross it under the conditions likely to prevail, they had to be prepared for the hazards of whichever route lay before them, in such a manner as not to increase their nervousness but to give them a sound confidence without making them overconfident or leading them to take real hazards lightly. There were briefings for crews as a whole, and separate briefings for pilots, navigators, and radio operators.

It was found that many men had difficulty in remembering all they were told, and that there was a certain proportion whose attention incurably wandered. Some even went to sleep. Most briefings, of necessity, covered long distances and contained too many items of information for some listeners to retain. This problem was helped in part by the folders and maps which were issued, but only in part.

To insure attention and retention, the Command embarked upon an ambitious plan for motion-picture briefing. This idea originated with General C. R. Smith. Pare Lorentz, the famous director of documentaries, was commissioned a major and placed in charge of the Overseas Technical Unit. He built up a staff of motion and still photographers, sound men, and writers of narration which was a real concentration of talent, and established a studio for final production of the films in Hollywood. A B–24 was equipped with a special plate glass nose and plate glass side-gunner's windows — the bombardier's greenhouse must have been an uneasy sort of place to ride in during a landing. In this plane the unit traversed all the Command's routes, recording them as the pilot sees them, recording exactly the landfalls, approaches, and landings to be made. They flew around, and photographed, the venemous, fast-moving, narrow thunder-tempests of Brazil, the major fronts, the confusing fjords of Greenland, the mountain peaks of the Hump. With a sound track in flyers' language and animated maps, and supported by really beautiful still pictures around the walls of the briefing rooms, they produced films which no one could help but watch and remember. These films were true works of art, which was why they were so successful.

When everything at last was ready, the aircraft was dispatched. The bomber taxied to the starting point, the engines were run up with extra attention. The men on board were conscious of a special feeling in their stomachs. "The ritual, as rigid as the Mass, reaches its Benediction: '688 — 688 — this is the tower; your cruising altitude is 8000 feet; wind is southwest, fifteen; good luck; over.' 'Tower, this is 688; Roger, thank you and out.' " [1]

The ever-recurrent, ever-miraculous event of 55,000 pounds or so lifting itself into the air occurred. The lighted runway of the last base on the mainland swirled beneath them as they made their procedure turn, then dropped behind. The plane climbed steadily to its assigned altitude, then the tone of the engines changed, more purring, less aggressive, as she levelled off. The land ended, and under them was the wine-dark, inimical sea.

From the base a departure message went to the next base, and to the traffic control center. At various points, cards with a model name and serial number on them were moved to new positions. At the coast, the watch on the ready crash-boat checked the bomber's departure. Radar followed it. Where there were islands, or where ships were stationed on watch — "check points" — the aircraft reported.

"This is six six eight, altitude eight thousand feet, wind southwest, ten miles per hour. All well."

"Roger. Good luck."

"How's the fishing down there?"

At check points or at assigned reporting times when it called, first to its departure point, later to its destination, the traveller

---

[1] "The Flight Plan," manuscript study of tactical ferrying by the Historical Unit, Pacific Division, A.T.C. now in A.T.C. and Air Force archives. This very valuable monograph was principally the work of Staff Sergeant Greene.

was told of any changes in the weather ahead. If the weather looked really bad, the plane might be rerouted to another base. In case of trouble, the long-range search planes were ready, and an ocean-encircling communications system could mobilize every resource. Thus the system ran, overseas and overland, until at last, feeling rather cocky, the men set their aircraft down at the last A.T.C. base, from which they would make a short hop to that other base which would be their starting point for stranger and more terrible flights.

This was the "control of overseas tactical ferrying," the function which developed out of the sad scramble of X Mission. My description is greatly summarized and simplified, to give only the high spots of the methods by which some 50,000 combat aircraft were sent to the theaters of war with an over-all accident rate running around two per cent. Thus by the hundred, without mishap they made such pinpoints as Ascension and Kwajalein, and by the thousand passed through the strange, exotic weathers of the great world.

There were special variations, of course. Attack bombers crossing the South Atlantic flew in company with heavier aircraft which carried radio operators and navigators. When possible these mother ships were flown by Ferrying Division crews. In moving A–26's (the small, fast bombers which first came into fame in the hedgehopping operations in Normandy) to Hawaii, where the distance was so great as to leave small margin of safety, not only was the weather read with the most intense care for certainty of favorable winds, but one of the Command's navigators was put on board each ship. As there was no provision for a navigator in the cockpit, he did his work under disagreeable conditions. P–38's, the twin-engine, long-range Lockheed fighters, and later the "Black Widow" night interceptors — the grimmest looking of all aircraft — were convoyed across the oceans in fair numbers. The Ferrying and North Atlantic Divisions, in conjunction, successfully performed the notable experiment of convoying a number of single-engine P–47's to the United Kingdom via Greenland and Iceland, but the experiment was not repeated, although no plane was lost and only one suffered any real damage.

The safe movement of the tactical aircraft was as essential a part of the Air Transport Command's mission as the safe flight of its transports or of the planes delivered by its own crews. For this as much as for its other uses it embraced the network of communications and of weather stations, helped to build up the trans-oceanic traffic controls, sent the long-range weather observing planes out over its routes, established its check-points, and held its rescue service well-oiled and ever ready.

Perhaps the maturest, smoothest execution of this function was in the movement of the 20th Air Force's B–29's from California to the Marianas, carried out without a single loss. Their departure point was Mather Field near San Francisco. Wanting to see something of tactical ferrying other than merely from the ground, and having, too, a yen to go up in one of these great beauties, I made arrangements to go over to Oahu as a passenger in one.

The B–29 on which I went across had assigned to it the call code "Fox one five two nine." Fox, for F, was the letter assigned arbitrarily to a certain number of aircraft taking off that night. The figures were the last four of its serial number, 46–1529. The crew was atypical in that the commander, Major C. J. van Vliet, was an older man, being in his late twenties. He had been a B–29 instructor for a year or more in the States, and now at last, in May 1945, was taking his ship over for the big push against Japan. The co-pilot, Smitty, came from Flatbush.[2] He was a lieutenant, and in his mixture of seriousness, skill, and slapdash, more characteristic of combat pilots.

In addition to the two pilots, the officer complement consisted of the bombardier, navigator, and radar officer. The enlisted men were the radio operator, flight engineer, and three gunners. I met the pilots and navigator at the five-thiry briefing, the final instructions before take-off, when they were given their call numbers and the latest data on weather. The flight plan would be 9500 to 10,500 feet, to avoid adverse winds. Check points to be picked up as one left the coast, assuring

[2] Texans were not as predominant in the Air Forces as is commonly supposed. The general impression derives from the fact that whenever a Texan is present, everyone is made aware of the fact.

that one was on course, were gone over again, as well as the
stations kept by three Navy vessels along the 2400 mile route.
The approach to Oahu was reviewed, with the exact procedure
along fixed lanes which would ensure not being suspected of
being enemy aircraft. They were also given the procedure
they must follow in order to identify themselves to the West
Coast radar and defense patrols if forced to turn back.

Van Vliet accepted me with much the same hospitality a
ship's captain extends toward a guest. Under it, in him and in
the others, lay some curiosity about the odd phenomenon of a
ground officer, to them distinctly elderly, being assigned to
them as a passenger.

After briefing there was nothing to do but eat supper and
get some sleep — if one were minded to sleep. Take-off for
Fox 1529 was set at twenty-four hundred hours — midnight
exact. This would take full advantage of night atmospheric
conditions and bring the plane to Oahu at early daylight.

Shortly before midnight we met in the terminal, a big
hangar, and picked up the equipment we had checked there.
Van Vliet told me he had noticed that my canteen was empty,
and had had it filled. This was characteristic not only of him
but of other good plane commanders. When it is time for serious business, they watch all the details.

We went out to where the plane stood in a line with its
fellow giants, the starlight gleaming on their bright upper sur-
faces. An officer came out and advised us that head winds had
been reported, and therefore the tanks were to be topped off
with extra fuel. We would not take off for another hour.

We went to the snack bar, where most of the crew ordered
fairly hearty suppers. Everyone sat at the same table, there
was no question of separating officers and men. They seemed
immensely young. Most of their heads were covered with the
semi-transparent fuzz of recent, close crew haircuts. They
kidded heavily. Everyone went by nicknames. From kidding
they would switch to technical questions of the flight, and back
again. In their talk there were woven recurrent, slight references to ditching which betrayed their fundamental nervousness.

Tentatively, they let me into their talk. They were partly feeling me out, partly expressing a natural good manners and friendliness. Finally Smitty asked me the inevitable question, "How do you feel about crossing the ocean?"

I should, of course, be a little scareder than they. The others were listening, not obviously, casually. I said, "Well, I've crossed the Atlantic six times."

"You have?"

There was a little motion of relaxation among them. It was somehow wonderful that this Kiwi could have done that. It was reassuring. I was no longer just an oddity, I was a sort of good-luck piece. They were glad to have me along.

Van said it was time to go to the plane. When we reached it, he lined us up, and gave us his instructions. Apart from assigning my take-off position in the radar compartment, he merely repeated familiar matters, but he did so with seriousness and care. Here you had the other half of the relationship between a good plane commander and his crew, the real discipline and responsibility of command. This is a matter to which bomber pilots give considerable thought. The democracy, the blending of the whole crew in fellowship, is an essential; it must be united with complete discipline. The commander has a very nice balance to maintain. The general success with which this was done in the Air Forces, the instant, absolute obedience which the pilot, speaking as commander, gets from the men who kid and horse around with him in idle moments on the ground, by a system of behavior not covered in the military rules but worked out from habitual American team relationships, is a lesson in the true art of command which staff officers and trainers would do well to study.

We pulled the propellers through four turns apiece, two men at a time on each blade, then climbed aboard and took our stations. Everything was strictly business. The cockpit check was made, over the intercomm each man reported from his station, the plane taxied to the end of the runway. The engines were run up, one after the other roaring sweetly. Fox 1529 was cleared for take-off. With the extra gas in her tanks, she weighed some 140,000 pounds, and she needed a lot of runway to become airborne, but Van was no three-hundred-hour pilot. He lifted her so skillfully that the only way you could tell that she had left the ground was by the markedly smoother motion.

There was a little talk on the intercomm then, more when we cleared the coast. There was a feeling of finality about that. We were over the ocean now, committed. Half an hour later the radio operator, overanxious to establish contacts which he was not due to make so soon, began to get worried. I could hear Van quieting him. At the proper time, Sparks got his answers, after that he was happy.

I should not care to be a radar officer. The narrow, cluttered compartment aft of the middle of the fuselage is a nightmare of wires and gadgets. It is windowless. Only the amazing eye of the scope looks out on the world, interpreting the unseeable in bright dots and blobs on the screen. It was interesting to pick up the last islands, a boat, and later, the first of the Navy's watch vessels, but it occurred to me that it would be a grim business sitting in that blind tunnel while the flak was exploding just outside and the fighters diving in.

Travel on a bomber is a very different thing from on a transport. That little incident of Van's filling my canteen was significant. You cannot just stroll down a wide passage to a water cooler. Combat discipline was maintained, which meant that every man wore his pistol, knife, first-aid kit, canteen, parachute harness and Mae West, uncomfortable though the gear was. The parachute pack (we were using the chest parachutes) was kept always at hand. Later on, when the bombardier came forward to his position after taking a nap under the navigator's feet and did not bring his pack with him, the commander sent him back for it immediately. There was no fooling in these matters.

The only place in which a man can stretch out straight to sleep is in the tunnel above the bomb bay from the radar compartment, waist gunner's positions, and the after gun turret to the forward area which contains the forward turret, navigator's and engineer's positions, and the flight deck. A man sleeping in the tunnel is likely to be wakened time and again, to climb out and let someone pass him. The hole is just wide enough to let a man through, not on all fours, but on his belly. The crew members, accustomed to their plane, did manage to sleep in remarkable positions, twined around assorted obstacles.

The flight deck of a B–29, with its wide area of glass like a hemispherical greenhouse, is a dream. Half the world lies open to you when you sit in one of the pilots' seats. We watched the day beginning, the west ahead of us lightening and the stars paling in response to the greater brightness growing behind us. The gentle mountains of Oahu came into sight in the morning light. Satisfaction moved through the crew, the intercomm became lively. They had passed through a kind of initiation, proved themselves and their plane, to which as yet they had not given a name. They felt an assurance which no number of training flights could engender. Smitty claimed his seat. I crawled back to the radar compartment, to listen to the exchanges with the control tower at John Rodgers field and the ritual of landing. As he had taken her up, so Van set her down, without a jar, like a leaf gliding onto the runway.

We crawled out, dirty, tousle-headed, sleepy-eyed. They went off to their transient quarters, I to Pacific Division headquarters. On the way, while the hum of the engines slowly died from my ears, all I could think of was what a grand bunch of young men they were. What a grand bunch, and they were going on to the shooting war, not twelve, but sixteen and eighteen hours of that cramped, fatiguing flight, with, in the middle of it, the run through death, the lottery in which no virtue or skill or courage is protection against the final loss. I seemed to ache with wishing them safe passages and a sure return home.

XXI

PRIVATE AIR FORCE

THE SPECIAL FUNCTIONS of a strategic air transport system call for an organization which differs strongly from the standard organization of the Air Force. At the beginning of the war, all branches of the Army Air Forces were divided into flights, squadrons, groups, and wings, corresponding to the companies, battalions, regiments, and brigades of the infantry. These units, especially groups and lower, were fairly well fixed in size.

A complete separation ordinarily exists between flight and ground units. A bomber squadron, for instance, consists of its commanding officer and his staff, and the flight crews. Such a unit can pick itself up bodily and fly itself to any given point. On arrival at a base, it depends upon the ground personnel stationed there for all "housekeeping" services, issue of supplies, and maintenance and repair of its aircraft. In the air forces stationed overseas, command of the flying and non-flying organizations comes together in the air force commander. Within the United States, in most instances it lies in the commanding general of the Air Force.

This organization is excellent in general. It ensures the compact mobility of the fighting organization and relieves its commander of a mass of distracting responsibilities. It depends, of course, upon willing teamwork between the two classes of units.

In 1941, when it was proposed that the Ferrying Command establish ground squadrons of its own, the proposal was rejected. The Command required no type of service different from the standard ones, and could more effectively carry out its then limited mission with the usual procedures. It needed only "control officers," stationed at the bases through which its aircraft generally passed, to expedite their passage, report on the progress of the planes, and exercise general supervision over its pilots.

In 1942 the situation changed rapidly. The great quantitative increase in ferrying and the allied in-service training program called for bases exclusively devoted to serving the Command. So did the rapid increase in the volume of its transport activities. Techniques with which the men trained in standard Air Forces training were unfamiliar then became necessary. The maintenance of a transport, for instance, is different from that of a bomber. This lies not only in the difference between models, but in differences of function. A bomber ground crew and the related repair shops for higher echelons of maintenance will need to be thoroughly familiar with repairs to the skin of aircraft, as it is expected that they will frequently return shot up. Those who take care of transports will have relatively little need for that skill, but must be expert in dealing with engines which accumulate flying time rapidly. At such points as Natal in Brazil, where both ferried aircraft and transports took off across the ocean, the mechanics had to be extremely versatile, able to give the most rigid inspections and to make at least simple repairs on a dozen or more different types.

The nature of the Command's activities also put its bases into the hotel business. Tactical and ferrying crews and passengers arrived in large numbers, for a meal or to remain overnight, sometimes longer when weather was bad or a large backlog had accumulated. At all points where cargoes or passengers transshipped or "originated," there had to be stationed men who were trained in priorities. Before specialists in administering and interpreting priorities and such related matters as reading waybills, interpreting code terms for destinations, and loading and unloading, were stationed all along the routes, there occurred lamentable instances of shipments sent to wrong destinations, or overlooked and left forgotten at way stations.

It became obvious that the Air Transport Command must control and staff its own bases, an innovation which was formally recognized in the General Order of June 20, 1942, which created it out of the Ferrying Command.

Even at that early time, the Command was also running into trouble with squadron and group organization. At one base, for instance, its principal activity was transport flying. It handled cargoes and passengers, and interpreted and administered priorities. The flight crews were assigned to the base, and lived there between flights. At a second base, the sole mission might be overseas ferrying. The number of transients to be lodged and cared for was smaller, cargo loading and priorities were minimal, the flight personnel were transient, and briefing and preparation of the crews for the long flight were much more elaborate. Functions and combinations of functions varied so that no two bases could be manned in exactly the same manner.

How could this variety be fitted into squadron organization? Colonel Richard C. Lowman, the Command's A–1, struggled manfully with the problem. Suppose you devise a squadron with a Table of Organization calling for two priorities and traffic officers, four enlisted clerks under them, two transient service officers, two briefing officers, so many cooks, bakers, mechanics, radio operators. . . . That squadron might serve the purposes of Base A, two such squadrons might serve Base B, which does the same job in twice the quantity, but how would you take care of the bases that fell in between, and still worse, of bases which required entirely different proportions of the various specialists? It proved impossible to work out an overall, standard air transport base squadron.

The Command then turned to a system of squadrons each made up of one type of specialist, from which detachments were sent to each base in the numbers required. For achieving flexible manning, this system was good enough, but it created a nightmare. A man cannot be completely cut off from the unit to which he is assigned. It must carry him, present or absent, on its rosters and reports, keep track of him, administer for him, attend to his promotions. Squadrons of specialists

such as priorities experts might have detachments of from two
to a dozen officers and men at twenty different places, all to be
carried on the books. The result was confusion, and, since the
paper work became so involved, a valueless overhead of men
who might otherwise be usefully employed, engaged in keeping track of the fragments.

It was difficult for men who had spent their lives in working
through long-established military procedures to get away from
the concept of the fixed unit with its Table of Organization.
They comprised the simple and generally effective way by
which the Army sets up manpower for almost any task. You had
companies or troops or flights, battalions or squadrons, organized for many different purposes. You could always create new
ones, with new "T/O's," calling for different proportions of
specialists and allocating a different assortment of grades. Each
such unit was further provided with an Organizational Equipment List and other tables, and from these and the T/O you
could tell at a glance how many men, with what skills, in what
grades, with what arms, vehicles, tools, machinery, tents,
rations, supplies, and equipment of every kind were needed
to produce the complete unit ready to take the field. You
could, moreover, immediately determine how many passenger
and freight cars, trucks, buses, or aircraft (or for that matter,
mules), or how much space in a ship, were required to move
the unit complete with equipment. The system was convenient, practical in wholesale application, eminently suitable
to most of the exigencies of war. It was also delightfully
thought-saving, and could be applied by even the oldest colonel.

Air Transport Command Headquarters was fortunate in the
number and calibre of its civilians in uniform. A committee
of these, notably Lieutenant Colonel James H. Douglas, Jr.,
Major Samuel E. Gates, and Captain Malcolm A. MacIntyre
(they all ended the war as full colonels), produced what was,
militarily, a revolutionary solution. The twin gods of the fixed
unit and the T/O were junked. There were no more groups
and squadrons, but only "stations." (The Ferrying Division
unofficially kept its old Ferrying Group designations because
of the traditions which had begun to cluster around them.)

For each station there was drawn up a "manning table," tailor-made to that particular base, subject to periodic review and to change whenever change might be indicated. In supporting their proposal, the committee pointed out that it was a military adaptation of civilian airline practice. The great difference was, of course, that having determined its needs, the airline's problem was only to hire the necessary help, while the Command had to justify each new demand to Air Staff.

The system was not perfected immediately. At first, the manning tables of each base were fixed, and the allotments of personnel were made by Air Staff according to them. This forestalled internal shifts between stations. Later, the "exact manning table" which showed how many bakers, and in what grades, should be stationed on Ascension Island, and how many historical officers there should be in Manila, were presented merely as the justification for the "over-all manning table" which gave the total of personnel, by grades and specialties, to be assigned to the wing or division. The sum of these, in turn, gave the "over-all manning table" for the Command. Once the over-all table had been approved, the Command and its subordinate units had wide discretion in shifting positions around.

The equipment lists and all the tables were now thrown hopelessly out of kilter. Equipment for each station, also, had to be individually calculated and justified. This situation was somewhat easier than in justifying the manning tables, as it was possible to work out standard ratios to numbers of personnel, aircraft assigned, and similar factors.

There was an element of courage in establishing a system such as this, with its arduous requirement of continuous recalculation of needs, in an organization which at the height of its empire controlled more than two hundred and fifty bases and two hundred thousand military personnel. It was proposed, and was accepted by Air Staff, because it was the only system which would work. While I have no direct evidence of the fact, I have little doubt that the effectiveness of this innovation had a strong influence on the higher staff. The A.T.C. station-manning table organization was put into effect in March, 1943.

In July, 1944, the Army Air Forces largely abandoned squadron organization for many of its non-flying elements, substituting for them A.A.F. Base Units, conceived somewhat as were the stations. In conformity, the Command's stations were redesignated as Base Units.

Even late in the war it was difficult for some of the authorities in Headquarters, Army Air Forces, to free themselves of the old concept of fixed units. In this they were affected by the combat forces, which properly retained their wings, groups, and squadrons. They wanted to know why the Command could not offer a standard base unit, why its line-up at Fairbanks was so different from that at Natal, why one base should be commanded by a colonel, another by a major or a captain. The Command waged a steady campaign of education, employing, finally, a group of very fancy charts prepared for it by O.S.S.

Outside of the Air Forces, where the conception of what the Command did and how it did it was even vaguer, old ideas died very hard. As late as 1945 the Command and General Staff School produced tables showing the personnel and equipment for ferrying and transport squadrons, groups, and wings, with exact data on the requirements for moving them by various means of transportation, although there had been no such squadrons or groups for nearly two years and the air transport wings (most of which by then had become divisions) varied in numbers from three to twenty thousand, and varied almost as violently in their functions and equipment.

It was common observation, as a matter of fact, that the staff of the Air Transport Command never did come to an end of explaining to authorities in the Air Forces, and even more in the Army generally, what the Command's job was, what services it could render, and how it worked. Its unique character seemed to repel comprehension. This was not merely a case of the alleged limitations of the military mind, the volunteers were equally slow to grasp this new thing. One may observe that many volunteers who attained senior rank were inclined to become even more "military minded" than the regulars. In all men, too, there is a tendency to brush aside the unusual.

To men outside the Air Forces, still unaware of the capabilities of aviation, the Command's claims as to its potentialities and as to the scope of its activities seemed fantastic.

Throughout the war, the Command was constantly experimenting with itself organizationally. As I have already told, it added to the usual list of major staff divisions a totally new one, Priorities and Traffic. It also reduced Intelligence to a minor position, under the title of Intelligence and Security. This change exemplifies the rôle that personalities sometimes play in the supposedly impersonal military world. A command which possessed a complete network of airlines and radio reaching all over the world from Washington, and which in many cases had the only American troops in various odd areas, was obviously in a position to render very valuable intelligence services. Lack of force at the top of its Intelligence Division resulted in a failure to develop these opportunities, and intelligence activities stagnated. Briefing, normally an intelligence function, was gradually usurped by operations officers in the field. In the big reorganization of 1943, the men at the top simply saw that their Command's intelligence work was unimportant as it stood and came to the conclusion that, since A.T.C. was not a combat organization, it did not need an assistant chief of staff, A–2. Intelligence was reduced to the secondary level.

After this reduction, much abler men took over within the division, notably Colonel Fred C. Morgan and his successor towards the end of the war, Lieutenant Colonel Robert Wright — the one who developed the Indian-China search and rescue program. These men saw the true possibilities in the Command, but they had to work against established preconceptions. Not until hostilities were ended did A.T.C. Headquarters and Air Intelligence see the light, and move to exploit this extraordinary network. About the time that Intelligence was restored to its proper position, the network had begun to dwindle and the opportunity was lost.

When the Air Transport Command was established as such in July, 1942, its former Foreign Division disappeared, being replaced by the first of its foreign wings. These wings, also, failed entirely to conform to the conventional conception of the air equivalent of a brigade. They were routes, or portions of routes, as from Florida to Brazil, from the west coast of Africa to India, or from California to Australia, under a single, local command. Some embraced many bases, some few. Their strength varied accordingly, just as their operations and equipment varied. The term "wing" is military, but in conception these units were more like portions of a great airline or railway system than like any known military establishment. The Domestic Division, as has been told, became the Ferrying Division. It, too, had strongly individual ways of doing things, a reflection both of its special mission and its commander's personality, one might say a private air force within a private air force.

In 1942 the Command experimented with an air transportation division, which when proposed sounded like a logical parallel to the Ferrying Division. It merely overlapped the foreign wings on the one hand and Headquarters Operations on the other. It was reduced to the Domestic Transportation Division, and later absorbed by the Ferrying Division.

In July, 1944, the foreign wings were raised to the status of divisions, and many later subdivided themselves into wings. At the Command's greatest extension the divisions were: North Atlantic, European, Caribbean, South Atlantic, North Africa, Central Africa, India-China, Pacific, Alaska, and Ferrying Divisions. All of them operated local services. Those at the "flyaway points," the edges of the United States, operated long-range transports, first those of the airlines under contract, then increasingly and in the later stages of the war, preponderantly, purely military flights by military crews. As in all other things, in this respect, too, the Ferrying Division was different. From the outset its ferried aircraft moved through the areas of other units. Later, it took over domestic air transportation, as well as a number of long-range foreign schedules or was made responsible for new ones, so that in both ferrying and transport its operations reached to most of the regions touched by the Command.

Thus the Air Transport Command took shape as it grew,

unorthodox of necessity. The Army Air Forces as a whole were constantly rearranging themselves during the war. After all, it was only shortly before that that the shackles were stricken from the old Air Corps, and it was not until after the shooting had started that its leaders had a chance to learn by trial just what form a great air organization should take. Commands and staff divisions were shifted and shifted again. This process was intensified in A.T.C., with the complete novelty of its task and shifting emphasis upon its functions. It was the lesser organization's good fortune that it set about its own experimenting at a time when the higher was also fluid and seeking better methods. Today, most of the men from civilian life have returned to it, many of the more important regulars who were at the top of A.T.C. have retired or gone elsewhere; there is a danger that the desire for conformity for its own sake and the absence of men who remember why the Command had to be so ornery and so different may lead to a loss of essential flexibilities.

XXII

THE EAGLE FLIES

ON THE END PAPERS of this book are two maps. The one at the front shows the tenuous routes of the newly constituted Air Transport Command on July 1, 1942, that at the back shows its routes at their greatest extension in 1945. To the latter I should like to add the routes of the Naval Air Transport Service and of the R.A.F. Air Transport Command, both for completeness, and to symbolize the fact that while the subject of this dissection is A.T.C. specifically, the interest of this narrative is not in a single organization's history, but in the making of a new age in which it had a share. To add the rest, unfortunately, would create a maze which could be followed only upon a very large map.

Go back a year earlier than the first map, to July 1, 1941. We could draw a line, then, from Montreal across the North Atlantic to Prestwick — a broken line, indicating intermittent flow, as when we show desert rivers — and another from Takoradi in Africa to Cairo, and credit both to the R.A.F. On that day Lieutenant Colonel Caleb V. Haynes took his modified B–24A off from Bolling Field runway on a record-making, anxiously followed flight to Scotland. Just a year later the Air Transport Command, heavily dependent upon civilian contract carriers, had routes which might be called at once timid and daring, via Brazil to Africa and India, from Maine to Scotland, from Montana to Alaska, from California to Australia, and down through Central America to Panama. Three years later it had become a mighty logistical tool, an important factor in every major plan. To those who were privileged to know its achievements free from the veil of censorship or the feathery generalizations of press releases, it presented a development of the Air Age which, barring the disaster of another war, would not be seen again in their time. The men who brought it into being, made it work, studied it, recorded it, looked upon their creature with mixed pride and awe. Not even the most familiar, the most daring-minded, could quite take in what this giant had come to be.

To grasp the fullness of what the war meant to aviation one must add to A.T.C.'s fleets the smaller, yet mighty, fleets of our Navy and the R.A.F., and superimpose on that aggregation the sky-blackening passages of the fighting aircraft in combat and the unending drone of training aircraft in the home skies.

For combat, ferrying, transport, the runways dotted the world with their narrow strips, the air was nervous with electric signals. Americans, American foods, medicines, candies, drinks, clothes, and customs were set down bodily about the world, in places which we have come to take for granted but which from the point of view of anything save such a war were improbable to the point of hilarity. Johannesburg, Asmara, Bangalore, Sidney — that Mohammedan paradise for airmen — and Kuling until the Japanese sacked it, were rest points for overstrained men. The Azores, towards which Olds and his staff had looked so longingly in vain, had become the world cross-roads they were predestined some day to be. At all the key points — Hawaii, Guam, Goose Bay, Gander Lake, Natal, Accra, Khartoum, Dakar, Fairbanks, Assam, Prestwick, St. Mawgans, Terceira, and so many more — the aircraft circled, landed, took off in their hundreds. There was not much for a bird to do but dodge.

The simile of any bird breaks down; the condor, the roc, are dwarfed. If this was an eagle, it was an eagle beyond all mythology, a host of eagles, or a bird with wings reaching from the top to the bottom of the earth, which, in passing, threw a shadow briefly over our familiar world. The shadow was beautiful, a sort of luminous shade, with a promise of great comforts and new wonders. In it there was also a chill; when it had passed it left a momentary shudder in the bones. It was the future. It had in it great good and great evil.

For good or evil, the men built and the planes flew. To tell what they achieved, what the physical size of just the one aspect of this new thing was, once again I must throw a bunch of figures on the page. At the peak, in the middle of 1945, east and west the Air Transport Command sent fifty-two flights a day across the Atlantic. The end of the line was no longer Prestwick but Paris — Frankfurt — Berlin. From the California coast twenty-one flights by military crews and seventeen by civilian set out daily across the Pacific, and the same number came in. In the peak period, 205,000 officers and enlisted men and 108,000 civilians served this Command alone. Their aircraft flew over 35,000 miles of domestic routes, 148,900 miles of foreign. In the peak month of ferried deliveries overseas, 2589 aircraft were ferried, while the domestic ferrying record stood at 9205. Transport was at its highest level in July, 1945; in that month 124,637 tons were carried, along with 274,934 passengers. These two activities, over the vast distances involved, result in the staggering figures of 174,131,863 ton-miles for cargo and 618,619,020 passenger miles.[1]

With the surrender of Germany came the time to shift our full strength against Japan, to fight that nation with both hands when up till then we had been using what had become a powerful left hand. In making this shift, the value of air transport in global grand strategy was proven. Well before the end of hostilities in Europe the arrangements began. When they ended, we had hundreds of thousands of troops in that continent. Some of them had seen their full share of combat and more, and had well earned discharge or stateside duty. Others were properly due for further service overseas. The return of the men of the first group to the United States would release many on duty there for service in the Pacific. In addition to

[1] With which I draw a deep breath. But add in the N.A.T.S. peak month in August, 1945, when 85,191 ordinary passengers, 8854 patients, and 11,040 tons of cargo were moved on their 53,250 miles of routes. Their maximum route mileage was over 76,000, and in their best ferrying month they delivered just under 5000 aircraft. If the R.A.F.'s records are added to these, we get a monumental movement of cargo and people by air which seems almost to clog the skies, and makes present-day commercial operations look like very small potatoes.

men, there were aircraft by the thousands, still in shape for further combat. A huge transfer was needed, in two stages, first from Europe to the United States, then on from there to the Pacific, with a pause for reorganization in between.

The more rapidly this could be accomplished, the sooner the war in the Far East would end. Surface transports must, as ever, carry the heavy bulk of men and equipment, but aircraft could do a great part. The Air Transport Command was handed three projects, the "Green," "White," and "Purple." The Green Project was, upon receipt of notice, to superimpose upon its established schedules over the Atlantic the movement of 50,000 men a month from the European Theatre to the Zone of the Interior. The White was to ferry, or control the ferrying of all the aircraft it was thought desirable to bring back — this, of course, without interrupting the flow of aircraft westward over the Pacific. Later the Purple Project would be added, which would be the carrying of 10,000 troops a month across the Pacific. A special project was not set up for the movement of the "White" aircraft to the new combat area; that would be merely an augmentation of existing ferrying activities.

The first two projects went into operation on May 1. For the movement of the soldiers towards home, the Command concentrated 227 C–54's and 150 C–47's, the latter running a shuttle between Miami and Natal. A portion of these were drawn from Troop Carrier squadrons from the E.T.O. The men who manned these had not had their new assignment properly explained to them when they took off across the Atlantic; they thought they were headed straight home. They were completely disgusted when they found themselves engaged in a new, arduous service almost entirely outside the States, and their disgust was embittered by the breaking up of their squadron organization. A.T.C. authorities claimed the break-up was necessary; I suspect that had they realized what its effect would be upon the men, or realized more fully the power and importance of their loyalty to their outfits, they could have found a means to keep the squadrons in being. The T.C.C. men were unhappy, but they flew. So did the Com-

mand's four-engine planes. Between the start of the project in
May and the fifteenth of September, 166,059 passengers were
brought home on this project. Shortly thereafter, Japan having surrendered, the project as such was terminated, and the
Command's commitment on its Atlantic services dropped to
10,000 men a month.

The troops who returned by this means were deeply impressed by the new form of transportation. Any reservations
some of them may have had about flying were overcome by the
prospect of so fast a trip to home. They were also struck by
the manner in which they were treated, many of them being
fresh from the haphazard impersonality, confusion, and miserable food and quarters of the replacement depots. The Air
Transport Command, proud of its standards, put forth great
efforts to handle this flood of transients at the points at which
they remained overnight as it had been accustomed to handling
transients throughout the war, and succeeded in this to a remarkable degree. The expressed appreciation of some of the
enlisted men was striking.

During approximately the same period, 5965 aircraft were
returned to the United States under the White Project. These
brought with them over 86,000 crew members and passengers.
Taking the two projects together, it is obvious that in those
four months there was a transatlantic passenger traffic which
would be sufficient to make a boom year for the peacetime
steamship lines.

The further development of the movement westward, into
the Pacific, to everyone's delight, was stopped by the surrender
of Japan. From then on, the regular flights eastward to California were loaded with returning men, men who knew that
they were coming home for keeps. Often enough they came to
the aircraft direct from the forward areas, still yellow with
atabrine, in their gray-green monkey suits, relieved just the
other day from the endless, deadly business of hunting down
Japanese hold-outs. They came from fox-holes or from tents
which were solid with tropical heat and heavy with the eternal
dampness, from open-air chow-lines and cold C-rations. The
big transports were a marvel to them. Those who were loaded

onto the "plush jobs," the C–54E's with the airline-type seats, could be seen incredulously fingering the plush. They had been so long away from anything like this. In the most modern of all wars they had lived like early savages. They did not know that enlisted men could have access to such accommodations. They were incredulous again when the flight traffic clerk offered them coffee or brought them a box lunch, the same lunch he brought to the colonel in the seat in front.

They climbed on board at the ends of the line, for a flight through a long morning to Guam, a chance to stretch their legs there, and then a solid ten hours over the emptiness of the Pacific, time enough to become bored, to have boredom die away a hundred times in the face of the thought of home, and after the transport had hurried into the westward-speeding night, to sleep, uneasily at first, then deeply, in the sound of the engines. They wakened to the sandy bleakness of Kwajalein, and dozed and turned and talked through nine hours to even more desolate Johnston. Day, night, and day, and at last Hawaii. Between them and the real United States, of which Hawaii was a sort of foretaste and sample, there remained only a slightly greater distance than a North Atlantic crossing. If anyone wants to know just how vast are the reaches of the Pacific, let him fly it.

At Oahu they lay over and got some sleep, before the final early morning departure. On this last leg excitement mounted, quietly, almost imperceptibly. Eleven to twelve hours of empty ocean, a box lunch, the very rare sight of a ship on the water. Always the sense of home grew stronger. Freedom of talk with such officers as might be on board increased. Coming in one time I sat next to a big, solid, blond, young combat infantryman. At first he was quiet. In mid-flight he began plying me with questions about flying. From then on we talked freely. The islands of the California coast came in view, then the coast itself, San Francisco, the Golden Gate. The men ran to the portholes like children, craning to one side and the other. They were not from here, but this was part of it. They could not see enough.

The landing warnings flashed on, "No smoking. Fasten

Safety Belts." Everyone took his place. We came over Hamilton Field, circled, waited our turn, came in. As the wheels jarred on the runway the infantryman, acting as if he could not help himself, threw off his belt and stood up. Others were on their feet, although taxiing as we still were at high speed, the going was bumpy.

Then the man cried out, in a half strangled, keen voice, one word: "America!" I have never heard it said like that before or since. That was all. It was enough.

That was at the end of the great days of the Air Transport Command. Truly, they had been great. It had carried everything and anything by air. I remember WAC's, nurses, State Department secretaries, Polish officers, British officers, a German major general and his staff, three Kamikaze pilots (meek, rather cute little fellows whom we watched closely even when they slept), colonels and enlisted men from the German front with the black look of combat on their faces, a Red Cross girl smashed up in an air raid upon Okinawa, four enlisted radio technicians bound for China, American ferry pilots flying for the R.A.F. — they were survivors of the original daredevil Atfero group, and good fun to be with — a Free French admiral to whom I gave a Hershey bar, a variety of brigadier generals, one of whom ranked me for the only clear space on the floor big enough to stretch out on, a variety of Navy officers and men, a Chinese general and his staff, the American adviser on foreign affairs to the Siamese Government, war correspondents, Australian infantry, a Canadian tank officer who was astonished at the quality of the K-ration I shared with him, a group of Brazilian air cadets, and a collection of tropical rats suffering from a rare and important disease, nursed by a civilian from Harvard. I have slept on the case containing a B–29 engine, on mail sacks (a coveted bed), the bucket seats of the C–54A's, the canvas, cot-like seats of the later models, on floors — once with a hundred kilograms of platinum for a pillow — on a large packing box containing I know not what for Calcutta, on a case of books in the overseas edition, and a crated stationary engine.

The cargo aircraft seemed more real, more truly part of the

picture, than the "plush jobs" with the passenger seats. Besides, I never could sleep decently sitting up, and I have long legs. In the cargo models, people adjusted themselves as best they could, there was more informality, more unity among the passengers. Blankets, and later the O.D. quilts, were handed out. A card game would start on a bit of floor space. As soldiers commonly do, many went to sleep right away. People draped themselves over the more comfortable areas of whatever cargo was on board, and the competition for floor space was keen. During daylight, many read or wrote letters. The long flights either originated in the dark or ran on into darkness. In the dome of the fuselage a few bulbs made spots of light, showing the rounded sides with their raw construction, emphasizing the cavernous effect of the big interior of the flying box-car. Under one light a group might be at cards. Beyond them an aircraft engine, symmetrically spidery, loomed in its crate. Nearer, a sleepless watcher, cocooned in a blanket, sat upright against one wall, seeming by a trick of light and shadow huge and inhuman. Figures sprawled here and there like the dead, except that they had a peacefulness, usually an innocence on their faces, which is not in the combat dead. Without insulation of any kind, the vibration of the motors was in everything against which you might rest, their sound was constant, at times heard, at times forgotten, a part of night and space and speed. It was hard to believe that you were airborne, resting upon that solid, scuffed, wooden floor. At times, in a bit of rough air, the plane would swoop and rise under you, generally its motion was so steady that it seemed to be stationary. You woke and slept and woke again, went to the tail end to see if any coffee was left, went to the cockpit for a smoke and a look at the instruments.

These flights were utterly unlike a trip on a commercial airliner. They had an infinitely greater quality of flying, of *aircraft* about them. The very crudeness of the plane's interior made you feel its power. It was strongest at night, and it was then, too, that you realized how very strange it was that you, of all people, should be hurrying thus to Khartoum or Prestwick, Brisbane or Bangkok. You realized the miracle of organ-

ization, technical achievement, construction, by which a slip
of mimeographed paper handed to you at your home station
could send you to the oddest parts of the world without thought
on your part as to where you would sleep or how you would
be fed, or what reservations to make to fly from one stopping
place to the next. The grub was sometimes good and sometimes terrible, the lodgings were the same. You were not sent
on a Cook's tour. But it was a never-ending miracle that, given
a piece of paper which said, as one of mine did, "Casablanca,
Paris, Calcutta, Manila, Tokyo, Hickam Field T.H. . . . authority to vary itinerary . . . " all you had to know was that your
immunization was up to date, your baggage did not exceed
sixty-five pounds, and that your plane would leave the airport
at Washington at 1155 hours. The rest was automatic. You
were under the wing of the eagle, and the eagle was full grown.

XXIII

BROTHERS IN ARMS

It is impossible to give broad treatment to any phase of air operations without some reference to relations between the Army Air Forces, or the present Air Force, and the Navy. During the war one could see how steadily the realities forced control of air transportation higher and higher, into a special committee of Joint Chiefs of Staff to which were added some top civilian officials, but always the control was split and made indecisive by the fact that the Army and Navy representatives could not outvote each other. When in 1945 this Joint Army-Navy Committee on Air Transportation sent a sub-committee to the Pacific to report on duplications and other matters, the report they turned in consisted of a carefully reasoned argument for unification up to the point at which it reached conclusions and recommendations. At that point it trailed off into minor recommendations for closer collaboration which amounted to an admission that, as when Mr. Pogue wrote to General Arnold in 1942, unification was impossible — in fact, that u — — n was a bad word, which the Navy delegation, at least, dared not use in reporting to its superiors.

Although we now have an independent Air Force, equal with the Army and Navy,[1] the Navy consistently frustrates any form of unification, so that today we are being asked to go to fantastic expense to support two competing air forces, the Air Force air force and the Navy air force. The admirals, forced at

[1] This equality is referred to by the amazing jargon word, "co-equal." I am still waiting for someone to explain to me in what respect "co-equal" differs from "equal."

271

last to admit that battleships are obsolete, have embraced the aeroplane that made them so and look to it to keep the Navy on top and to justify the continued construction of huge ships for their command, at a cost of millions of dollars. With a properly nourished Air Force, and the bases which we and our allies now control, we can strike anywhere in the world, yet the admirals would have us starve that striking power in order to build them aircraft carriers and equip them with planes, not for the Navy's normal and proper uses, but to serve the same purposes. In recent manoeuvres, the Navy itself demonstrated that its schnorkel-equipped submarines could sink its carriers almost at will, but that demonstration has not been allowed to weaken its demands, nor has it been called strongly to public attention.

The Department of Defense points to the present Military Air Transport Service as its prize example of unification. How unified is it? The Navy has to some extent surrendered command control over its long-range transports to the Air Force, but it has done so in such form that if the opportunity should arise, the Navy could take them back. The personnel from the Navy remain Navy personnel, in Navy uniform. Their aircraft remain Navy property, and can be serviced and maintained only by Navy crews. So little has the old N.A.T.S. been "unified" into the Military Air Transport Service that it was headline news when Navy transports joined the Air Force ones on the Berlin air lift!

The Navy is not alone guilty of duplication. Until the end of 1948, for instance, the Army also had a Navy. This has been removed from it by the Secretary of Defense's order assigning all water-borne transportation to the Navy, a highly proper step. But, significantly, the Secretary is still, at this writing, only "considering" assigning all land and air transport to the corresponding services. The Army does not particularly want to sail boats or fly planes, the Air Force does not desire to run ground offensives or operate submarines. The psychology of the Navy is a thing unto itself; throughout the war it cost us millions of dollars, and it is still doing so.

The battle between the services which see ground, air, and

water as the media of three closely co-operating arms, each specialized in its element, and the one which wants to be all three within itself, ran all through the war and still continues. Despite that battle, despite the fact that A.T.C. and N.A.T.S. were pieces considerably more important than pawns in it, the two organizations worked well together. N.A.T.S. maintained an office in A.T.C. headquarters for closer liaison. Priorities frequently were interchanged. Over and again, when one agency had cargoes to be flown exceeding its immediate capacity, it turned to the other, and the other responded.

This co-operation was made possible by, among other things, the friendly interchange which existed between the men at the top. It did not end there. As I can testify, N.A.T.S. officers knew that they could blow off to A.T.C. men, and be understood, as they could not with their own service, about the Navy's slowness to recognize what air transportation could do. Both groups were drawn together by their common belief in air transportation and their common battle for its recognition.

The relations at the top are beautifully exemplified by one interchange of correspondence. It happened that a certain regular army colonel, stationed on the West Coast, got a free ride from N.A.T.S. to the East when he had a leave. Before taking off, he breakfasted at the mess of the Naval Air Station at Oakland. The colonel was not pleased with the food served him, and made certain emphatic comments, which elicited the following letter from the West Coast N.A.T.S. Commander:

NAVAL AIR TRANSPORT SERVICE
AIR TRANSPORT SQUADRONS, WEST COAST
U. S. NAVAL AIR STATION
OAKLAND, CALIFORNIA

VR–WC/L20–1/Wn

11 March 1944

Colonel ——, U.S. Army,
2000 E. Main Street,
Dalton, Alabama
Sir:

Certain deficiencies connected with the Naval Air Transport Service at this base have been called to my attention in connection with your sojourn here yesterday, 10 March 1944. While our primary mission is to carry priority cargo, we do carry a few passengers and are ever solicitous towards the improvement of facilities for their comfort and welfare, especially those who are members of other branches of the Service.

For your information, and in explanation of some of the deficiencies noted, there are no officer messing facilities available here at the present time. We do provide space and a cafeteria system for transient officers using the facilities and food of the general mess at prices established for the subsistence of enlisted personnel. This arrangement has been generally satisfactory and the Commissary Department has been the recipient of many compliments from members of all branches of the Service for the quality and quantity of the food served.

It appears that the breakfast menu for 10 March was as follows:

> Fresh fruit
> Dry cereal with fresh milk
> Creamed chipped beef on toast
> Eggs to order
> Parker House rolls
> Coffee with cream   (Price .20¢)

The doughnuts which you requested do not ordinarily form a part of the breakfast menu for reasons which are obvious to those acquainted with the difficulties connected with the preparation of this product of the culinary art for a crew of 1100 men. We regret that it happened to be one of your favorite breakfast items. A thorough investigation has been conducted concerning your contention that the beverage served you was not coffee. Results of this investigation disclose that it was a standard brand of Navy coffee, brewed with a density which experience has proven is palatable to the average Navy man. You may, therefore, have our assurance that while the coffee was not "the kind that you may have been accustomed to" it was, nevertheless, *coffee*, and any substitution of a cereal product, such as Postum, has been proven to be beyond the realm of possibility.

While formerly mugs or cups, equipped with handles, were a standard Navy issue, the Navy Department has recently seen fit to provide cups not so equipped. Therefore, your criticism in this matter involves a situation over which we have no

control and are without power to correct. In this respect, our
Navy enlisted personnel may have cause to envy the mess
equipment employed by the Army, which apparently includes
cups with handles.

Be assured that all interested parties are quite apprehensive
concerning your comfort throughout the rest of your trip, yesterday, inasmuch as it is known that the facilities along our
transcontinental route do not approximate those afforded by
commercial airlines. However, it must be admitted that the
difference in passenger rates, and the resultant saving, tends to
compensate for any discomfort or lack of facilities, especially
in these days of high prices and priority preference which present certain problems to domestic leave passengers if they are
to travel by rapid means of transportation with the least possible cost.

If you have further constructive criticism to offer as a result
of your transcontinental journey, please be assured that any
deficiencies will be given due consideration, if corrective action
is at all possible.

JAMES E. DYER,
Captain, U.S. Navy,
Commander, Naval Air Transport Service, West Coast.

A copy of this letter was transmitted to the commander of
N.A.T.S., who in turn forwarded it to the Commanding General, Air Transport Command, with the following covering
letter:

NAVY DEPARTMENT
OFFICE OF THE CHIEF OF NAVAL OPERATIONS
WASHINGTON 25, D.C.

13 March 1944.

Dear Harold:

May I pass on to you a copy of ComNatsWestCoast letter of
11 March relative to the constructive suggestions of one Col.
——, U.S.Army?

As you may observe, our NATS business is lacking some of
the finer points of Army good customs and usages, and I
thought maybe it could be possible for you to assume some
mugs or cups equipped with handles in order that your Army
Colonels may enjoy the niceties to which they are accustomed.

Capt. Dyer's letter I found to be most interesting and I am
sure you will appreciate the sincere honesty and humor.

To date we have had no further criticism from one Col. ——
and accordingly we have assumed that the rest of our eastbound service was acceptable (we hope).

Very sincerely,

/s/ Don Smith

DON SMITH

Maj. Gen. Harold L. George, AUS,
Commander, Air Transport Command,
Pentagon Building,
Rm. 1844, Annex 1,
Gravelly Point, Md. [sic]

Copy to:

Capt. J. E. Dyer, USN
ComNatsWestCoast,
U. S. Naval Air Station,
Oakland, California.

On receipt of this letter, General George called in his deputy
chief of staff, who referred the matter to a specialist, and the
following answer was returned by A.T.C.:

1st Wrapper Ind.   AFATC/I&S/OLaF/swc

Hq AAF, Air Transport Command, Washington 25, D.C.,

15 March 1944

To: Captain Donald F. Smith, U.S.N., Director, Naval Air
Transport Service, Room 2951, Navy Department, Washington 25, D.C.

1. Your letter and the enclosed copy of letter from Captain
James E. Dyer to Colonel —— have been read with interest
and appreciation. These communications deal with problems
which are encountered from time to time in the Air Transport
Command as well as in the Naval Air Transport Service.

2. It should be recorded, however, that one of the first re-
sponses aroused in this Headquarters by Captain Dyer's letter
was a profound interest in the breakfast menu included there-
in. It is the considered opinion of those consulted that seldom have two thin dimes been made to cover so much. Also,
information is requested as to the density of the coffee, mentioned in the same connection. Is this tested with a hydrom-
eter, or judged by trained coffee-testers, or by observation of
the reaction which it brings about when administered orally
to a sleepy subject? It has been suggested that possibly the

desired density of coffee in any given instance is in direct ratio to the density of the consumer, and hence that a consumer of an exceptionally dense nature might fail to be pleased by a beverage which would seem ambrosial to most people.

3. A fondness for doughnuts is widespread among all the Armed Services and may be said to be an American Institution and one of the less destructible cornerstones of democracy. The best medical advice obtainable here, however, is that only in rare cases does this fondness develop into a vice or habit which cannot be suspended. We further concur with Captain Dyer's contention that, given Parker House rolls, the manufacture and distribution of 1100 doughnuts per day would be a poor substitute for creamed chipped beef, eggs to taste, cereal with fresh milk and fresh fruit.

4. Special consideration has been given to your suggestion concerning the provision of mugs or cups with one or more handles for the benefit of transient Colonels. Attention is called to the fact that in the enlisted messes and many officers' messes of this Command the use of mugs without handles prevails, as in yours, it having been found that handles, at best, were transitory attachments. A single handle may soon disappear as the result of enthusiastic washing and stacking. A cup, mug, chalice, or loving cup equipped with several handles will offer something to take hold of longer, but is also likely to create confusion in the mind of the user. Experience has shown that, under the stress of necessity, even field officers will develop the prehensile strength required to use a plain mug effectively and without letting it fall to the table, ground or lap. Older field officers may use two hands, and this is also recommended for beginners.

5. In view of the considerations set forth in the last paragraph above, our suggestion is that transient field officers passing through or guests of your West Coast Stations be briefed in the use and appreciation of the local crockery and provender. In the case of company and of general officers it will usually be found that their intuition will suffice.

6. We trust that these comments and suggestions may prove helpful.

[s] H. L. GEORGE,
Major General, U.S.A.,
Commanding.

XXIV

MISSION SEVENTEEN

SOUNDNESS OF TECHNIQUES, maturity of experience and procedures, are proved by the ability of the practitioners to deal with unexpected, difficult, even excessive demands. Two undertakings of the Air Transport Command towards the close of the war demonstrated conclusively what such an organization could achieve, and the high level that the skills and knowledges had reached. They lifted the curtain a little farther upon the future, for startling glimpses of what aviation will be able to do, in peace or war, when the need arises.

The first of these undertakings was the carrying of the American and some of the British representatives to and from the Yalta Conference. Quantitatively the mission was a minor one. In view of the extraordinary preciousness of the cargo, the short notice given, and the complexity of the difficulties involved, it was a perfect test of methods, skills, and equipment.

That a conference was to be held at Yalta seems to have been known to the White House early in December, 1944. I do not know what preliminary warning may have been given to General George in that month. A.T.C. Headquarters received fairly specific information at the turn of the year, and on January 2 placed Colonel Ray W. Ireland, its Assistant Chief of Staff for Priorities and Traffic, in charge. The code name for this mission was "Argonaut." [1] Following its usual practice, A.T.C. gave it the secondary name of "Mission Seventeen" for internal use.

[1] As the Argonauts actually went to the Crimea in quest of the Golden Fleece, this may have been a pretty classical reference, but it was an incorrect procedure in assigning a code name.

On the fifth, General George called upon his Intelligence Division (which, as I explained in Chapter XXI, had been relegated to a subordinate position) for all information available on the enemy order of battle, airfields, aids to navigation, anti-aircraft dispositions, and other pertinent matters, for an area covering Greece, Bulgaria, Rumania, Russia along the Black Sea, and the northwestern part of Turkey. There was, of course, no explanation of the reason for this broad request. The matter was turned over to Lieutenant Colonel J. Kirkman Jackson, Chief of the Informational Intelligence Branch. That branch kept files of all information that came its way on airfields anywhere at all, still, it was hardly equipped to cover this assignment by itself. It called upon the Office of Naval Intelligence, Air Intelligence, and the O.S.S. In forty-eight hours of intense, unrelenting work, Colonel Jackson and his staff — which included some of the most intelligent and attractive young ladies I have ever met — produced the desired study.

On the twelfth of January the Joint Chiefs of Staff advised that the service to Yalta would begin about the twenty-fifth, and about that time gave an approximate list of the people to be carried — the President, Mr. Byrnes, the Joint Chiefs of Staff, Admiral Leahy, Secret Service men, and various others. Thus it seemed that the Command had thirteen days in which to get ready. Actually, there was a little more time. The President would go by boat to Malta, which was the rendezvous, and from there would fly — for the first time — in his special C–54, the *Sacred Cow*.

On the thirteenth the British asked for one C–54 to carry certain members of their delegation from Washington.

The list of problems to be solved, the difficulties inherent in the mission, are staggering. Yalta, a former summer residence of the Czars, is on the Crimea. The air base is at Saki, eighty miles away. Heavy winter weather could be expected there in January and February. The easiest approach to Saki would be from Teheran, where A.T.C. had an establishment, but flight from there required crossing mountains which would force the planes to high altitudes. In view of the age and health of some of the passengers, it was felt that the altitude would be dangerous. Hence it was decided to rendezvous at Malta and come in from the Mediterranean.

This approach offered plenty of problems. Yugoslavia and Crete were still in enemy hands. In Greece, fairly lively fighting was going on between the British and rightist Greeks on the one hand, and the leftist Greeks on the other. Bulgaria and Rumania were occupied by Russian troops, and the Russians were notorious for attacking Allied planes. The route could be worked out to pass entirely over the seas until it reached the Dardanelles, then it had to cross Turkish territory. The Turks were jealous guardians of their borders. A special arrangement had to be made with them, to let the aircraft pass.

Everything had to be conducted in top secrecy with trimmings. Top secret matters are always difficult to handle. The number of persons to whom any explanation or hint can be given of what is afoot is strictly limited, and the procedures in handling messages are cumbersome, of necessity. As the North Africa Division of the Command had a large part to play in the mission, its commander, Brigadier General James S. Stowell, and certain of his staff were informed. Only those base commanders who would be directly involved were told anything at all. If a plane carrying Argonaut passengers should be forced to land at any other base, the passengers and crew were to remain on board until the pilot had gone to the C.O. and explained matters. There was an elaborate procedure worked out for guarding the planes where they did land, and for guarding the passengers and protecting them from observation.

To protect radio communication, a special code of five hundred words was worked out. Malta was "Errand," Saki was "Umbrella-Bird," the President was "Sawbuck." In order to avoid having a single code name for a given aircraft repeated in a series of progress messages, which might betray the plane's movement if the Germans should break our cipher, each flight's name was changed daily. Thus Flight 1 was "Naseberry" on January 16, "Series" on the seventeenth, and "Featherwood" on the eighteenth, the day on which it actually left Washington. Messages were first put into this code, and then ciphered.

As an extra precaution, the manufacturer's serial number

was painted out on the *Sacred Cow,* and the serial of a C–54 engaged in routine services substituted.

The matter of communications involved more than the problems of a code within the cipher, and top secret handling. As the big rendezvous was at Malta, the British were to handle communications. The British channels were overloaded. In relaying cipher messages, the American practice is simply to pass them on as received. The British practice is to decipher them, paraphrase them (that is, alter the arrangement and wording of the text so that it no longer furnishes a clue to the original cipher), and recipher them. The delay involved is considerable. A.T.C. headquarters alone handled seven hundred top secret messages in the course of the operation; the load at Luqa must have been comparable. The British announced that they would be unable to handle the North Africa Division's administrative messages. On January 23, Major Arthur Sherry of that Division reported, no answer had been received to a trial Operational Priority message sent from Casablanca to Malta on the twenty-first. (Operational Priority is the highest in communications.) The situation was somewhat improved when the British installed additional channels.

On January 25, Major Sherry reported that communications with Washington were faster than with Malta. As to Saki, he wrote, it was "little better than trying to communicate with the hereafter."

To make this problem easier, the Russian Government required that twenty-four hours' advance notice of each incoming plane be received *at Moscow*. This fitted the Russian pattern of extreme nervousness over having any foreign plane cross its borders or the territory it occupied without permission from the very top. Whatever the reasons for agreeing to a conference on Russian territory, the Russians found it hard to relax their uneasiness over allowing alien planes to come in. A.T.C. knew this uneasiness well, and was well aware of the danger which confronted any aircraft which came over Soviet territory unannounced or which deviated from its assigned corridor. No regular A.T.C. service ran into Russia. Transfer points for cargo, passengers, and aircraft were well outside the

Russian borders, at Teheran and Fairbanks. The fact that Russian representatives were stationed all along the Alaskan route as far as Great Falls, Montana, did nothing to alleviate their country's fear. When the plan for shuttle-bombing between the British bases and Poltava was agreed upon, it was with the greatest difficulty that the Command secured permission to run a small, essential, supporting schedule from Teheran to Poltava, and to carry American personnel on certain administrative flights within Russia.[2] To the Command, the requirement of twenty-four hours' notice to Moscow was a new version of an old headache.

It must be remembered that the actual take-off of aircraft is rendered uncertain by weather, and sometimes by mechanical troubles, either of which may result in prolonged delays. Such delays would require a new message. This operation involved much more than the flights of a fixed number of aircraft carrying the President, the Prime Minister, and their staffs to Saki. There have to be survey flights in advance, and a variety of supporting flights, including a courier service. In case of some unforeseen need, it was essential to be able to send a plane in on short notice. The channeling of "warning messages" through Moscow meant that the North Africa Division would have to communicate either with our embassy in London or with Washington. In the former case, our embassy would turn the message over to the Russian embassy, which would forward it to Moscow, which in turn would communicate with Saki. In the latter, the War Department would turn the message over to State, which would send it to our embassy in Moscow, which would give it to the Russians. In either case, the message not only had to be relayed at several points, but to pass from the military to the diplomatic and back again. It is little wonder

---

[2] The Poltava service was definitely adventurous for many reasons. Among other notable incidents was the refitting of a strafed C–87 with wheels from an entirely different model as an emergency job to put it back into operation. This compares with C.N.A.C.'s famous achievement in the course of the retreat from Nanking, of repairing a DC–3 by putting on it one wing of a DC–2, an earlier Douglas model. The resultant hybrid, which flew, became famous as "the DC–2½."

that the A.T.C. men on the spot reported that this requirement was "an almost intolerable handicap." Happily, on the
twenty-second of January, Russia completely reversed herself
and gave blanket clearance to mission aircraft for Saki.

Fourteen C–54's, including the President's plane, were prepared for the mission. All leaves were cancelled for the 503d
A.A.F. Base Unit at the National Airport. This unit provided
eleven of the Mission Seventeen crews, out of its famous
"Special Mission Squadron." The rigid inspection to which
each plane was subjected occupied the time of fifteen men for
two days. At that time there was a shortage of C–54 spare parts,
yet it was essential that everything be available, all along the
line, to make about any repairs that could be imagined. The
503d sent planes around the country, requisitioning parts. A
4000-pound repair kit was placed on each aircraft, 5000 pounds
of spares were forwarded to Africa, to add to the stockpile
which the North Africa Division was building from its resources. Peter was robbed to pay Paul all along the line; it was
an epic of dog-robbing.

The kind of people who would be passengers on these flights
out-VIPped the VIPs. Bucket seats, box lunches, would not do
for them. Colonel Robert N. Hicks, A.T.C.'s quartermaster,
borrowed electric galleys with which hot meals could be prepared on each plane. He secured eight hundred pounds of
special, de luxe rations for each one. In addition he procured
such items as sleeping bags for all the Saki contingent, aerosol
bombs, a collection of gifts for the Russians, and six hundred
rolls of toilet paper. Hicks managed all this on five days'
notice.

The *Sacred Cow* was equipped with an elevator to allow the
President to ascend and descend. There was always concern
lest it get out of order. A sectional ramp was built, which
could be carried ahead to each landing place on another plane.
The principal British transport was the *York*, modified from
the Lancaster bomber much as the C–87 was from the B–24.
Like the C–87, it was a high-winged monoplane, with its
fuselage setting close to the ground. Naturally, then, Luqa
Field did not possess the high, movable stairs necessary for em-

barking passengers on C–54's. A supply of these was gathered and delivered there and to Saki.

The North Africa Division furnished the base personnel for Luqa and Saki, and provided items such as engineering and maintenance equipment and jeeps, a fork lift, and two bicycles for Saki. It was responsible for seeing that American daily papers (I do not know which ones) arrived there with the greatest promptness. The Division's C–46's and C–47's were to provide courier and support service. Six C–46's, carrying aircraft engineering equipment, mechanics, and spare parts, were "seeded" among the mission passenger planes, so that if one had trouble between Luqa and Saki, and had to land, a flying workshop would land with it.

The courier service was a sizeable item. Radio communication was not enough, there must be fast and frequent means of transmitting documents between the United States and Yalta. The courier aircraft were based at Cairo and Casablanca. Their route took them north across Turkey, calling for another set of permissions and the establishment of a corridor. Selected courier officers were provided to ride with the planes. At Casablanca the documents were transshipped to or from the four-engine, transoceanic aircraft.

At first it was thought that the Command would be in charge of the stationing of search and rescue ships and aircraft along the whole route. To its relief, however, the principal burden across the Atlantic was taken over by the Navy, while the Mediterranean Allied Air Force took charge in the Mediterranean. The Command's own search and rescue squadrons at the Atlantic stations, of course, were included in the organization.

Available information showed that bad weather was fairly common in midwinter over the Crimea. After a good deal of negotiations, the Russians gave consent to the use of Poltava as an alternate field in case Saki were closed in, and to the placing of some personnel and supplies there.

The Russians required special identification cards for each American on the mission, with clear distinction between those allowed only at Saki and those who should have access to Yalta.

The procurement of an adequate supply of these cards seems to have been fouled up, and there was a continuous crisis in regard to them. In view of the nature of the conference, this requirement was not only proper, but necessary.

It can well be imagined that every agency concerned in the conference, British, Russian, and American, was taking its precautions to ensure security. Of necessity, the Command was deeply involved in this, detailing Lieutenant Colonel William Conway of headquarters Intelligence to supervise this vital matter. Colonel Morgan, the Chief of Intelligence and Security, himself went to North Africa to lay the groundwork and indoctrinate his people there. The Command's responsibility began with the first assembling of aircraft and men at the National Airport, it continued through the arrival at its base and the departure of each load of passengers, and reached across its bases at Bermuda and the Azores, across North Africa and on to Cairo, and thence to Saki itself. Colonel Conway was later decorated for his successful execution of his important duties. The secrecy which surrounded this entire affair was close to perfect.

It is worth recalling what other major activities the Command was engaged in, in the latter part of January, 1945. It was embarking upon an ambitious project, involving heavy movements of personnel, supplies, and aircraft to India, which was to bring the tonnage over the Hump to China up to 50,000 per month. The North Atlantic main line had been extended into France and evacuation of wounded from there was at a peak, while outward from the United States it was flying the greatest possible quantities of supplies including such vital items as refrigerated whole blood for transfusions. Southwest Pacific Wing Headquarters had been established at Leyte in the Philippines a few weeks earlier, a direct route now ran across the Pacific to Leyte, in urgent support of the bitter fighting in those islands. With the fighting at last going well along the German frontier, plans for the great redeployment against Japan were being perfected, and the Command was preparing to be ready for the vast undertakings of the Green and White Projects as soon as it should be called upon to carry them out.

It continued, of course, its usual services to the various quarters of the globe. All this and Yalta, too.

At this point a dog called "Blaze" was shipped via A.T.C. from New York to California. Someone in the White House, a member of the President's family, I believe, telephoned Colonel Ireland and asked to have Elliot Roosevelt's dog carried. Colonel Ireland, overwhelmingly busy, turned the matter over routinely to the appropriate priorities officer in his division. Somewhere along the line someone, I have no idea who, gave the dog an "A" priority (equivalent to the overseas "1"), because the request came from the White House. As a result, the dog bumped two enlisted men en route home on furlough after long tours of overseas duty. The press found out about it, and quite understandably raised a howl.

The howl did not die down. Columnists and politicians took it up. There was a clamor for explanations and a head to chop off. General George could have taken responsibility, in his capacity as Commanding General, but that would have been received as camouflage. The unfortunate man actually responsible could have been thrown to the wolves, which would have been sheer cruelty. Colonel Ireland, well enough placed to take it, obscure enough to be convincing, accepted personal blame. Having done this, he departed, as scheduled, for North Africa, where he was urgently needed to continue running Mission Seventeen.

A cry went up for Colonel Ireland in person. When the Command announced that he had departed on an urgent, secret mission, there were bitter paragraphs about the abuse of security to protect an officer who deserved to be disciplined. The appropriate House and Senate Committees decided to investigate.

It was funny enough in its way. Men in N.A.T.S. had good, clean fun calling up A.T.C. acquaintances and asking solicitously how the Animal Transport Command was getting on. Some good cracks were passed in headquarters. Obviously, nobody's dog rated an "A" priority; nonetheless, it was, or should have been, a tempest in a teapot. The incident was tailor-made for those who hated the President and thought it fair tactics to get at him through his family. In the middle of all the intensely important and delicate undertakings I have listed, I have seen the top staff of the Command, seriously worried, devoting precious hours to the problem of defending their organization.

General George went personally to the Congressional committees. It happened that headquarters had just finished a rather full, graphically, even dramatically presented report of its activities (not including the Yalta mission, of course), for the eyes of General Arnold and one or two other very high people. General George took this report with him, and when the gentlemen of Congress had gone over it, they readily saw how utterly insignificant was the foolish business of the dog. Some of the columnists, however, determined to secure a more efficient prosecution of the war, continued intermittently belaboring what I hope I may be excused for calling a dead dog for some time afterwards.

One good thing came of this incident. Members of the President's household had been a trifle too free about calling up one or another officer of the Command and using the White House's prestige to secure small favors. Such requests from such sources are very difficult for the ordinary man to refuse. Now a single, rigid channel of communication was established, and the A.T.C. staff was forbidden to act upon requests from the White House unless they came through that channel, which ensured screening.

The route determined on for the actual flights from Malta was south of Sicily and over the Ionian Sea to Kythera, then northeast to the north tip of Andros Island, north to 40° 30′ north, 25° 45′ east, thence northeast to Enez 150 miles west of Istanbul, across Turkey to Midye, then over the Black Sea to Saki — a total distance of 1360 miles. The first advance 2-engine flights did not follow this route, but lay over at Hassani Airport outside Athens, waiting for word that the Turks had notified their anti-aircraft to let the American planes by, until January 19. While they were at Athens, some shooting was going on between the two groups of Greeks and the British. The hotel in Athens then occupied by the A.T.C. contingent was its fifth,

as the others had been so shot up or bombed as to be unin-
habitable. The shootings and bombings were not directed at
our people, but were simply the result of their being in a cross-
fire. Ordinarily, shooting stopped when the A.T.C. convoy
started out for or returned from Hassani, and the American
flag was respected by both sides. It was difficult, however, to
keep the British and the government troops from using the
roofs of the hotels our men occupied as points to shoot from.
One British gunboat, over-quick to see red in a flag, did fire
upon an A.T.C. convoy along the coast, hitting a jeep and
killing an officer. The usual amends were made, but as in the
case of the B–24 shot down over Murmansk, that does not
bring back the dead.

The advance flights took off on the nineteenth and reached
Saki without incident. By that time, the tentative departure
date for the conference members from Malta was February 1st.
The dispatching of the mission aircraft themselves from Washington was not a simple matter of sending fourteen aircraft
out on a single flight plan. Various flights had different plans
according to requirements. The first four were to go through
to Saki before February 1st, and then to return to Malta for
the rendezvous. Others were to pick up passengers at one or
another point along their route.

Nor was the manning of them simple. The crews were hand-
picked. The aircraft carrying the most important personages
had two first pilots and a co-pilot. On the President's plane the
pilots were Lieutenant Colonels Henry T. Myers and Otis F.
Bryan. Myers was General George's aide, a delightful person,
and one of the best pilots living. He is still today the presidential pilot. I do not know Bryan personally, but he is
famous among airmen, and if anyone can be rated as *the* best
of all pilots, it is he. A T.W.A. executive, he held a reserve
commission, and used to be called to active duty for occasions
such as these. Such was his reputation for flying the great of
the earth that calling him up, in itself, had to be handled with
secrecy. Madame Chiang Kai-shek insisted on being flown by
him whenever possible.[3]

[3] Mme. Chiang has a strongly regal streak. She was greatly annoyed
when she and the Generalissimo were flown to Cairo one time in a twin-

Flight 1 of the mission proper took off from Washington on January 18th. The pilot was Lieutenant Colonel Edward N. Coates, the same who commanded the C–87 shuttle across the Sahara to Oran. It proceeded without special incident, landing at Saki on the twenty-second. From there it flew back to Malta to wait for "D-Day," which now was set definitely ("God willing and the weather prevailing fine") for February 2. Flight 2 made the same trip with equal success. Flight 3, which was the *Sacred Cow* itself, shaved the edges of adventure. It departed Washington on January 21, carrying Harry Hopkins, who got off at the Azores. At Casablanca it picked up A.T.C. personnel, including Colonel Ireland and General Stowell, and took off direct for Saki. The trouble then being experienced with communications asserted itself, for the plane reached its destination ahead of its arrival message. Myers was in the left-hand seat. The weather was bad. Myers let down through the clouds right over Saki, and made so fast a straight-in landing that the Russian defense contingent never had a chance to train their guns on his plane. As I have noted before, a C–54 looks like the German heavy bomber, Focke-Wulfe 200, and the Russians would have shot the plane down if they could have.

I have made remarks several times about the quickness of the Russians in attacking Allied aircraft coming over their domain. I am willing to make them again, and extend them to the cold-blooded murder perpetrated by the Yugoslavs on August 19, 1946, when they shot down a transport which had lost its way. We may call it "trigger-happiness," but we cannot help suspecting an element of plain policy in it. In this case, however, even had they destroyed the *Sacred Cow*, we should have to absolve them. If the Germans got wind of the conference, slipping in an F–W 200 is just what they would be expected to try, and the Russians could take no chances. Warning messages in advance were essential. The fault here lay en-

engine plane, feeling that four engines were more suitable to their dignity. I have known generals who suffered from the same ailment, demanding — and not getting — C–54's where a Cessna or a Beechcraft would do splendidly.

tirely with faulty communications in an operation in which communications were vital.

The fourth of the C–54's which made the advance trip got further into trouble. It went slightly off course in thick weather. When the pilot, Major James S. Sammons, let down through the clouds to see where he was, he came within range of Crete, and was promptly fired at by the Germans there. He climbed up in a hurry, but even so he got a few flak holes in the fuselage.

On the first of February, to its great relief, A.T.C. was asked to take charge of communications. As it was much too late for the Command to install radio equipment, it arranged to make use of the radio of the U.S.S. *Catoctin*, a minesweeper which had arrived at Saki.

By noon of February 1 all of the Argonaut Mission aircraft were at Luqa Field, the American ships consisting of the fourteen C–54's and a C–87 which had brought Ambassador Harriman, as well as the "workshop" C–46's. Altogether there were thirty R.A.F. and American four-engine planes on the field, an impressive crowd. Thirty-two P–38's were ready at Andros, where they would pick up the main part of the parade and escort it to Saki. Weather reports were coming in from the destination at last. They were discouraging — ceiling zero, and cold fronts moving across the Black Sea.

The cruiser *Quincy* with Mr. Roosevelt aboard arrived the morning of February 2, to find H.M.S. *Sirius* with Mr. Churchill already at anchor. The two leaders boarded their planes late that evening. These planes were parked together. Around them was a double ring of British sentries, and inside that our Secret Service men were clustered about the *Sacred Cow*.

M. Harriman's C–87, Flight 17, was the first dispatched, taking off at 2230 (10.30 P.M.) Greenwich time. Others followed at precise, ten-minute intervals. Flight 10, which was to carry General Marshall, was scheduled to depart at 0030 (half an hour after midnight). It was the fixed rule that no passenger could board his plane less than twenty minutes before departure. Just twenty-one minutes before, the general arrived from

Valetta and boarded his plane. Flight 3 with the President took off at 0230, the last C–54 was air-borne at 0340. The departures were timed so that all planes would come over the Black Sea with ample daylight left for landing at Saki or, if necessary, at Poltava.

The convoy, with the P–38's escorting it from Andros on, stretched for 1300 miles. Flight 17 was due to land at Saki at 0515 on February 3; it landed at 0521. The *Sacred Cow* was due at 0910 and landed at 0912. No plane, British or American, was more than ten minutes off its estimated time of arrival, and many of them landed on the very minute. The Russians were frankly and openly astonished.

The worst was over, as far as the Command was concerned. It's all a matter of perspective. Mr. Byrnes in *Speaking Frankly* devotes two lines to this operation, which is a form of compliment to its smoothness. I devote none to the actual conference, which was none of the Command's business.

The President was due to leave Yalta the morning of February 12, to fly down the Red Sea to Deversoir for his conference with Ibn Saud. On the evening of the eleventh, inspection showed a possible defect in one of his plane's engines. The men at Saki did a remarkable job of exchanging it for the engine of a cargo C–54 overnight, and the President took off at 7.50 the next morning.

The aircraft went to Yalta in one single convoy. They came out by ones and twos, following a variety of routes according to the assignments of their passengers, but flying into known territory, to American-manned bases with familiar equipment and procedures. It was some time before the last of the Argonauts came home, but once the President had left the Crimea, everyone concerned could relax. Mission Seventeen had been performed with almost miraculous smoothness, and the Air Transport Command could well be proud.[4]

[4] This account is nothing but a thin extract from a remarkable, detailed, and complete military study under the same title, made by two able civilians of the A.T.C. Historical Branch, Mmes. Marian March and Maxine Radsch.

XXV

FLIGHT TO VICTORY

EARLIER I REMARKED that General MacArthur finally dreamed up the fanciest of all the special missions in which the Air Transport Command was ever engaged. This was nothing less than flying the first waves of the occupying forces to Japan from Okinawa. This operation was given the code name of "Baker Sixty" by MacArthur's headquarters, and was regarded as a subdivision of the larger plan, "Blacklist" for the Occupation first of Tokyo, then of the rest of Japan. To the Command, it was known as Mission Seventy-Five. Like Mission Seventeen, it was a test and a proof of the maturity of military air transport, and even more than the earlier mission, it was a glimpse of the future, a preliminary sketch of great and terrifying possibilities.

In actual fact, the germ of the idea seems to have originated with General Arnold, who on August 3, 1945, suggested to General MacArthur that a greater use of aircraft might be made in the Blacklist plan. In the early part of August, Brigadier General Alexander was engaged in terminating the Southwest Pacific Wing of A.T.C.'s Pacific Division. There was no longer need for extensive services between Australia and the Philippines, the supply-line reached straight westward across the Pacific. Once it had been decided that the next attack would be direct upon Japan, rather than against the Japanese in China as first proposed, prospective work for the Wing dropped sharply. Therefore, when MacArthur's General Headquarters called Alexander in on August 9, he represented an organization which was already partially dissolved.

Alexander communicated with Major General Ryan, commanding the Pacific Division, and on August 11 General Ryan placed him in control of Baker Sixty. On that day, also, Alexander radioed A.T.C. headquarters, giving them the first notice of a plan which, "B–Day" having been set for August 26, required on the face of it the concentration of some two hundred C–54's at Okinawa by that time, with all the other preparations to be made for a tremendous move. MacArthur's plan called for the flying in of the advance elements of General Headquarters, Headquarters of Army Forces, Pacific Area, of the 8th Army, and of the Far Eastern Air Forces, plus the 11th Airborne Division, reinforced, all to be followed by the 27th Division.

General MacArthur was accustomed to operating within his own empire. It did not, apparently, occur to him to lead off by notifying the War Department of his project, he just started arranging it. When A.T.C. queried the General Staff and Air Staff on August 12, no one had heard of Baker Sixty. On that day MacArthur sent a radio to the War Department, and on the thirteenth it instructed the Command to go ahead with the project.

As the project developed, there would be 20,000 troops and about 2000 tons of matériel and supplies to be carried a distance of slightly over nine hundred miles. With all its resources, the Command alone could not handle the job. To its fleet were added 272 C–46's and 100 C–47's from Far Eastern Air Forces' Troop Carrier arm. At that time the Pacific Division, which had been greatly strengthened in preparation for the "Purple Project" of moving 10,000 men a month to the combat area from California, had 154 C–54's. Thirty-three were drawn from the North Atlantic Division and 38 from the North African — all that could be spared while the "Green Project" continued — 12 that had been destined for the India-China Division were diverted, and 12 more secured new from production. Thus a total of 249 four-engine transports were assembled in the Pacific. All the trans-Pacific schedules flown by military crews were cancelled, leaving some seventeen daily flights by Consairways and United to handle that traffic. As westbound military flights came to Manila, they were inspected and sent north to Okinawa, the first C–54 reaching there on August 14. Eastbound flights received their inspection at Hickam Field on Oahu, and then proceeded on their new mission. Altogether, the Command assembled 187 C–54's at Kadena Airfield on Okinawa, with fifteen more in reserve at Manila, Guam, and Saipan.

Kadena Field had been prepared for B–29's, which had been due to begin operations from there on August 15. It now was placed under the command of Lieutenant Colonel James W. Luker. It was he, it will be remembered, who commanded the A.T.C. operation on Okinawa from the time of the first landing on. Fittingly, now he was in charge of the final, triumphant undertaking. By the time "B–Day" was at hand, he had 200 ground personnel and 3000 air crew members under his supervision.

At Manila, General Alexander rebuilt his wing organization, drawing staff from his remaining bases. A.T.C. Headquarters secured the loan of Major General Lawrence S. Kuter, and sent him to Manila as General George's personal representative. There were only thirteen days from the day that the War Department had given the Command the go-ahead signal, and in that time not only did the men and planes have to be assembled, the necessary supplies, including enormous quantities of gas and oil, be brought to Okinawa, but the whole organization for the operation had to be created.

On the 19th of August Colonel Earl J. Ricks, the Wing's Deputy Chief of Staff, flew Lieutenant General Tokashira Kawabe and his staff from Ie Shima to Manila for the surrender and occupation arrangements, and on the twentieth flew him back. On the twenty-fourth he brought the Russian delegation to Manila. This latter was the trickier of the two missions, as Ricks had to land in Siberia, and he ran into the familiar problems of failure of the Russians to answer his signals, doubt as to whether or not to land, and fighter planes nervously buzzing his aircraft.

As everybody knows, "B–Day," the beginning of the occupation of Japan, was postponed from August 26 to August 30, because of a typhoon. The extra breathing space was by no means unwelcome to the Command. On August 28, fifteen C–54's and Thirty Troop Carrier aircraft took off from Kadena Field to carry one hundred and fifty officers and enlisted men of the 5th Air Force and 12,000 pounds of gas and oil to Atsugi Air base outside Tokyo. With them went Lieutenant Colonel Marion Grevemberg, who was to be A.T.C.'s commander there.

On the thirtieth, Mission Seventy-Five began. The first C–54 landed at Atsugi at 0604 in the morning, the last took off from there at 1719 — nineteen minutes past five in the evening. All day long the planes left Kadena at three-minute intervals; for eleven solid hours the A.T.C. planes were airborne at an average rate of fifteen to the hour. They flew along one line, the Troop Carrier aircraft along another, to avoid overcrowded channels. On the first day 4000 personnel and 3000 tons of cargo were landed in Tokyo.

Japanese construction being what it is, by the end of the second day the runway at Atsugi was failing. Thereafter, for the remaining nine days of the mission, it had to be repaired each night.

Altogether, 3646 flights were made in those eleven days, to carry 23,456 pasengers and just under 2000 tons of cargo. The cargo included 924 jeeps, 267 other vehicles, including heavy trucks, 2348 barrels of gasoline and oil, nine L–4's (light liaison planes), and several tractors and bulldozers. There were no accidents or crashes. A man was killed at Kadena Field, but the occurrence had no connection with flying.[1] By September 12th the mission was completed.

On return flights, over 7000 prisoners of war were flown out. One load of these consisted of Army nurses captured on Bataan. The nurses, skin and bone when they were set free, were expedited back to the United States via Saipan and Oahu. Word of the nature of this load of passengers went ahead of the plane. At each stop the local garrisons pooled their resources, the precious rations of beer, the almost unprocurable cokes, the hoarded cigarettes, the scarce delicacies, the packages from home, so that, whether the plane stopped for half an hour to

[1] As usual, in this case I know of at least two sets of figures for the operation, which conflict at various points. The ones I give are mostly those of Lieutenant Carson Sheetz, the Wing Historical Officer.

refuel or remained overnight, there was always a banquet awaiting them. Afterwards, the men at the various stations told with pride how much the long-starved women had eaten. They had deprived themselves for weeks to come, and they were delighted to have done so.

Mission Seventy-Five was an impressive achievement. Perhaps the most impressive part of it was the assembling of so large a number of transports — certainly the largest massing of such aircraft the world had ever seen — on such short notice, and the implication of reserve power in the Command's maintenance of its normal services throughout the world except for a fifty per cent reduction across the Pacific.

Yet Mission Seventy-Five also was evidence that the Air Age, properly speaking, had not yet arrived. Early in the war the Germans had carried out a successful, purely airborne invasion of Crete across about 160 miles of open water, against a weak and disorganized enemy. We had had since then various massive drops and glider-landings of airborne troops in conjunction with surface operations. Given a distance of a thousand miles, which still would span no major ocean, this great concentration of transports, facing no opposition, could land only 4000 troops and their accompanying supplies in one day. This number, or the total number finally delivered, would have been helpless in the home territory of any major country retaining an army in being. This great air movement was a very effective way of moving the first wave of occupation troops to a surrendered capital; under combat conditions, air transport over such distances could serve only as an auxiliary — potentially a very powerful, possibly even a decisive auxiliary — to surface attack. The day of major invasions by air from distant nations had not yet come.

The equipment used, Douglas DC–4's and DC–3's and Curtiss Commandos, was even then obsolescent. The time is not far off when these aircraft, which served so nobly, will be buried in the past along with the square-rigged frigates from which Commodore Matthew C. Perry forced open the doors of Japan nearly a century earlier. It is in the light of what the successors to these veterans will be that Mission Seventy-Five takes on its full significance.

XXVI

THE EAGLE IN THE DOVECOTE

A LITTLE LESS than a hundred years ago American clippers came close to dominating the commerce of the seas. For ships to meet the threat, England, the great seafarer, turned to the Yankee shipyards, where a Scotsman from Newfoundland taught the world to build the most perfect sailing vessels of all time.[1] It took a great war to restore us to a similar position, or rather one in which the first place in commerce of the air is ours if we wish it, as well as first place in military air power.

Wisely used, the war's gifts to aviation are not for any one nation alone, but for all the world, a means of mutual aid, of exchange, perhaps even, if we can disarm our prejudices and bring our narrow souls abreast of our mechanical skills, a means of understanding and friendship. I have tried to give some idea of the routes, the great air highways, which are our legacy from the time of battle. They were built by no one nation alone; everyone had a hand in making them. Certain Americans, "Indian givers" (which Indians, incidentally, are not), may snarl about reverse Lend–Lease; the fact remains that the leap forward to a physical world equipped for heavy air commerce between almost all lands was made by the concerted effort of many nations.

Today, some of the once great routes are silent. The birds

[1] In our infatuation with our own times we commonly overlook the fact that, even under optimum conditions, few modern, scientifically designed, racing sailboats have ever equalled the speed records established by the clippers, also under optimum conditions. No sailing vessel exists today capable of maintaining, day in and day out, the speeds across the Atlantic and the Pacific which were usual with the clippers.

fly them undisturbed. There were great centers, such as Accra and Julianehaab, which we named so often, which were so solidly and completely built, and through which our traffic ran so heavily, that we thought of them as permanent. When they were abandoned, one felt almost a shock. In the speed of those crammed years, the desertion of one of the major bases after two or three years of use gave us the same feeling of a changed world that a man ordinarily receives when the fixtures of half his lifetime disappear. Such places were needed only because of specific military situations. As the enemy was confined to ever smaller areas, the military routes correspondingly swung to the permanently useful points. They stand ready now, capable of handling far more traffic than the present state of aviation can economically support. They are like a voice calling for a great interchange which is frustrated, strait-jacketed, by archaic nationalism.

So long as nationalism continues, we are committed to a two-fold endeavor: at once to strain every nerve to find the succession of formulae which will keep prolonging peace, and at the same time preparing with equal effort for the day when no formula will serve. In the second part of the endeavor we are now, not in good shape, but still in a position to put ourselves in good shape fairly rapidly if we make up our minds to do so.

When the fighting ended our armed forces crumbled away. On the overseas bases the great aircraft stood in ranks with their shining wings, the very portrait of power, but the Air Forces lay prostrate and helpless. The Air Transport Command, for which there was still a mountain of immediate work to do, sickened with the rest. The mail did not get through to Japan, General MacArthur thundered, the homeside newspapers screamed, Congress threatened. At Guam, the centerpoint of all the Pacific routes, five mechanics remained to keep the aircraft flyable. Every time a transport took off, the pilot prayed heartily that the maintenance had really been done. For months the whole Command held its breath, waiting for disaster.

We like to think of ourselves as adventurous, descendants of people who struck out for the New and unknown World in search of their dreams, descendants of the pioneers who moved ever westward into distant, unknown regions. Our military history shows us as a people with an overwhelming craving to go home. The shabby record of the Revolutionary militia, the regiments stacking their arms and turning north while the Union army marched past them on the way to Bull Run, bespeak a strange frame of mind. We seem to think it a terrific thing to ask a man to defend his country or to train himself in case he should have to defend it. If he has entered his country's service when it was in danger, no matter how unwillingly, how purely because his alternative was jail, and no matter what the nature of his duties, he feels that forever after the whole nation is in his debt. More remarkable, most of the nation, instead of considering that he has merely discharged the great debt he owes to it, agrees with him. Even while the fighting continued, the Americans cried to come home as did the men of no other nation. When it ended, their crying echoed to the heavens, with Congress and the public cheering them on. In a burst of sentiment and self-indulgence we destroyed our ability to defend ourselves, and so far we have made no serious move to restore it. Perhaps the most dangerous aspect of the atomic bomb is that the politicians can exploit it as a justification for keeping their country weak.

The blame does not lie entirely with the troops. It must be shared by military leaders who did not believe it necessary or even useful to teach the soldiers why they were where they were. It goes further than that, to a ramshackle educational system and to the parents, who, between them, could not teach their sons to know and understand the world which surrounded that sweet land for which they so longed. The children have been taught to love their mother, but the love they learned does not include willingness to make personal sacrifices to keep her safe and great.

For all our errors, fate is being indulgent to us. It offers us a chance we have not earned. We can keep our nation strong with much less effort than has been required of the great countries of the past. Our position, flanked by the seas, plus the development of air power — including that aspect of it which is the concern of this book — enables us to rely heavily upon that power for our safety, and accordingly makes it possible for us to maintain less of a standing army, while the fantastic expense of an old-style, ocean-dominating Navy has become clearly superfluous. The establishment of a true Air Force has given us the essential framework, if we can make up our minds to fill it.

So long as we must continue to anticipate war, we must keep our eagle, ready and able to strike effectively at a moment's notice. We shall not again have others to hold the enemy while we laboriously get ready.

Mission Seventy-Five showed that, even with the equipment we then had, we could under favorable circumstances deliver a sizable striking force nearly a thousand miles by air. Already that equipment is being superseded. Among other transports, the Air Force is now testing Convair's [2] XC–99, which can carry 100,000 pounds of cargo or 400 equipped troops a distance of 8100 miles at a speed exceeding 300 miles an hour. Forty of these monsters could pick up a full division in California and fly it, non-stop, to Nanking in approximately twenty-four hours. Truly, Mission Seventy-Five fades into the archaic. They could take off from our Atlantic bases, drop their troops over the nearer parts of Europe, and return. The XC–99 is a close relative of the new B–36, which has a range of a full 10,000 miles — quite capable of taking off from Hawaii, dropping a load of bombs on the Asiatic mainland, and flying back, and of making deep raids into Europe from the Atlantic coast.

What this team of aircraft means in striking power, if the Congress will allow us to have enough of them, is obvious enough, and comforting in a grisly way. We have them coming up bigger, faster, with greater range. Jet-propelled heavy bombers and transports are just around the corner. Nor can we flatter ourselves that we are the only nation in the world that is making technological advances in aviation. With or without atomic bombs, very powerful, even paralyzing, lightning attack comes daily nearer.

2 Convair is the new firm name of Consolidated Vultee.

Our first hope is that there may never be an attack. For the world in general, the poor second is that one's own nation may get in the first blow. For the United States, this second can be realized only under most unusual and unlikely circumstances. Not only do we hate war and move towards it with the greatest reluctance, but our Constitution has been carefully, and wisely, framed to make it impossible for the military, including the President, to declare war. The Armed Services may strike only if Congress authorizes, or if they are attacked.

If a war comes, it is likely to come in one of two ways. The one we fear most is a sudden, deadly assault upon the continental United States. Such an assault will probably be initially from the air, accompanied by atomic bombs and other refinements of modern civilization. Along with it will probably come attacks upon whatever of our outposts, east or west, provide us with the bases from which to counterattack effectively deep into the enemy's country. The purely air attack will of necessity be followed by invasion, from the air, from the water, or more likely from both. To save ourselves we shall need, of course, the combat aircraft, to intercept the attacking planes, to seek out and destroy the launching places of the flying bombs, to counterattack the enemy's own centers. We shall need, also, to supply and maintain the bases from which we counterattack, wherever in the world they may be, and we shall need absolutely to move our ground troops, our rescue services, our equipment, to threatened or attacked points within the United States and beyond with the greatest possible speed and flexibility.

It is more likely, and somewhat less terrifying in prospect, that war will begin by our involvement in some matter overseas which will lead to some outpost being attacked. It is probable that for a very long time to come a major enemy will feel the need of clearing us out of Europe, or of establishing himself closer to us in the Pacific, or of establishing himself in South America, in order to get within satisfactory striking range of our mainland. We may then again have the luck of fighting the worst of the war outside of our borders. That is, we may have that luck if we are in a position to pour heavy reinforcements into the threatened area almost instantaneously.

It will be noted that in these last, depressing paragraphs I assume the importance of ground troops. We always have our comfortable de Severskys, who tickle the public by telling us that the latest gadget, with just a few improvements (which neither they nor anyone else know how to devise), has outmoded everything else, and we can send the Army home for keeps. I think I am reasonably air-minded, yet I agree thoroughly with the best military authorities, that we have not yet found a substitute for the Infantry and the Artillery. What we have done is to provide them with a terrific ally in the air, and the existence of that ally demands that the rifleman and the cannoneers be able to travel at the same speed. If all efforts are unavailing and we are, some day, subjected to something which will make Pearl Harbor look like good, clean fun, we shall more than ever need a fully developed air transport arm.

Let us suppose for a moment that on December 7, 1941, we had had a going air-transport organization equipped with one hundred C–99's. Allowing, say, four days to assemble troops and issue them the barest essentials of overseas equipment, these could then have been picked up wherever they were concentrated within the United States, and within six days two full reinforcing divisions could have been set down at Manila. Fighter aircraft, crated for boat delivery to Britain, could similarly have been flown to the Philippines, which would have enabled us to offer some adequate resistance to the Japanese air attack. The possibilities are stupendous. We might have chosen, for instance: to send one full division plus ten of these aircraft (with an interior volume equal to ten railroad cars each) loaded with fighter aircraft and spare parts to the Philippines, all arriving there by December 13. The fighters, of course, would then have to be assembled. At the same time or more quickly we might have landed a brigade plus artillery on Guam. By then we should have achieved extensive concentrations of troops on the West Coast by rail — or under modern conditions, by rail and by twin-engine transports — so that within possibly three, certainly not more than four more days, we could have repeated the dose. This bit of dreaming, entered into in order to illustrate what may happen in the future, omits consideration of enemy fighter interception of our transports. It assumes that as early as the thirteenth it would have been possible to get to Manila and Guam without serious opposition. Thereafter, the transports would probably have to make a detour to the south, and depend upon the reinforced fighters in the Philippines to protect their actual landing. Transposing this imaginary operation to modern times, we have to assume that we shall already have good fighter cover and anti-aircraft at the delivery point.

However the fighting starts, providing the initial defense is effective — that is to say, provided we wreak as much havoc upon the enemy as he has done upon us, the whole thing partaking of the nature of a suicide compact — then it would be foolish to expect a short war. For many years it has been the fashion to predict that, in view of the increasing dreadfulness of the weapons everyone possessed, wars would become short. The tendency seems to be the other way, and the next war may prove that H. G. Wells, in *War in the Air,* was an accurate prophet.

If, then, the two sides manage to disembowel each other to a point of approximate equality, we may expect the same old hammer-and-tongs business with assorted modern trimmings. We are likely to face all the logistical problems we faced in World War II, only with a new, deadly emphasis on speed. Having survived the initial blast, we shall move into a second phase of further developing our air transport beyond present imagination.

For all of these situations, we cannot rely on our commercial airlines, important as their contribution will be, any more than we could solve our problem with them in the last war. The Air Forces have always worked closely both with the airlines and the aircraft producers, and they must continue to do so, but the necessary military transports must be on hand, not on order, and the number of personnel on active duty must be, not just a nucleus or a cadre, but sufficient to operate an adequate, minimum system while the reserves come in. These reserves, in turn, must be ready to enter upon their full duties at once.

Considering what this means takes us into the commonplaces of preparedness, matters the importance of which is obscured by their familiarity. "An adequate, minimum system" in this case means enough aircraft, general equipment, and men to ensure the mobility and striking power of the combat forces we shall have on hand. If the reserves are to be able rapidly not only to join their organizations but to proceed to operation, they must have adequate experience in this type of operation with the types of aircraft then in use, and this experience must not have become too stale. To be able to enjoy the economies and protection which air transport makes possible, we must have an air transport arm engaged in active operations in peacetime, large enough to not only keep the standing force up to the minute, but also the reserves or national guardsmen in their training periods. Back of this basic force we must have ready for use the aircraft and other equipment corresponding to the full reserve strength, which will become available at the same rate as the reserve strength of other arms becomes ready for action.

This air transport arm, as all the lessons of the last war so emphatically showed, must be a single unit under the control of the highest level of command. There is still a tendency to parcel it out, even in the staff of the Air Force itself, and as we have seen, the Navy has not yet consented to honest union of its air transport arm with the Air Force's. The function of this unit is *strategic*. It must be in a position to concentrate its strength in one direction, or divide it, unequally or equally, in two or more, as the top strategists decide. If a considerable part of our strategic equipment is broken down on a Troop Carrier basis, turned over to the individual control of assorted tactical units, its value will be destroyed.

All weapons tend to grow obsolete rapidly in this age of invention. This is especially true of aircraft. The Air Forces, as I have said, have always worked closely with the airlines and the manufacturers. The new Air Force must continue to do so. When it was a question of maintaining continuous planning and experimenting in combat aircraft alone, so different in many ways from transports, the interests of the Air Forces differed at many points from those of men primarily interested in commercial aviation. The great development of airborne supply brings the two groups much closer. The commercial carriers still largely emphasize Pullman-type passenger service; the military must have cargo aircraft, which of course can also carry passengers, but without luxury. These are largely differences of internal structure, models of the same types, but they are truly differences between *models*. That is to say, the efficient military variant of a successful airliner cannot ordinarily be produced by modifying the airliner, but must be built in its military form on the production line.

What this means is illustrated by many examples from the last war. For instance, as noted, a large number of Douglas DC–3's from the airlines were taken over by the Army. To adapt these for war use, they were modified into C–53's. Each modification took about a month and cost some $30,000. The result was a hybrid, unable to handle as heavy a cargo, nor to stand as rough use as the C–47, the pure military type. Similarly, the first DC–4's available, the C–54's, were aircraft originally designed for airline use. Not until separate production lines — in this case a separate factory — were established to manufacture the C–54A did we get an allround, satisfactory military plane in this type.

The air transport arm, then, must be able to work closely with the designers as well as with the commercial carriers in the development of better transports. Through this affiliation we can approach economy through basic types suitable for both uses. We may reach further economy, as in the case of the XC–99 and the B–36, through a type partially adaptable three ways. At present, commercial air freight will not support itself on a significant scale. Either the Air Force must be free to buy adequate numbers of transports, or we must enter on the manifold political and other difficulties of heavily subsidizing the airlines to go into the freight business.

All this represents a tremendous outlay, but in this case the nation gets a rebate. Our combat aircraft must be maintained in large quantities, with all the attendant personnel and bases, occupied in constant training flights which return to the nation nothing — except safety. The scale and nature of the air transport arm's peacetime operations must primarily be determined by the need for keeping it well-trained and experienced. In this training, however, it can engage in productive activities. For many years to come, it seems, we shall have sizable bodies of troops in the former enemy countries. Even after they have all been withdrawn, we shall have military and naval establishments scattered over the Pacific, at points in the Arctic, the Caribbean, along the Panama Canal. Wherever units are stationed, there arises a steady movement of personnel between those stations and the Zone of the Interior. Men whose service has expired or who are due for rotation, and their replacements, the exchange of whole units, men on leave or returning from it, make a heavy traffic. There will always be a movement to and fro of assorted specialists on temporary duty, inspectors, staff officers and commanders, and some medical cases.

These people in transit are a total loss, and an expensive one. With forces overseas of 400,000 men, a reliable calculation is that, using surface transport, 60,000 men will be in transit at any one time. To illustrate what this means let us take a major, who in the peacetime Army would probably have at least twelve years' service, being sent to the Philippines on a tour of inspection. Extracting him from the center of the country, and not from the ever-likely Washington, we allow a hundred dollars and two days for his rail travel. We imagine that he has crossed the Pacific in one of our fastest boats, in ten days, and we can figure about two hundred dollars as the cost of that passage. If to this we add his pay, his idle time on the round trip (altogether twenty-four days with, miraculously, no delay at all at ports of embarkation), would cost the taxpayers some seven hundred and fifty dollars, including transportation, but not including the considerable item of per diem or mileage allowance. Unmarried majors are rare: during this period his dependents would be allowed another hundred and fifty dollars, more or less.

The Naval Air Transport Service has worked out a comparison between costs of air and surface transportation over the Pacific for the seven months from January 1 to August 1, 1947. In that period 14,339 naval personnel were carried in boats. Average pay of the officers carried was twelve dollars a day, of the enlisted men, six. Average time in transit was 10.5 days for officers and 11.1 days for men. Total number of man-days consumed in surface travel was 359,594, and the total salary paid while these people were en route was the handsome sum of $2,205,014. Had all of these people moved by air, their time in transit would have been 4.6 days, the salary paid would have amounted to $512,145. The saving in salary alone would have been $1,692,969. Projecting the figures over a full year, air transport would have saved 474,209 man-days and $2,904,606. This is for the Navy in the Pacific alone.

With the equipment we were using in 1946, General George calculated that the 60,000 men in transit in connection with an overseas force of 400,000 would be reduced to 10,000. With the type of aircraft now coming up, the economy in manpower would be much greater. Even with the older equipment, on the basis of the Navy's study, we should have a yearly economy of more than $11,000,000, between the Navy and the Army's occupying forces. In addition, through the reduction in idle man-days, we should actually increase our military strength.

Carrying bulk freight by air is still an extravagance. Nonetheless, by using aircraft which in any case we must keep in operation, to carry all the passengers they can find and filling up the chinks with freight, we can substantially reduce the cost of maintaining a truly competent air transport arm.

Along with the active use of the aircraft come the communication and weather services. These can, and should be, made to serve commercial operations as well as military, and can be kept in a state of high efficiency as a mixture of civilian and military activities. The Civil Aeronautics Authority and Board, and the Air Transport Association, long collaborators with the military, provide the ready means for such interplay.

Properly handled, our military air transport system should continue in peace to be somewhat what it was in war, a fruitful, positive contributor to the progress of American aviation

as a whole. If we have the dreaded misfortune to be again involved in war, it should not be necessary once more for the
Air Force, the commercial carriers, and the manufacturers to
perform a frantic miracle of pulling themselves up by their
bootstraps. If it should be, we shall probably not be allowed
the time for the miracle to be consummated. In the event of
war there is no alternative; we must be able to put the remarkable team which these three groups represent to immediately
effective use. In the last war one used to see over the desks of
some officers, or put forth in public relations releases, a boast-
ful, rather childish slogan which was to a surprising extent
realized: "The difficult we shall do immediately, the impossible will take us a little longer." In the next war there will
be no "little longer."

It is less than fifty years since Kittyhawk. When that first
curious crate managed to hoist itself briefly off the ground, we
had little idea what it might portend. The meaning grew
greater and greater. Between the first blitz over Poland and the
smashing of Hiroshima and Nagasaki, we saw its awful power.
We have seen it as an instrument of unlimited terror, miti-
gated slightly by errands of great mercy.

The capacities of aviation before this war impressed us all
and captured our imaginations, but other than in relatively
localized use, we saw little more than a demonstration of far
future potentials. Now we have partly realized those potentials,
and we have infinitely speeded up the process leading to full
realization. Just as aviation during the war tipped the balance
of China's ability to stay in the war, so today it holds for us
the city of Berlin, and in so doing is changing the course of
history. We have changed the world. Optimistically, we say
that we have eliminated the barriers between nations. So
we have, and with that we have destroyed the old safeties.
Everybody, everywhere, is open to attack. Our world today as
never before in all time offers the crown to the ruthless, the
treacherous, the quick. The nations live today in the sordid
hope of getting in the first lick.

Is this all we have to show for the realization of one of our
oldest dreams? Perhaps not. Once again we are making plough-

shares out of swords — somewhat hesitantly. For luxury or for important business, people fly about the world. They will do so more and more. Nations speak to each other today as never before, voluminously, easily, just as their members today are beginning to visit each other. So far these advantages have proven sterile. The visitors have blind eyes. The speakers cannot hear. Still, they are our hope. No mechanical device of man, from the stone axe to jet propulsion, has been merely good in itself. It has been good to the extent that man has chosen to use it well. It is for us now, one by one, and by nations, to make travel lead to mutual understanding, and convert the mechanical transmissions which we call "communication" into the true communication of minds.

Aviation, world-encircling, world-shadowing aviation has come into being as the creature of war. Therefore, out of its parentage, it bears upon it the marks of the birds of prey. Like it or not, expensively and fearfully, we are forced to keep this weapon ready and even to improve upon it. It is the emblem and insignia of man's internal failure before God, which upon pain of death we must wear until either we destroy ourselves with it or we break out of our own self-created littlenesses.

THE END

INDEX

A–20, delivery of to Russia, 102, 104. *See also* Kit Project; Attack Bombers
A–26's, ferried to Hawaii, 247
Abadan, 103
Abbey, Maj. Edward A., 96, 98
Accra, 17, 18, 28, 194, 230, 263; abandonment of, 298
Aden, 146
Adler, Brig. Gen. Elmer E., 43, 64
Admiralty Islands, air evacuation from, 237
Africa, 2; regular service started across, 28. *See also* Central Africa, North Africa, *and* Subdivisions
Agra, 65, 119
Aircraft, transport, in hand Dec. 7, 1941, 2; procurement and characteristics of, 74–80. *See also* Designations of individual models
Air Corps Ferrying Command, *see* Ferrying Command
Air Corps, subdivisions of, *see* Respective titles
Air evacuation of sick and wounded, 177, 229–239; advantages of, 230; C–47 force-landed on Bellona Island, 237; early use of hospital planes, 230; first flight, 230–231; flight nurses, 231, 232, 235, 236, 237; flight attendants, 231, 235, 236, 237; from France, 285; future of, 238–239; from Leyte, 217–219; loading of patients, 234–235; N.A.T.S. part in, 236; from Okinawa, 223–226; Okinawa statistics, 226; opposition to, 230; planning for, 230; problems of, 230; procedures in European Theatre, 233–236; psychiatric cases, effect on, 234; short range, 233–237; statistics, 236; technicians, *see* Flight attendants; techniques of, 232–233; types of patients handled, 234
Air Evacuation Wing, 231
Air Force, independent, 271, 300. *See also* Army Air Forces; Unification
Airlines, 82; collaboration with A.A.F., 303; contracts with, 30–32, 73, 90–99; contribution of, 7; conflicting demands upon, 59; domestic airlines in overseas operations, 73–74; in future war, 303; in Hump Operation, 118; limitations of in 1941, 8; policy of armed forces towards, 31, 88; President's power to take over, 31; ratio of contract to military crews, 218. *See also* Names of individual lines
Air Lines War Training Institute, 108
Air Maintenance Command, 13, 58
Air Matériel Command, 106
Air traffic control, 144–145; on Hump

Route, 123; Pacific, 197; Transatlantic, 145
Air Transport Association, 1, 8, 209, 307
Air transportation, division of among agencies, 33; economy of, 307; strategic, *see* Strategic air transport; Troop Carrier and A.T.C. compared, 191–192; unified control of, *see* Strategic air transport
Air Transport Command, as instrument of Army policy vs. Navy, 222; co-operation with N.A.T.S., 273; established, 60; "fireball" service to Assam, 65; First Ferrying Group, 52, 86, 87; First Transport Group, 123; 503d A.A.F.B.U., 283; greatest extent of, 4–5, 263–264; intelligence capabilities neglected, 259; makeup of, 165–179; operational training units, 49; organization, evolution of, 253–261; organization, manning table system, 257; Overseas Technical Unit, 245–246; at end of 1942, 101; "Special Mission Squadron," 283; special requirements, 254; unique character, 258; widely misunderstood, 258–259
  Headquarters staff divisions: Intelligence and Security, 259, 279, 285; Operations, 69; Personnel, 179; Plans, 94; Priorities and Traffic, 67, 68, 69, 208, 259, 278, 286 (*see also* Priorities)
  Operating wings and divisions: listed, 260; varied nature of, 258, 259–260. Air Transportation, 260; Africa-Middle East, 61, 92, 195; Alaskan, 61, 260; Caribbean, 61, 124, 167, 260; Central Africa, 150, 260; Central Pacific, 220; Domestic Transportation, 260; European, 126, 136, 232, 260; Ferrying, 15, 61, 63, 114, 256, air evacuation by, 236, air transport by, 260, Fifth Ferrying Group, 129, P–47's ferried to Britain, 247, relations with Director of Women Pilots, 133–134 (*see also* Ferrying and WASP); India-China, 90, 125, 172, 260, 293 (*see also* Hump); North Africa, 260, 280–284, 293 (*see also* Mission 17); North Atlantic, 61, 260, 293, P–47's ferried to Britain, 247; Pacific, 167, 212, 219, 292, 293; Siberian, 104; South Atlantic, 61, 260; South Pacific, 61; Southwest Pacific, 155, 162, 167, 212, 220, 285, 292, relations with G.H.Q., Southwest Pacific Area, 212; West Coast, 220
Airport Development Program, *see* Pan American
Air Service Command, 30, 63, 106; air

311

livery of grenades to Solomon Islands, 209
Consolidated Aircraft, 75; modifications of Liberators, 33. *See also* C–87; LB–30; B–24; Liberator; Buccaneer
Consolidated Vultee, *see* Convair
Constellation, Lockheed, *see* C–69
Continental Air Force, 137
Continental Airlines, 73
Contract carriers, *see* Airlines
Convair, 300; *see also* C–99; B–36
Conway, Lt. Col. William, 285
Crashes, of aircraft, 144, 191–200; B–17 on Ice Cap, 195; B–25 en route to Hawaii, 197; C–54 in Dutch Guiana, 193–194; C–54 leaving Iceland, 195–196; C–87 between Accra and Natal, 194–195; C–87 that flew by itself, 199–200; caused by buzzing, 198; causes of, 192–193; collision of B–24 and C–46, 198–199; P–38's on the Ice Cap, 193; passenger plane out of gas, 196–197
Crete, airborne invasion of, 280, 296; German flak on, 290
Crews, *see* Tactical; Ferrying
Crimea, weather over, 279, 284, 290. *See also* Mission 17
Crimson Route, *see* North Atlantic
Crowell, Maj. James, 149–150
"Crystal" (Arctic weather stations), 149–150
Curtiss-Wright, 76. *See also* C–46

Dakar, 96, 263
Dally, Capt. Benjamin H., 195
Dardanelles, 280
Darwin, 44
Davis, Lt. Col. Richard, 208, 210
DC–3, Douglas, 78, 79; conversion to military use, 305; in Hump service, 87; moves to stop production of, 74–75; obsolescent, 296. *See also* C–47; C–53
DC–4, Douglas, *see* C–54
Decorations, automatic, 176
Delta Airlines, 73
Deversoir, 291
Directorate of Air Transport, 207, 210
Director of Women Pilots, 131, 134. *See also* Cochran, Miss Jacqueline
Discipline, of flight crews, 249–250
Doctrine, *see* Strategic air transport; Command control
Doolittle, Maj. Gen. James H., 95
Douglas Aircraft Corp., 74. *See also* DC–3; C–54
Douglas, Col. James H. Jr., 32, 168–169, 256
Dunlop, Lt. Bernard W., U.S.N., 201
Duplication, by Army and Navy, 272
Dupont, Captain Felix A., 13
Dutch Guiana, 194
Dutch Harbor, 8
Dyer, Capt. James E., U.S.N., 273–276

Eastern Airlines, 73

East Indies, early operations in, 42–44
Egypt, 1. *See also* Cairo
Eighth Air Force, early deliveries to, 108, 182
Eisenhower, Gen. of the Armies Dwight D., 63
El Alamein, 84–85
Eleventh Airborne Division, 293
El Fasher, 26
El Obeid, 9, 21
Elwes, Capt. Orval, 194–195
Emmons, Maj. Gen. Delos C., 12
Enez, 287
Engineer Corps, Army, 38th Regiment of, 83–84
Engineering, in Hump Operation, 118–119
England, *see* Britain
Espiritu Santo-Auckland shuttle, 209

Fairbanks, 102, 106, 263; Russians stationed at, 104
Falconer, Maj. Richard E., 155–158
Far Eastern Air Force, 221, 293
Farmer, Lt. Col. J. J., 208–209, 210
Ferrying Command, 129, 175; Atlantic Division, 22; Domestic Division, 46–47; established, 11–12; Foreign Division, 46; in June, 1942, 53; organization of, 253–254; Western Division, 14
Ferrying, control of, 72; crews, 244; domestic, procedures for, 18–20; first domestic delivery, 17; first foreign delivery, 21; first transatlantic delivery by R.A.F., 9; pilot procurement, 48–50; pilot qualifications, 48; pilots, classes of, 49; pilot shortage, 47; pilot training program, 48–50; pilot training, relation of pursuit ferrying to, 135, 137; "Project 32," 44; tactical, control of, 39–41, 54–55, 96, 248–252. *See also* Ferrying Division *under* A.T.C.; WASP
Fifth Air Force, 221, 295
Fighter aircraft, *see* Pursuit aircraft
Fiji, 16
Finland, occupied by Russia, 190
Finschafen, 214–216
Flexibility, problems of, 70–71
Flickinger, Lt. Col. Don, 202
Flying, combat, nature of, 190; transport and ferry, nature of, 191–192
Flying Tigers, 87, 113. *See also* Fourteenth Air Force
Focke-Wulff 200, 188, 289
Fort, Miss Cornelia, 133
Fourteenth Air Force, 89, 114. *See also* Flying Tigers
France, A.T.C. services extended to, 285
French West Africa, 95; surrenders, 96
Funafuti, 207
Funk, 1st Lt. Benjamin I., 43–44

Gander Lake, 22, 263. *See also* Newfoundland

Wideawake Field, *see* Ascension Island
Wilder, Lt. Col. Henry, 65
Willkie, Wendell, 104, 171
Women pilots, 48; British use of, 129;
casualties of in A.T.C., 139; evaluated,
139–140; Navy's interest in, 130; in over-
seas ferrying, 135. *See also* WAFS;
WASPS
Wright, Lt. Col. Robert, 201–202, 259

"X" Mission (air delivery to the Philip-

pines), 4, 35–41, 96, 242, 247; first plane
dispatched, 38; losses, 38–39

Yalta, conference at, *see* Mission 17
Yellow Sea, 225
Yerwa, 148–149
Yontan Field, 223, 224, 226
York transport, 283
Yugoslavia, 280; transports shot down by,
289